Death by HR

How Affirmative Action Cripples Organizations

Jeb Kinnison

Library of Congress Control Number: 2016955985

Cover photo: Shutterstock

Death by HR

How Affirmative Action
Cripples Organizations

Jeb Kinnison

Author's Note

Like most programmers, during my career as a software engineer I dealt with HR as little as possible. They seemed pleasant enough, though their obsession with collecting signed paperwork was odd. My career started thirty or more years ago, and mostly at smaller companies—and I understand that HR requirements are now worse. It can be harder now to get a hiring manager to see you and your portfolio of work face-to-face, especially if you're older.

In Silicon Valley, I mostly managed money for wealthy technologists. No longer in engineering myself, I got a look at the VC and management community. HR was always considered a necessary evil, ideally put off as long as possible. Usually the first HR manager hired was a smart, no-nonsense woman whose husband worked elsewhere in tech, and she would single-handedly manage personnel with the help of contract payroll services and benefits managers. But at some point in the growth phase, the hiring of more HR employees would begin—and they weren't as accomplished, or as motivated to make the enterprise grow smoothly. It was just a job for them.

Researching this book, I was astounded at how many examples there are of absent, incompetent, or even criminal employees of large government bureaucracies like the VA and EPA who keep their jobs, paychecks, and pensions after years of malfeasance. In the private sector, HR is under pressure by unions, the Dept. Of Labor, or the EEOC to apply civil service-style standards to all employees, especially those of protected classes. As this dysfunction creeps into private business, the hard-working and competent lose heart and commitment. The entire economy slows and the US becomes less growth-oriented and more status quo-preserving. It's not surprising that US family incomes stopped growing significantly two decades ago.

A corrupted system built on staggering piles of debt and regulations from Washington, with asset values artificially propped up by central banks holding interest rates near zero, is going to fail—and probably soon. It may be too late to stop the decline—but keep your friends and family safe, and keep your skills sharp. A crash, if it comes, will provide an opportunity to rebuild the right way, with more freedom and less regulation.

Introduction

This book is about the new Age of Incompetence, with brain-dead, unaccountable employees holding sinecures at the heart of our government agencies and regulated institutions like banks and hospitals, protected by affirmative action and union policies. The rot is spreading as pressure from state and federal regulation of companies has increased, empowering an internal compliance bureaucracy—Human Resources (HR)—that has devalued the best job candidates and employees and promoted affirmative action and diversity over team productivity.

The result has been ever-more-costly failures and a steep decline in organizational performance. From the mortgage meltdown that brought down the world's economy in 2008, to the disastrous launch of the healthcare.gov website for Obamacare, major segments of business and government in the US have grown more expensive and less competent over the past few decades. Billions of dollars of waste in government contracts for IT projects, boondoggle weapons systems, and deadly service failures at the VA are in the news every day. Public schools are widely seen as mediocre, and in the poorest urban districts they are failing to provide a decent education for the students who need good schools the most to make up for bad family backgrounds. Costs for regulated services like schools, colleges, medical insurance, drugs, courts, prisons, and infrastructure like roads and bridges rise far faster than inflation, while time to complete major projects stretches out to decades, and many fail completely and are cancelled after billions have been spent. And the rot is spreading as government pushes businesses to adopt similar employment policies, with HR enforcing government mandates that compromise competitiveness and give overseas companies the advantage.

This book will trace the factors that have hobbled growth and damaged organizational competence. Government regulation has led to HR departments that actively sabotage the hiring of the best candidates for jobs, with by-the-book mediocrities placed in positions of responsibility.

Silicon Valley and the tech industries are the next targets. If you're a manager at a tech company, I'll suggest some ways to protect your people from HR and its emphasis on credentials and affirmative action (AA) over the best fit for a position. Corporate leaders need to be sure their HR departments are managed to prevent infiltration by staff more interested in correct politics than winning products. And I'll show why appeasement of diversity activists is a dangerous strategy that may make your organization a target for further extortionate demands.

The idea for this book came from the author's personal experience seeking a mortgage from a major bank in 2012. The amount of paperwork required was enormous, and every detail of every account had to be documented multiple times. Unexplained, lengthy delays took months. This was true everywhere in the country, as every lender had to sell new mortgages they had originated to one of the government buyers—Fannie, Freddie, or the FHA, which were the ultimate funding for nearly all mortgages, and where crackdowns on the low-documentation ("liar") loans and sub-prime loans had led to an overreaction.

After months of drama and repetitive responses to their information requests, the loan was funded just in time to complete the purchase of my house. All seemed well, but I got a letter one week later demanding proof of insurance, which had already been provided to the bank and approved by Fannie Mae, who had approved and purchased the loan. I had been working with an executive-level expeditor (one key sign of problems is that the bank had to set up an office of expeditors just below upper management to act as a sort of ombudsman, helping customers navigate its own impenetrable bureaucracy), so I got him on the phone, and he set up a conference call with a VP in their servicing division, a woman of a protected class—with an uneducated accent, and unable to respond to either the expeditor or me with anything but simple stonewall statements—"That's just how we do it, Sir. Those are our procedures,

Sir." She wouldn't concede that her bank had just days earlier originated and sold the loan to Fannie Mae based on proof of insurance being provided. Both I and the expeditor gave up trying to talk about anything with her, and the bank dropped the matter after that. While it's true that the VP title at a bank is handed out to thousands of managers, her apparent lower-than-average intelligence and lack of interest in responding with logic was a sign that the bank was employing deadwood in supposedly responsible positions.

I started to investigate and discovered that this was not an isolated incident—because affirmative action policies have placed mediocrities at major decision points in most large companies, government agencies, and highly-regulated institutions like schools and hospitals. A small percentage of deadwood can be routed around, but over time feedback effects from the generalized lack of accountability and lowered standards for performance cripple the institution. This is the cause of the failure and extreme cost overruns of almost all large government projects and a tolerance for incompetence so long as policy manuals are followed to the letter. This effect is largest in government and public education, but also visible in larger companies where HR departments are coming to be staffed by progressives who believe in removing non-progressive thoughts and people from the workplace. In high tech, women and minorities dominate HR in part because companies wanted to balance their male-and-Asian-heavy engineering staff to make their numbers look better, but now are just realizing they've created an internal enemy to product quality and excellence in staffing engineering teams. (A corporate manager comments: "How do you know HR is lying? Their lips are moving…")

This book will focus on the situation in the US, which was until recently more resistant to the bureaucratic disease and thus had a healthier economy and a more dynamic labor market than Europe. The onset of top-down sclerosis by Federal regulation and micromanagement has reduced US growth to the same stagnant levels seen in Europe, for much the same reason: educated by public schools to believe they need permission to do anything, young people stop trying to do anything, and wait for someone to help them. The increasing numbers of untouchable diversity hires in positions of responsibility has inhibited accountability, and the inability to fire employees after even the most egregious malfeasance has spread from civil service and union shops into major corporations—since some cannot be held accountable for incompetence, no one is; and the continuing presence of employees who coworkers know are shirkers, incompetents, or even criminals reduces the morale of those who are good at their jobs and work hard. The dysfunction varies by industry and company, with the worst-hit in heavily-regulated sectors like banking, education, and healthcare, where government either controls every element of the business or pays for most of the product. Sectors which until recently were relatively free of deadwood, like high tech, are now under attack by the diversity activists, who want more hiring of less qualified people to make high tech workforces more representative—which would mean discriminating against better candidates who are white, Asian, Indian, male, etc.

This book will also look at a few other countries that have tried various forms of affirmative action policies to demonstrate that while these places are culturally very different, the divisive and socially damaging long-term effects of AA preferences are visible in every country where it has been in place for longer than one generation.

Affirmative action—which substitutes the lower standard of "good enough" for "best" in hiring new employees, setting the bar low enough so that affirmative action hires can meet it instead of seeking out the most qualified candidate—is not the only labor regulation crippling organizational productivity. State and federal regulation and micromanagement of economic activity continues to increase, complicating and delaying every public and many private projects. Whole sectors of the economy are weighed down by regulation; new medical devices and drugs cost $billions to get through corrupt and scientifically-antiquated FDA studies and approvals processes, which results in high prices for new medical technology. Routine services like dental cleanings and hair braiding are illegal in many states unless done under supervision of a cartel of state-certified practitioners; four states even outlaw residential decorating services unless licensed. Hazards of toppling armoires aside, the state is easily captured by motivated business groups to outlaw new competition for their business, and under the pretense of protecting consumers, allowing professional cartels to charge much more for services.

Labor laws are similarly gamed by politically-influential unions and power-seeking bureaucrats. Minimum wage laws outlaw lower wages for unproven or new workers, and restrictions on firing as in Europe make it less likely companies will take a chance on hiring a full-time worker rather than a temp or contractor. The long-term result of Euro-style labor protection is Euro-style high unemployment, especially in young, inexperienced workers, who are thereby kept from ever gaining the experience that would make them valuable enough to hire despite the additional rules and costs imposed by the laws. People accept that education costs money and that students may be paid less for internships or even pay outright for classes, but forget that most occupational skills are acquired in the workplace, in the first years of employment. By outlawing lower wages and at-will employment, labor laws are keeping young people from important learning experiences and ruining their chance to start on a career ladder.

Until the Roosevelt administration and the New Deal, the Supreme Court had held back many attempts to regulate private business, ruling them unconstitutional overreaches. But after Roosevelt threatened to pack the court with new justices who would approve his regulatory agenda, the Supreme Court bowed to his wishes. In a series of cases, the newly Progressive-leaning Court expanded the Commerce Clause to allow federal regulation of almost all economic activity. In *Wickard v. Filburn*, 317 U.S. 111 (1942), the court ruled that a farmer could be fined for growing wheat on his own land for his own animals' consumption because he would otherwise have had to purchase wheat in the market, which a 1938 agricultural control law regulated. After this, the court rarely found any Federal regulation of contracts or commerce to be unconstitutional, despite the clear intent of the framers that such Federal power over commerce was intended to prevent states from creating trade barriers and discriminating against the products of other US states.

As a result, laws and regulations on commerce of all kinds—and labor specifically—have expanded, and the staffing levels of Human Resources departments and administrations at colleges and hospitals have ballooned to meet bureaucratic requirements. Federal fingers are now in every pie, wasting resources and deadening initiative, since a lawsuit or negative attention from the NLRB, EEOC, Dept. of Education, HHS, EPA, and other enforcement agencies can destroy or damage a company or institution. HR and administrative staff approve of the progressive control agenda—which gives them power and status—and when free to drift leftward serve as an internal fifth column dedicated to enforcing progressive standards on their own organization and its workforce.

Companies serving an international market find themselves battling foreign companies who don't have as many burdens, especially in Asia. The US advantage of a productive workforce and innovative technology is gradually worn down by the time and money spent fighting bureaucrats. Mediocre managements take current rewards for themselves but ignore the future, eventually failing. Foreign companies take over markets, one by one, as US companies dragged down by unions and mediocre key employees lose revenues and eventually abandon markets.

Governments have expanded the areas they control while the Civil Service, union, and affirmative action rules imposed on their workforces have reduced their effectiveness in their most critical functions. From deaths caused by bureaucratic malfeasance at the VA to killer cops rarely punished and kept on the payroll by the efforts of police unions, this lack of accountability makes it difficult to remove incompetent or criminal public employees and makes it impossible for even motivated elected officials to reform public services. The rising debt and costs for every public project mean failing services, rampant injustice, and decaying infrastructure are not being addressed. As a result, US competitiveness is declining vs. countries with better-managed public services. And public anger and cynicism as the years pass and each new group of elected officials fails to fix any of the problems they promised to fix is leading to a dangerous disregard for the law and a desire for a dictator who will sweep aside the checks and balances of a Republic.

Because there are so many examples of malfeasance and incompetence in government's control of commerce and labor regulations, I was forced to leave most of that material for the next book, which will focus on government. Entire books have been written about the costly failures of the Drug War, public schools, affirmative action, and police militarization. This book will focus on the creeping spread of this atmosphere of **consequence-free failure.** The hubris of central planners and their capture by special interests, acting in concert with well-meaning but naive do-gooders who think they can vote their way to a better world, has brought us the diseases of socialism by taking away authority and accountability that let businesses succeed or fail. The pleasant-sounding ideal of equality of outcome—which killed hundreds of millions of people as the activating principle of Marxism-Communism—is actually the enemy of individual freedom, accountability, and achievement. The decline of excellence as a primary goal leading to profit and growth has not come because people like failure and mediocrity, but because they were sold a fairy tale about how government could make everything fairer and make everyone happy through the workings of laws and regulations. The result has been a lot more unhappiness and civil strife as the unintended consequences have swamped whatever good was intended. And the level of hypocrisy has risen as politicians promote the message that everyone is a victim and that someone else —"the 1%," corporations, Republicans, foreigners, Muslims, blacks, the Koch Brothers, the Jews, whoever works as a scapegoat—is responsible for keeping them down.

High tech, one sector where the US led the world and generated immense new wealth, has now been targeted as the next area to be regulated. Activists and demagogues are attracted by money, and with more than half of the US private economy now controlled by government regulators, it was inevitable the parasites would look toward the remaining healthy sectors for their next fix. Calls for diversity quotas in tech company workforces, video game characters, and open-source software projects are early warning signs. HR departments in most tech companies serve as the political commissars of regulation, and HR departments in tech are staffed by lower-paid employees who have little understanding of the technology but a lot of interest in screening out even the best prospective employees who don't fit the narrow diversity mold. Managers who want the best teams and the fastest, coolest products are resisting these HR apparatchiks, and I'll show what you can do about it if you work in tech.

The next battlefield after high tech is discretion in hiring—which the activists believe must be limited to force employers to hire any candidate "qualified" for a job as soon as they apply. Only a few radicals are proposing this kind of blind hiring now, but continuing successes in getting firms to bow to their diversity demands will result in a list of new demands. Seattle has already passed an ordinance requiring landlords to rent apartments to the first applicant who qualifies—next what counts as qualified will come under their control, and government-sponsored Section 8 and protected class tenants will be deemed qualified no matter what their credit reports and criminal records show. And similar movements in hiring—supposedly to prevent discrimination by eliminating management choice of who to employ—are coming soon.

There are many people working hard in HR to promote the interests of their organization, but their efforts are often blunted by the prevailing HR culture that substitutes buzzwords and feel-good social goals for promotion of productivity and excellence:

> ...Most HR organizations have ghettoized themselves literally to the brink of obsolescence. They are competent at the administrivia of pay, benefits, and retirement, but companies increasingly are farming

those functions out to contractors who can handle such routine tasks at lower expense. What's left is the more important strategic role of raising the reputational and intellectual capital of the company—but HR is, it turns out, uniquely unsuited for that. Here's why:

HR people aren't the sharpest tacks in the box. We'll be blunt: If you are an ambitious young thing newly graduated from a top college or B-school with your eye on a rewarding career in business, your first instinct is not to join the human-resources dance. (At the University of Michigan's Ross School of Business, which arguably boasts the nation's top faculty for organizational issues, just 1.2% of 2004 grads did so.) Says a management professor at one leading school: "The best and the brightest don't go into HR."

Who does? Intelligent people, sometimes—but not businesspeople. "HR doesn't tend to hire a lot of independent thinkers or people who stand up as moral compasses," says Garold L. Markle, a longtime human-resources executive at Exxon and Shell Offshore who now runs his own consultancy. Some are exiles from the corporate mainstream: They've fared poorly in meatier roles—but not poorly enough to be fired. For them, and for their employers, HR represents a relatively low-risk parking spot.

Others enter the field by choice and with the best of intentions, but for the wrong reasons. They like working with people, and they want to be helpful—noble motives that thoroughly tick off some HR thinkers. "When people have come to me and said, 'I want to work with people,' I say, 'Good, go be a social worker,'" says Arnold Kanarick, who has headed human resources at the Limited and, until recently, at Bear Stearns. "HR isn't about being a do-gooder. It's about how do you get the best and brightest people and raise the value of the firm."[1]

If you are familiar with the content in a section—say you have already studied the problems with affirmative action at length— please skip to the next. I try not to assume that every reader has been paying attention to all of these areas, so filling in the background and the issues is valuable for those who haven't. Also, some parts were posted in draft form online, so if you're a regular reader of JebKinnison.com, they will be familiar.

Part One

Death by HR

1: The Great Enrichment

This book is about HR's role in damaging team effectiveness by enforcing labor regulations and affirmative action thinking in organizations, and thus hamstringing business productivity and growth. But first we need to see the even bigger picture: the Great Slackening of recent years comes after a long period of powerful growth and change which started in Europe but swept most of the world, transforming stagnant, poverty-and-disease-ridden societies into a thriving, world-spanning technical civilization—the Great Enrichment. We refer to the culture that laid the foundation for this miracle as Western Civilization—though it's not especially Western any more as many elements have been adopted in the East.

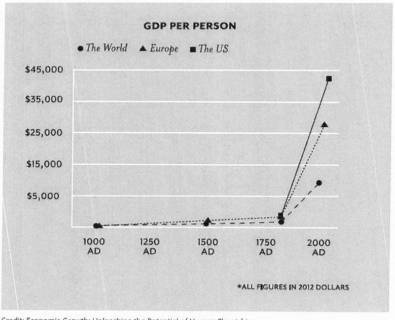

Credit: Economic Growth: Unleashing the Potential of Human Flourishing

As wealth has grown, those protected from life's harsher lessons by being born to great wealth and privilege have turned to sabotaging the very freedom and free markets that created that wealth—but that is nothing new in the world, where it has long been folk wisdom ("clogs to clogs in three generations"[2]) that the first generation of family wealth is generated by driven and productive founders, the next by not-so-driven conventional maintainers, and by the third generation, wealth is dissipated and pampered decadents run the family business into the ground if they are still in charge. Something similar happens to entire cultures unless leadership transfers to newer and hungrier elements as older generations grow wealthy and forget hunger, and the Great Slackening can be viewed as the consequence of the clinging to power of a wealthy elite who unconsciously act to keep down threats to their status from the new fortunes that might arise if free enterprise is allowed to grow unchecked.

Human status is relative, and those unwilling to work hard to keep their already-high status tend to rely on keeping down threats from nouveau riche others, which requires nothing more than political contributions and unthinking support of the status quo government, which will happily regulate away threats of competition. This is certainly bad for hard-working, newly-middle-class strivers, but it's also bad for society as a whole, stifling those who might have created the new technologies and businesses of a brighter future.

Economist Deirdre McCloskey has written some great books delineating the culture that produced the Great Enrichment. Her latest, *Bourgeois Equality: How Ideas, Not Capital or Institutions, Enriched the World*,[3] recaps the cultural features that allowed billions of people to escape poverty in the last few centuries. Her paper "The Great Enrichment: A Humanistic and Social Scientific Account," summarizes:[4]

> From 1800 to the present the average person on the planet has been enriched in real terms by a factor of ten, or some 900 percent. In the ever-rising share of places from Belgium to Botswana, and now in China and India, that have agreed to the Bourgeois Deal—"Let me

earn profits from creative destruction in the first act, and by the third act I will make all of you rich"—the factor is thirty in conventional terms and, if allowing for improved quality of goods and services, such as in improved glass and autos, or improved medicine and higher education, a factor of one hundred. That is, the reward from allowing ordinary people to have a go, the rise at first in northwestern Europe and then worldwide of economic liberty and social dignity, eroding ancient hierarchy and evading modern regulation, has been anything from 2,900 to 9,900 percent. Previous "efflorescences," as the historical sociologist Jack Goldstone calls them, such as the glory of Greece or the boom of Song China, and indeed the Industrial Revolution of the eighteenth century in Britain, resulted perhaps in doublings of real income per person—100 percent, as against fully 2,900 percent since 1800.

What needs to be explained in a modern social science history, that is, is not the Industrial Revolution(s) but the Great Enrichment, one or two orders of magnitude larger than any previous change in human history. If we are going to be seriously quantitative and scientific and social we need to stop obsessing about, say, whether Europe experienced a doubling or a tripling of real income before 1800, or this or that expansion of trade in iron or coal, and take seriously the lesson of comparative history that Europe was not unique until 1700 or so. We need to explain the largest social and economic change since the invention of agriculture, which is not the Industrial Revolution, not to mention lesser efflorescences, but the Great Enrichment.

In explaining it, I have argued, it will not do to focus on capital accumulation or hierarchical exploitation, on trade expansion or class struggle. This is for two sorts of reasons, one historical and the other economic. (I do not expect you to agree instantly with all of these. I list some of them here only as place-holders, and invite you to examine the three thick volumes marshalling the quantitative and humanistic evidence. I mean only to open the issue.) Historically speaking, neither accumulation nor exploitation nor trade or struggle is unique to the early modern world. Medieval peasants in Europe saved more, in view of their miserable yield-seed ratios, than did any eighteenth-century bourgeois. Slave societies such as those of the classical Mediterranean could in peaceful times see a doubling of real income per person, but no explosion of ingenuity such as overcame northwestern Europe after 1800. The largest trade until very late was across the Indian Ocean, not the Atlantic, with no signs of a Great Enrichment among its participants. Unionism and worker-friendly regulation came after the Great Enrichment, not before. Thus world history.

Economically speaking, capital accumulation runs out of steam (literally) in a few decades. As John Maynard Keynes wrote in 1936, the savings rate in the absence of innovation will deprive "capital of its scarcity-value within one or two generations." Taking by exploitation from slaves or workers results merely in more such fruitless capital accumulation, if it does, and is anyway is unable to explain a great enrichment for even the exploited in the magnitude observed, absent an unexplained and massive innovation. The gains from trade are good to have, but Harberger triangles show that they are small when put on the scale of a 9,900 percent enrichment. Government regulation works by reducing the gains from trade-tested betterment, and unions work mainly by shifting income from one part of the working class to another, as from sick people and apartment renters to doctors and plumber. Thus modern economics.

What then? A novel liberty and dignity for ordinary people, among them the innovating bourgeoisie, gave masses of such people, such as the chandler's apprentice Benjamin Franklin, or the boy telegrapher Thomas Edison, an opportunity to innovate. It was not capital or institutions, which were secondary and dependent. It was the idea of human equality. Egalitarian economic and social ideas, not in the first instance steam engines and universities, made the modern world. One history of Western politics," writes the political philosopher Mika LaVaque-Manty, citing Charles Taylor and Peter Berger (he could have cited most European writers on the matter from Locke and Voltaire and Wollstonecraft through Tocqueville and Arendt and Rawls), "has it that under modernity, equal dignity has replaced positional honor as the ground on which individuals' political status rests."

Out of common-law Northern European traditions, then, came the
rule of law and equal treatment of all, at first just landholding men,
but then every citizen of all stations, sexes, and races. Hard-won
freedoms and respect for the individual gave each person enough
security in their person and property to motivate them to work
harder, since they could retain the fruits of their labors and hope to
advance themselves and their heirs with less fear of theft by the
powerful. This is related to the decline of the "Culture of
Honor" (which relied on aggression and violence to maintain
individual property and status) and its replacement by the "Culture of
Dignity," which replaced violence and theft with the rule of law and
property rights. No longer could a higher-status warrior simply kill
and confiscate the property of a lesser-status person who had blocked
his path or insulted his status; disputes were resolved peacefully by
compromise, or taken to court to be judged by law.

Now there have been many earlier civilizations that had the rule
of law and at least some theoretical rights for the people—those who
weren't slaves, at least. But until the 17th century, no Great
Enrichment occurred because kings, nobles, clergy, or warriors could
rewrite contracts and restrain trade as needed to keep others from
rising to threaten their power. As McCloskey says:

> Liberty and dignity for all commoners, to be sure, was a double-sided
> political and social ideal, and did not work without flaw. History has
> many cunning passages, contrived corridors. The liberty of the
> bourgeoisie to venture was matched by the liberty of the workers,
> when they got the vote, to adopt growth-killing regulations, with a
> socialist clerisy cheering them on. And the dignity of workers was
> overmatched by an arrogance among successful entrepreneurs and
> wealthy rentiers, with a fascist clerisy cheering them on. Such are the
> usual tensions of liberal democracy. And such are the often
> mischievous dogmas of the clerisy.

> But for the first time, thank God—and thank the Levellers and then
> Locke in the seventeenth century, and Voltaire and Smith and

Franklin and Paine and Wollstonecraft among other of the advanced thinkers in the eighteenth century—the ordinary people, the commoners, both workers and bosses, began to be released from the ancient notion of hierarchy, the naturalization of the noble gentleman's rule over hoi polloi. Aristotle had said that most people were born to be slaves. "From the hour of their birth, some are marked out for subjection, others for rule." Bishop (and Saint) Isidore of Seville said in the early seventh century that "to those unsuitable for liberty, [God] has mercifully accorded servitude." So it had been from the first times of settled agriculture and the ownership of land. Inherited wealth was long thought blameless compared with earned wealth, about which suspicion hung. Consider South Asia with its ancient castes, the hardest workers at the bottom. And further east consider the Confucian tradition (if not in every detail the ideas of Kung the Teacher himself), which stressed the Five Relationships of ruler to subject, father to son, husband to wife, elder brother to younger, and—the only one of the five without hierarchy —friend to friend. The analogy of the king as father of the nation, and therefore "naturally" superior, ruled political thought in the West (and the East and North and South) right through Hobbes. King Charles I of England, of whom Hobbes approved, was articulating nothing but a universal and ancient notion when he declared in his speech from the scaffold in 1649 that "a King and a Subject are plain different things."

The ability to freely question old ways, and to improve a trade or production process by innovation then eliminate the old ways of doing things—and the old fortunes—by outcompeting them, trading the new products to distant lands, is what started the Great Enrichment off with the bang of the Industrial Revolution. Printing, steam power, mass production, standardized parts, and engineering science made it possible to innovate, spread the new ideas broadly and preserve them in libraries around the world, and invest the profits from innovation into even more innovation. The explosive growth of productivity allowed billions of people to escape hardscrabble rural subsistence farming for urban living and increased the number of people wealthy enough to think about science, art, and design instead of short-term survival.

Thomas Piketty's *Capital in the Twenty-First Century*[5] (2013) was a best-seller promoting a fashionable theory that the rate of return on capital had been greater than economic growth in recent years, which automatically increased concentration of wealth and therefore inequality. Seized on by redistributionists to justify new taxes on wealth and new subsidies for the poor, it seemed to mechanistically explain increasing inequality as the result of automatic processes which could be counteracted by redistribution without harming the engine of growth.

Piketty's explanations were disputed, and MIT economist Matthew Rognlie demonstrated that most of the excess capital accumulation—the enrichment of the wealthy—that Piketty had discussed came from outsized real estate price increases around the world, due primarily to elite control over land development that artificially increased the scarcity and price of prime real estate, notably housing.[6] Piketty's theories were no longer as useful to promote larger government, since government control of real estate development and regulation of other economic sectors like energy and healthcare began to look like the source of the increasing inequality. The heretical notion that it was control by the elites of the commanding heights of government that was actually raising prices and squeezing out the middle class began to spread....

Is the Great Enrichment over? Certainly it continues to expand into newly-opened territories like China and India, where the old Communist Party and Indian bureaucracies are giving ground to freer enterprise and mass movement of rural folk into the cities is transforming life. But in the developed countries that once led the world in innovation, countervailing forces of regulation and central planning are slowing and stopping growth.

This is now being called the Great Stagnation, or as I'm calling it in its corporate form, the Great Slackening. The rise of the administrative superstate in the US and the EU has given the already-powerful a tool to suppress threats from below, and under the guise of protecting the people, it's making the people poorer and more dependent while limiting their freedoms.

In the US, the decades after WWII were marked by high growth and technological innovation. Rebound from recessions was quick, and reforms like the deregulations of the Carter era (trucking, railroads, airlines, interest rates on savings, and the breakup of the AT&T monopoly on phone service) and the tax simplifications of the Reagan administration lifted growth. Waves of labor-saving innovations increased productivity rapidly—computers first eliminated most manual record-keeping, then automated processes and streamlined production and logistics.

But each successive wave of recovery growth from recession has been weaker. This graph from the Center for Economic Policy Research charts the recoveries from the recessions of 1981, 1990, 2001, and 2007.

Index of Real GDP Since Start of the Recession for the Last Four Recessions

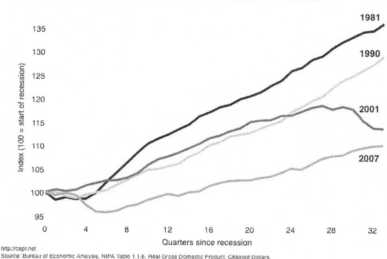

http://cepr.net
Source: Bureau of Economic Analysis, NIPA Table 1.1.6. Real Gross Domestic Product, Chained Dollars.

The weak growth for the quarter puts this recovery even further behind any prior recovery at the same stage. After eight and a quarter years, the economy is only 10.1 percent larger than its pre-recession level of output. A more typical recovery would have seen at least twice as much growth.[7]

Economist Tyler Cowen has coined the term "The Great Stagnation" for this gradual decline in growth and economic dynamism. His book *The Great Stagnation: How America Ate All The Low-Hanging Fruit of Modern History, Got Sick, and Will (Eventually) Feel Better*[8] was published in 2011, after the shaky recovery from the recession of 2007, but before we knew the stagnation would continue.

His major point is that the US post-WWII took advantage of one-time advantages and opportunities: most of the industrialized world had been crippled by war, and unskilled unionized workers could take advantage of their position to win seemingly stable, high-paying manufacturing jobs while the technologies developed in the Depression and WWII decades were rapidly incorporated into production processes. When the rebuilt rest of the world began to catch up and compete directly, much of the easy profits for both US companies and workers were competed away, and technologies developed since have been adopted around the world quickly. The backlog of new technology waiting to be incorporated into production is gone, and meanwhile the overhead of law, regulation, and web of intellectual property (patents, trademarks, and copyrights) has grown complex, to the point where innovation in products may be retarded by legal tangles.

The description of his book, *The Great Stagnation*:

> America is in disarray and our economy is failing us. We have been through the biggest financial crisis since the Great Depression, unemployment remains stubbornly high, and talk of a double-dip recession persists. Americans are not pulling the world economy out of its sluggish state—if anything we are looking to Asia to drive a recovery. Median wages have risen only slowly since the 1970s, and this multi-decade stagnation is not yet over. By contrast, the living standards of earlier generations would double every few decades. The

Democratic Party seeks to expand government spending even when the middle class feels squeezed, the public sector doesn't always perform well, and we have no good plan for paying for forthcoming entitlement spending. To the extent Republicans have a consistent platform, it consists of unrealistic claims about how tax cuts will raise revenue and stimulate economic growth. The Republicans, when they hold power, are often a bigger fiscal disaster than the Democrats. How did we get into this mess? Imagine a tropical island where the citrus and bananas hang from the trees. Low-hanging literal fruit—you don't even have to cook the stuff. In a figurative sense, the American economy has enjoyed lots of low-hanging fruit since at least the seventeenth century: free land; immigrant labor; and powerful new technologies. Yet during the last forty years, that low-hanging fruit started disappearing and we started pretending it was still there. We have failed to recognize that we are at a technological plateau and the trees are barer than we would like to think. That's it. That is what has gone wrong. The problem won't be solved overnight, but there are reasons to be optimistic. We simply have to recognize the underlying causes of our past prosperity—low hanging fruit—and how we will come upon more of it.

Cruft (a term from MIT hackers for useless, complicated leftovers that have accumulated) has grown around our laws and practices, with vested interests blocking change and dynamism through legal means and bureaucracy. New technologies continue to change our lives and speed up work, with the Internet and web starting in the late 1980s and mobile apps and smartphones now connecting people on the go. Yet productivity does not appear to be increasing, and while there is a lot of improvement in living standards that doesn't show up in GDP (no one enjoyed waiting in teller lines at the bank, for example), all of that freed-up time is going somewhere else, and most people's working hours aren't shrinking, and their incomes aren't rising much.

Occasionally a sector will be disrupted (the current buzzword for innovation that suddenly makes a stable sector of the economy unstable) and the efforts of the status quo defenders become more obvious, as with Uber and other ride-sharing services, which had cut into the business of cab companies in many cities before the taxi industry roused itself to try to outlaw them. Few understood the system as it had been, with its taxi commissions, high-priced medallion licensing, and cabbies forced to rent cabs from medallion holders who made the lion's share of the money. The taxi medallion system grew up over many decades, originally to keep gypsy cabs and jitneys—low-priced, unregulated, and occasionally dangerous—from serving the needs of the poor and incidentally crowding the streets of Manhattan, where a free market in taxi services would have resulted in a tragedy of the commons in the form of continuous gridlock. Taxi commissions supposedly protected the safety of riders, but they also restricted the market for local transportation, raising the price and reducing service. Medium-sized cities, low-income and low-density suburban areas adopting taxi regulations tended to end up underserved. The benefits of Uber-like services were so apparent so quickly that most politicians were forced to bow to the fait accompli, and the prices of taxi medallions giving the owner the right to operate a city-approved taxi fell dramatically:

> To own a cab in New York, you need a medallion—a metal shield displayed on the vehicle's hood—and there are a fixed number issued by the New York City Taxi & Limousine Commission (TLC). Until very recently, medallions were a good thing to have a lot of. In 1947, you could buy one for $2,500. In 2013, after a half-century of steady appreciation, including a near-exponential period in the 2000s, they were going for $1.32 million.

> Then came Uber. Since the arrival of the car-by-app service... taxi ridership is down, daily receipts have declined, and drivers are idling —or going to work for Uber. Add it up, and desperate medallion sellers are trying to fob off their little tin ornaments for as little as $650,000.[9]

But that kind of disruption is rare, as more and more economic activity is regulated and new entrants are kept out by the need for government approvals. Products and services from our most heavily-regulated industries—healthcare, education, energy utilities, cable and broadcast entertainment, housing, and finance—have seen outsized price increases without much increase in quality in recent decades, with government regulations either limiting competition or subsidizing consumption (or, as in the case of education and healthcare, both.) Routing around these government controls is starting to happen—household solar panels, Internet entertainment streaming, and homeschooling with online instruction from the likes of the Khan Academy[10] show what is possible when freed from monopoly providers. But breaking the grip of the vested interests on some of these sectors—like the NIMBY restrictions on new housing in the cities controlled by Progressive political machines, or the failed public K-12 schools in urban districts—will take more time and effort.

Virginia Postrel's book, *The Future and Its Enemies: The Growing Conflict Over Creativity, Enterprise, and Progress* (1998)[11] described two opposing philosophies working against each other: stasists, who prefer a regulated and controlled status quo offering predictability in a society mostly closed to new thinking, and dynamists, who accept instability, innovation, and change allowing higher growth and creative achievement:

> Postrel argues that these conflicting views of progress, rather than the traditional left and right, increasingly define our political and cultural debate. On one side, she identifies a collection of strange bedfellows: Pat Buchanan and Ralph Nader standing shoulder to shoulder against international trade; "right-wing" nativists and "left-wing" environmentalists opposing immigration; traditionalists and technocrats denouncing Wal-Mart, biotechnology, the Internet, and suburban "sprawl." Some prefer a pre-industrial past, while others envision a bureaucratically engineered future, but all share a devotion to what she calls "stasis," a controlled, uniform society that changes only with permission from some central authority.

> On the other side is an emerging coalition in support of what Postrel

calls "dynamism": an open-ended society where creativity and enterprise, operating under predictable rules, generate progress in unpredictable ways. Dynamists are united not by a single political agenda but by an appreciation for such complex evolutionary processes as scientific inquiry, market competition, artistic development, and technological invention. Entrepreneurs and artists, scientists and legal theorists, cultural analysts and computer programmers, dynamists are, says Postrel, "the party of life."[12]

Where are the jetpacks and the flying cars dreamed of in the 1960s? Disney's 2015 movie *Tomorrowland*[13] suggested our shared pessimism had slowed progress and endangered the future, but it failed to address the source of the exhaustion and defeatism: the many regulations that now prevent an energetic entrepreneur from putting his or her new idea into practice in the world. People who tried to do something differently have found their way blocked, and their lives are often destroyed by vested interests using the legal system to delay their projects and drain them of energy and capital. Every effort to build something new becomes a political effort requiring that you not only interest customers, but also pay off politicians and rent-seekers who see their interests threatened. The compliance overhead in growing from a small business to a large business is now so large that most people who might try are discouraged and stick with what already works for them. It's far safer to work for a government or big corporation than to try to start a business. The result for our economy is stagnation and declining growth.

The decline in new business formation from 1978 to 2011:[14]

Figure 1.

The U.S. economy has become less entrepreneurial over time
Firm Entry and Exit Rates in the United States, 1978-2011

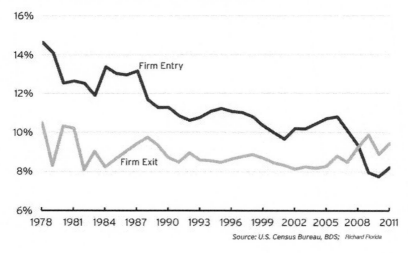

Source: U.S. Census Bureau, BDS;   Richard Florida

Figure 2.

Business dynamism has been steadily declining over the last three decades
Job Reallocation Rate and Trend, 1978-2011

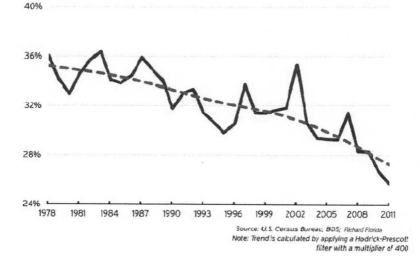

Source: U.S. Census Bureau, BDS; Richard Florida
Note: Trend is calculated by applying a Hodrick-Prescott
filter with a multiplier of 400

It's ironic that the free world outcompeted and ultimately broke the
Communist central planning systems of the USSR and China, with

both Russia and China now authoritarian mixed kleptocracies with at least some freedom for private industry, yet the US is now tied up by central-planning bureaucrats. Regulations are crippling growth and favoring larger corporations that support politicians through favor-trading and campaign contributions. Every small loss of economic freedom and increase in corruption has been accompanied by government-funded propaganda to explain how much it benefits The People. And The People have awakened to a hangover of enormous debts and poor job prospects, having been slipped a mickey of miseducation and dependency.

The French have a term to describe their tendency to let a centralizing state control business activity: *dirigisme,* "to direct." Progressives have gradually molded the US population to more closely resemble the French in looking to the state to decide economic matters, and borrowed many of the ideas of the welfare state and public education from German models. The bureaucracies they spawned tend to grow, and those employed to write regulations will never run out of ideas for new and more detailed specifications of how everything should be done. Because Progressives believe wise rulers (themselves) can make better decisions on every choice less enlightened citizens might make—and it's their duty to improve society by improving people, for their own good. As C. S. Lewis said:

> My contention is that good men (not bad men) consistently acting upon that position would act as cruelly and unjustly as the greatest tyrants. They might in some respects act even worse. Of all tyrannies, a tyranny sincerely exercised for the good of its victims may be the most oppressive. It would be better to live under robber barons than under omnipotent moral busybodies. The robber baron's cruelty may sometimes sleep, his cupidity may at some point be satiated; but those who torment us for our own good will torment us without end for they do so with the approval of their own conscience. They may be more likely to go to Heaven yet at the same time likelier to make a Hell of earth. This very kindness stings with intolerable insult. To be 'cured' against one's will and cured of states which we may not regard as disease is to be put on a level of those who have not yet reached the

age of reason or those who never will; to be classed with infants, imbeciles, and domestic animals.[15]

Suppose your children have learned well from you and their teachers and set out to start an innovative business, or just a food truck. If they fail because they couldn't persuade customers to pay for what they offered, then they will be forced to deal with that reality and try again with a better product. But if they fail because someone told them what they wanted to try required permits and approvals, and in trying to get them they lost interest after weeks, months, or years of delay and bureaucracy—or discovered that big business competitors had rigged the system so they couldn't get those approvals—what do they do? To survive they will have to settle for a job working for one of the "approved" businesses that have paid off the pols to get approvals. And what happens when they observe their friends fail, bankrupted and gutted by a corrupt crony capitalist system? They learn to keep their head down and wait for approval or an influential protector before venturing into business for themselves. It was always risky to strike out on your own—but when the book of rules has grown to the point where no business can avoid violating at least some, the only businesses that survive are those who can stay small enough to be ignored or those who pay off the enforcers.

While this book will touch on overregulation and bureaucracies, there are already quite a few studies and books on each of the affected industries—books on the failures of public education alone number in the hundreds. This book is primarily about labor regulations and their costly and productivity-draining intrusion into hiring and employment practices. Employer fears of exposure to lawsuits led to extensive delegation of control over hiring and firing decisions to HR departments. Government-enforced unions, Civil Service rules, and increasing efforts to require equality of outcome while devaluing excellence are reducing growth now and may doom us to a second-rate future as other countries not so crippled outcompete us. The US can return to a high-growth, lower-inequality path, but only if these sectors are unlocked and allowed to innovate in both process and personnel. Freedom to work and trade as we choose—and not as Washington dictates—will keep us free, and give our children the future we dreamed of.

Both lower-level managers and executive offices need to push back against the tide of government regulations and the runaway HR departments that enforce them. It is entirely possible to keep HR acting in a company's interest by hiring the right HR executives and managers, with an attitude of keeping the company out of legal trouble while not compromising excellence or tolerating deadwood staff who happen to be of a protected class. Regulators will make an example of any company that openly resists their directives, but passively resisting—fulfilling all the requirements for paperwork and policy documents while in practice hiring on merit alone—is a healthy response that will preserve your competitiveness.

From a *New York Times* article on the Obama Administration's flood of new regulations:

> The Obama administration in its first seven years finalized 560 major regulations—those classified by the Congressional Budget Office as having particularly significant economic or social impacts. That was nearly 50 percent more than the George W. Bush administration during the comparable period, according to data kept by the regulatory studies center at George Washington University.

> An army of lawyers working under Mr. Obama's authority has sought to restructure the nation's health care and financial industries, limit pollution, bolster workplace protections and extend equal rights to minorities. ... And it has imposed billions of dollars in new costs on businesses and consumers....

> In its final year, the administration is enacting some of its most ambitious rules, including limits on airborne silica at job sites, an overhaul of food labels to clarify nutritional information, and a measure making millions of workers eligible for overtime pay.... executive power has expanded steadily under both Republican and

Democratic presidents in recent decades...

> The new rules built on the legislative victories Mr. Obama won
> during his first two years in office. Those laws—the Affordable Care
> Act, the Dodd-Frank Act and the $800 billion economic stimulus
> package—transformed the nation's health care system, curbed the
> ambitions of the big banks and injected financial support into a
> creaky economy.... In May, Mr. Obama was asked by a farmer in
> Elkhart, Ind., to justify the "dramatic increase" in government
> regulations that affected his business. "I'm not interested in
> regulating just for the sake of regulating," Mr. Obama responded.
> "But there are some things like making sure we've got clean air and
> clean water, making sure that folks have health insurance, making
> sure that worker safety is a priority—that, I do think, is part of our
> overall obligation."
>
> Infuriated Republicans describe many of the new rules as
> unwarranted, resulting in "less jobs, less businesses, less prosperity,
> lower take-home pay," in the words of the House speaker, Paul D.
> Ryan. Business groups, also incensed, have challenged a number of
> new regulations in court, delaying them or preventing them from
> taking effect. Some economic experts worry that the accumulation of
> regulation is contributing to the economy's persistent sluggishness.
>
> "The big issue that I grapple with is that the regulatory state keeps
> growing," said Robert Hahn, an economist and a regulatory expert at
> the Smith School at the University of Oxford. "And as it keeps
> growing, when does it become too much?"[16]

A comment there makes the case for economic stagnation as a result
of this regulatory explosion:

> The tidal wave of regulations are a hidden tax on many levels. I have
> family in the HR business. They tell me a large percentage of their
> recent hiring is for people just to monitor, enforce and report on
> regulatory requirements. They also describe the frustration with
> complying with regulations that not only overlap but contradict each
> other.

Plus the regulations tilt the playing field for larger companies. For example, suppose a new reg required 5 full time employees for compliance. Imagine the difference in bottom line effect on a firm with 100 employees versus one with 1,000.[17]

The next book will cover the government side of this overregulation. This book will deal with the specific problem of HR and its enforcement of damaging policies like affirmative action, minimum wages, and degree and certification requirements as a substitute for merit.

3: Process Optimization and Specialization

Why do large companies exist? Hollywood film studios used to be vertically integrated[18]—that is, most aspects of production were completed by direct employees of the studio, with even screenwriters and actors under long-term contract. This allowed the studio to put together productions rapidly and under direct control, shooting on their own lots and cranking out enough product to keep costs down and quality up. Vertical integration kept down the costs of negotiating with each supplier / worker and guaranteed availability of unique resources, like the services of major stars and expensive soundstages.

The Hollywood studio system has since been broken up, and many productions are completed by dozens of business entities handling separate parts of the project. Agents and producers package projects and a thriving ecosystem of specialized contractors do much of the work; at the end of every special-effects blockbuster film you'll see dozens of firms credited.

Big companies stay vertically integrated when a new product or industry takes off and there is limited support from outside contractors, or when legal and regulatory burdens make it difficult to reliably contract out parts of the work. In countries where influence with the government is the only way to operate without harassment, large firms that have apparently unrelated businesses under one ownership—conglomerates—are the most successful form. In South Korea, these firms (called *chaebol*)[19] were seen as national champions and had the political pull necessary to survive in a corrupt, influence-peddling environment; improvements in transparency and the curbing of corrupt influence after the Asian debt crisis of 1997 resulted in reform of the chaebol system and broke up the ownership of large segments of the Korean economy, which has improved the country's growth record and competitiveness.

Mature industries with highly-developed contract labor markets tend to outsource many more functions, which lowers the carrying costs for the industry as a whole—an in-house special effects division, for example, will either be over- or under-utilized much of the time, and it's a natural evolution from seeking outside business for slack periods to being spun off as an independent concern when there are large numbers of independent special effects firms with different areas of expertise. As a contracting market develops, it then becomes practical for even a small team to start their own firm, further atomizing the market.

The classic pamphlet "I, Pencil"[20] explains the story of the simple graphite-leaded wood pencil's production as a mute symphony of coordination and cooperation by suppliers and producers who have organized spontaneously under the free market system to produce a product not one of them fully understands. All of its component materials and the machines needed to manufacture the pencil come from different suppliers who have developed the constituents independently, specializing in, say, the paint for the exterior, or the rubber eraser. Time and many instances of contracts fulfilled lead to trust between suppliers, and competitive markets hone each supplier's quality and price to hold down the cost of the completed product.

What happens when trade barriers go up? Say the best producer of rubber pencil erasers is in Malaysia, and a protectionist Congress slaps a high tariff on products from Malaysia....

The price landscape the US-based pencil manufacturer sees changes when Malaysian erasers leap in price because of the new tariffs, and a US-based supplier now appears to offer a better deal on erasers, so the manufacturer orders from them instead. Unfortunately the unfamiliar supplier has a lower quality product at a higher price, and the pencil manufacturer and the new eraser supplier spend days negotiating payments and terms. The resulting pencils have to be priced higher and consumers notice the erasers don't work very well, and begin to consider other brands of pencil instead....

Relatively free trade allows multinational networks of the best and most-efficient suppliers to capture the benefits of specialization globally. The world's auto industry, for example, benefitted greatly in the end by combining innovations from Japan, Germany, and the US. Autos manufactured anywhere today source parts from multiple countries—which becomes most noticeable when, for example, the dangerous failure of airbag components made in Mexico by major supplier Takata of Japan spreads to include recalls of upwards of fifty million cars from at least twelve different car companies.[21] Atypical disasters aside, the availability of low-cost and reliable components from overseas has brought US-manufactured cars up to increasingly-high global standards and allowed US final assembly plants to remain competitive despite their higher labor costs.

When trade barriers are lowered, there is often short-term pain for less-competitive, formerly-protected industries, as there was for the US auto giants in making the transition to a global market. But high trade barriers and closed markets mean higher prices and a lack of competition to keep the domestic industry honest—and if the protected products are a large component of national consumption and a capital good necessary for other industries as well, like autos and trucks, the entire economy of the protectionist country will grow more slowly and become less competitive in international trade. A return to high trade barriers for the US, like the Smoot-Hawley Tariff Act of 1930,[22] would lower the quality and raise the prices of many US-made goods, making them less competitive in global trade even if no other countries retaliated by raising their tariffs. Just because there are still countries with high tariff and other barriers doesn't mean the US, as one of the greatest beneficiaries of the global free trade system, should also shoot itself in the foot. In the 1930s countries stumbled into a worsening Depression by such short-sighted actions which harmed everyone, and contributed to the strains resulting in WWII.

Similarly, it is damaging when any government acts to limit or over-regulate trade between its citizens and its companies. The US Constitution addressed the issue of trade barriers between the various States by giving the power to regulate "interstate commerce" to the Federal government, intending to prevent the kind of tariffs and barriers that Britain had used to benefit their own industries at Colonial expense from springing up between the States.

Today France is in the throes of strikes and disorder as its Socialist government tries to reform its labor regulations to allow for a freer market in labor.[23] Current regulations there make it so difficult to fire or lay off employees that companies do everything they can to avoid hiring regular full-time employees, and most young people are forced into the undermarket of contract and temporary labor to gain employment. Youth unemployment rates over 20% in many parts of Europe are crippling their career development, in large part due to overregulation. Entire economies grow more slowly when special-interest regulation favors the few insiders who already have secure positions over the young outsiders.

Trade liberalization and the global spread of freer markets produced the greatest improvement in global living standards the world has ever seen, the Great Enrichment, with higher living standards than ever dreamed of for middle classes in the developed world, and billions of people lifted out of poverty outside it.[24] The increasing prosperity and health of these populations defused the population bomb that was supposed to have produced famine and war by the late 1970s.[25] Technological innovation and capitalist investment fed more people and found more resources and energy at lower prices. Growing wealth created a demand for clean air and water, and a supply of new emissions and cleanup technologies that have improved the local environment of every country that has completed the transition to both democratic governance and capitalism. The countries that tried to maintain their centrally-planned economies were outcompeted, and every one has either reformed or collapsed into poverty.

But the temptation to control an organic free-market economy to benefit special interests is always waiting, and those special interests (whether private industries or public employee unions) are good at funding campaigns and lobbying legislators to have laws written in their favor. US courts have been all too willing (since the Supreme Court's 1937 "Switch in time that saved nine," which bowed to to FDR's desires[26]) to allow Congress and state legislatures to regulate private contracts and trade by presuming any regulation which had a "rational basis" was constitutional. This great expansion of opportunities for graft resulted in the growth of an overbearing administrative state, a permanent shadow government of tenured bureaucrats and administrators who are so protected by Civil Service and public employee unions that there is no accountability and only limited desire to serve the public who pay all the bills. Meanwhile, the economy grows more and more slowly, as some industries like banks are bailed out and protected while others are harassed by regulators. Small businesses and community banks are crippled by costly regulatory requirements and labor rules like the ACA, while costs rise in every sector heavily regulated by governments—and those sectors (healthcare, education, banking...) lobby for special loans and subsidies. Young people are told they must go to college, taught that government and nonprofit services are the most moral career choices, then saddled with student loan debt and a slack labor market when they graduate—if they graduate.

Let's imagine for a moment that a Freedom of Contract Amendment exists—a freedom implied by common law and precedent until 1937, but smothered by Progressives eager to mold the people toward a scientifically-managed, centrally-planned future, which as we have seen does not work. People would be free to sell their labor under any terms they wish. Other than Civil Rights Act protections against discrimination, employers would be free to seek out the best employees for their teams and organize them and pay them in whatever way is agreeable to both employer and employee. The impossibly complex jumble of fringe benefits and 401Ks and stock plans and options created by complicated tax incentives goes away when the tax system is simplified. It's a dream, right? Freedom to achieve without being "helped" by a politician with his or her hand out for a contribution, or sued by a lawyer wanting to retroactively apply antiquated 1930s labor regulations designed for factories to white-collar employees...

A bright future doesn't come with thousands of pages of laws and regulations dating back to the last century and designed to hold a tottering status quo in place. It comes out of individual striving, strong growth companies, and new technologies, and an American people free to mold themselves as they wish. The access to all of the world's knowledge we now have via the internet means education can be flexible and nearly free for those who are motivated, and trapping our children in failed urban schools or mediocre and ideologically-driven public universities wastes their time and our tax money.

[Note that the current mechanism for negotiating and implementing "free trade agreements" looks very much like the dysfunctional process now used to write new laws—opaque, lengthy, written by committees and tailored to special interests. That's certainly not a good thing, and opens the process to corrupt influence-peddling. I'm defending the general principle of free trade here, and often these deals are mixed, a net positive for the US economy while containing many objectionable parts.]

A bucket brigade. Ten people who pass buckets down a line from one to the next, always succeeding in passing it along in one second, so one bucket per second is moved from one end to the other.

There are two types of worker: fast and slow. Fast workers can pass along one bucket per second, while slow workers take two seconds.

Suppose one worker on a bucket brigade of ten workers is slow and takes two seconds; in that case, every person after them in the chain has to wait two seconds for the next bucket, and production is *halved* at one every two seconds. The chain can produce no more than its weakest link.

Recognizing this, the chain is reformed: the slow person is cut out, the rest reach a little extra, but can only pass a bucket every 1.1 seconds. Still, by leaving out the weakest link, production is increased from one every two seconds to one every 1.1 seconds, with everyone working a little harder. The slow worker is idle.

Now suppose there are five slow people. The fast five can't reach far enough to move the buckets from one end to the other; the best they can do is form a team of eight, three slow and five fast, and production is decreased to one every two seconds. The fast people, reaching a bit further, can produce at one per 1.3 seconds, while still limited by the slow to one per 2 seconds speed. Two slow workers do nothing.

But then: the brigade leader realizes the fast five can move at 1.3 per second then split the buckets between two lines of two slow people each, alternating. This allows the fast people to work at their higher speed of one per 1.3 seconds, passing the bucket alternately to each slow line. Not limited by the slow, total production is now one per 1.3 seconds.

Now imagine hundreds of bucket brigades. Each brigade leader is tasked with recruiting and paying the team members, then taking payment for the buckets moved (Production) and disbursing it to team members at the agreed-to rate of pay.

For simplicity, we'll assume the payment for each bucket delivered is the same, $0.05. The resulting model starts to look like firms in a competitive industry. The talent pool is continuously refreshed with new people with no performance record; some of them are strong and coordinated even at first, while others learn over time to move faster and more surely. Some will always be slower, or unable to focus on the task, or lack coordination. The brigade leader is Management: their job is to decide what work to do, how to do it, and with what workers.

Brigade leaders have a variety of strategies to choose from. The obvious strategy is to go after those workers who have demonstrated how productive they are previously, and offer them higher pay. A brigade with all fast members will move the full one bucket per second, or 28,800 per eight-hour day. At the end of the day, the brigade leader collects $0.05 per bucket, or $1,440, and if each worker is paid the same, they can be paid $140 each, enough for food, shelter, and clothing in our simple model's factory town. (We'll assume our brigade leader also works the brigade line for now, and collects a little off the top for the extra job of managing it.)

But another brigade leader tries to fill her crew with the best workers and discovers only a few are available. She decides on a different strategy: hire some cheaper and slower workers and hire more of them, then use her organizational skill to set up the line to produce as much as possible with the workers she has. She is able to hire five fast workers for the competitive $140/day salary, but also hires four slower workers at $80 a day each, so her payroll is 700+320=$1,020 a day, and by using her fast workers in a single line then having her slow workers split into two lines which alternate handling the buckets coming from the fast line, production is slower than the all-fast team at 1.3 seconds per bucket moved versus the fast team's 1 second per bucket moved, so in an eight-hour day her team can produce only 22,154 buckets vs the fast team's 28,800, and they are paid only $1107.70 for their output. But that's more than she's offered to pay her workers—so she can collect an additional profit and put to use workers who would otherwise be shunned as slow. Those workers, true, are paid less—and perhaps they have to live near the railroad tracks in smaller, cheaper rooms and eat less expensive meals—but they have work which keeps them fed and healthy, and companionship as they work, and the opportunity to get better with time and practice so that their pay can be raised.

This simple model shows how important it is to be able to pay workers in accordance with their productivity in any business, and how management can reorganize the flow of work to use those who are less productive.

This model also has the feature of the real-world job market requiring each worker to prove their worth before commanding their fair salary. A new worker with no experience will tend to get paid much less than even the slow workers, then rise in pay to the level commensurate with their productivity as it is recognized and becomes common knowledge; a brigade leader (manager) who fails to raise that worker's pay will find that worker has been hired away by another brigade at a higher rate. And those workers who slowly get more productive will eventually find their new skills recognized in pay, or also be hired away.

Now suppose the town's mayor comes by and discovers some of the workers are paid less for the "same" job of moving a bucket from one hand to the other. The mayor has been watching MSNBC, and reading Marx, and finds this intolerably unequal—so he returns to Town Hall and has the Town Council pass a law fixing a minimum wage of $120/day. They believe workers will thereby have more money to spend and the town will boom as all these new dollars are spent.

The result is different. All of the strategies managers have used to organize their teams to use less-productive workers are defeated—the only way a brigade can make it is if every worker is fast. All of the slower workers are let go, and teams scramble to reform with only fast workers. Since there aren't enough fast workers to go around, there are fewer brigades, and the town's total production falls. Even some brigade leaders are out of work, and none of the remaining brigade leaders will take a chance on a new worker who might cripple their production. The brigades that remain are doing well, and perhaps a shortage of the product even increases its price and thus the profits of the brigade leaders/owners, which allows an increase in the remaining workers' $140 pay to $150.

But the town is full of unemployed workers, and they demand relief from the Town Hall, who already took responsibility for their welfare by ruling low pay illegal. Retail businesses are suffering as the total spending of the town's workers falls. More shop workers and owners also find themselves unemployed.

We'll end our parable here, before the mayor announces a new job retraining program or decides to attract a major-league sports team by borrowing money to build a new stadium.

Most work is vastly more complicated than a bucket brigade, and it is generally more difficult to tell which workers are the most productive when you look at more abstract products like software or engineering design. If a less-competent worker occupies a key role in a modern software development team, that software will not only be produced more slowly, it may never work at all. Managers often can't tell whose failures are damaging a team's work output until it is too late, and it is far harder to tell whether a new hire is going to be a valuable addition, or a regrettable mistake.

It's also important to note that most workers can succeed in some environments while failing in others; the fit of a worker to a position and team can vary widely. A worker who actually detracts from team performance in one job is often much better suited to another job, which is why it's better for both employee and team if bad fits are quickly removed. The bad fit can go on to be a valuable addition to some other team. Being fired is widely seen as a negative, but it should not be—unless it becomes a habit. Many European countries make it difficult to fire anyone for any reason, which only makes it harder for young people to get a good, stable job since employers are punished for taking a chance on new employees by being stuck with any mistakes.

Software is a special case where some programmers are hundreds of times more productive[27] than others, and some are actually negative producers—bottlenecking their teams, derailing meetings, and demanding management attention while making other team members less productive. Fred Brooks wrote *The Mythical Man-Month*[28] about the mistaken belief of managers that a programming project could be sped up or rescued by adding more programmers. He came up with Brooks' Law: "Adding manpower to a late software project makes it later."

The highest-quality programming projects are generally designed and prototyped by a single visionary or a very small team, and as more programmers are added, the clarity of design and implementation are lost and the code balloons in volume and is more prone to errors. When the programmers are mediocre and there are many of them, as in most government-contracted software projects, the entire effort may collapse and be scrapped after millions (or billions—note the many examples of catastrophic failure in government IT projects, including healthcare.gov) of tax dollars have been spent. This is just the most extreme consequence of bureaucratic project management; in many other fields, the consequence of mediocre team members is low productivity, poor quality, and wasted effort, but the result may function well enough—for government work.

In the United States, we inherit much of our Constitution and political thought from English common-law models. Throwing off the tyranny of inherited privileges, every citizen was deemed equal under the law, with basic rights that were not to be trampled by government; government's role was to defend those rights against infringement by others, whether other citizens or external states. In Enlightenment England, the Crown came to be viewed as the abstracted ideal of government power to be used only for the mutual benefit of all citizens. The US Revolution further clarified this doctrine by eliminating the Crown and replacing it with the written Constitution.

So whence came the impulse to take from some citizens to give to others who had been treated unfairly? One of the early movements in the English Civil War, the Levellers of 1645-46,[29] were intellectual forebears of the idea of redistribution. They wished to remove the special rights of nobility and landed gentry, and make all citizens equal under the law, a radical thought at the time. But of course the system they were rebelling against was, by our standards, a kleptocracy, with the privileged early warlords taking and holding landed estates which were the primitive support for the early centralized governments. In return for providing fighting forces and support for the Crown, local warlords were given title to large territories and worked the land using serfs, collecting taxes for the Crown. Under the feudal system, trade and industry were looked down on, and wealth could be stolen by authorized brigands from those who had worked for it, since power came from arms and ultimately could not be held without the protection of the Crown. So the tale of Robin Hood, seen today as stealing from the rich to give to the poor, was a story of a true social justice warrior, taking from the tax collectors and the wealthy thieves of feudal government, returning wealth to those who had earned it, the serfs and free citizens.

Much of the belief system of European-style Labor and Socialist parties dates back to the feudal days when the Balzac quote was true: "Behind every great fortune lies a great crime," which morally justifies efforts to redistribute wealth from rich to poor. The United States went further than England in establishing a system of free citizens, equal under the law, who could usually rely on the protection of their rights and property by the new government. Inherited titles and lands were less significant and power and wealth more broadly distributed and more often acquired through hard work and intelligent enterprise. Until recently, the US was home to great wealth generated primarily by free enterprise and innovation, and there was little moral justification for redistributive policies.

There are many places left in the world, however, where wealth is generated by government influence and corrupt monopolies, where business must bribe and pay tribute to pols, and where the wealthy support the corrupt government that has favored their special privileges. And some of that corruption is coming back to the United States as our corrupt pols have figured out how to peddle their influence to foreign powers and interests in return for contributions to their own power and campaign financing. The Clintons have been especially successful at this, with just one example being their Haitian exploits.[30] In the late 1990s, kickbacks from the Haitian telephone monopoly enriched connected Clinton Democrats at the expense of every poor Haitian family calling relatives in the US.[31]

Kleptocratic regimes grow very slowly if at all, with advances mostly due to imported technology. Individuals in kleptocracies know hard work that raises them to the level of being noticed will attract a stronger clan to steal what they have earned, often killing or exiling their victims. The explosion of growth in the West only came about because the rule of law and protection of property rights made keeping your own earnings and profits more certain; and the most ambitious people in poorly-governed countries around the world worked to reach the US and other liberal states to escape the suppression and theft of their homelands.

As this lesson has been buried under layers of permits and bureaucracy in the US, the rule of law has degenerated into rule of administrative law, with smothering red tape and overregulation. The black markets in labor and goods that are prominent features in kleptocracies are becoming more and more important here, with cash labor combined with social welfare payments keeping more people in the underground gray zone, dependent on government and trapped by the high price of going aboveground.

Growth has been steadily declining across the developed world, with central bankers trying to keep the game going by artificially pumping created cash into the economies and mispricing debt to force investment in more risky enterprises. This has inflated stock and property markets and made the already-rich richer at the expense of workers and savers. The levers of the power squelching growth and limiting new housing in desirable cities are held by an elite class of bureaucrats and attorneys, and the situation of young people in places like San Francisco and New York is analogous to the situation of serfs in feudal systems: they work hard and spend all of their income on bare survival, with a large chunk of their income going to rentiers. Like the Levellers, they wonder how the deck was so stacked against them by the previous generations, and call for a new deal. And like the Levellers, many see theft from the wealthy as just, never having been taught economics or the horrendous history of socialist regimes, because their schools are now dominated by progressives who indoctrinate them in the goodness of government solutions to the problems of global warming, pollution, and economic inequality.

The better remedy is removing most economic activity from the grasp of government. Having thrown off the monopolies imposed by Britain on tea, for example, the framers of the Constitution did not include regulation of commerce among the enumerated powers, and until the New Deal, it was common for the Federal courts to strike down state and local laws that tried to restrain commerce by granting monopolies or fixing prices. But since the New Deal—FDR's effort to centrally-plan the economy—the Supreme Court has allowed almost every kind of commerce to be regulated by Federal and State law, applying a rational basis test: if there is at least some chain of reasoning provided that connects the law with a general government purpose, the court has deemed the law constitutional.[32] This has given us restrictive zoning, rent control, local cable TV and telecomm monopolies, local minimum wage laws, licensing of even the most harmless services like hair-braiding, and set up legislators as the ultimate collector of tolls on business in the form of campaign contributions and lobbying.

Of course there are externalities requiring regulation; the most obvious example is pollution, which imposes costs on others that justify regulation. But laws that were originally promoted for the general welfare, like zoning, eventually were used to capture benefits for certain people—notably owners of existing homes and buildings —at the expense of others, notably newcomers and landowners. When the word "unregulated" began to be used as a scare word by popular media to imply danger in any commercial activity not regulated by a bureau or government, the triumph of the bureaucrats was complete; now we pay more and get less for everything from housing to medical care to cable TV and Internet service, because competition in those areas has been suppressed by law. Incomes are high for many of those employed in those sectors, but millions of young people are un- or under-employed because the businesses they might have worked for can't start up under such restrictive conditions.

Remember the bucket brigade model of teamwork? It demonstrated that giving a manager the freedom to pick and choose who would be on a team and what they would be paid allowed even those weak in some areas to be employed to complement the strengths of other team members. Taking away that freedom to choose—by imposing minimum wages or labor regulations—resulted in some people being unemployed who might otherwise have done well and gained skills over time.

The cog model of labor, as employed by unionists and government labor laws, sees jobs as slots to be filled by anyone who is "good enough"—who can function at some standardized level in the position. No worker is supposed to do much more than the standard amount of work, and hours are to be regulated by law to prevent abuse of workers by rapacious business owners. Much of the discussion of affirmative action (AA) and diversity assumes the cog model—when there are many candidates to choose from, one can simply declare a minimum competence requirement, then choose the candidates that further diversity goals from among that pool. These will typically not be the best candidates for the particular position and team environment, but team managers are not given a choice.

Signifiers of "good enough" that are seen as objective—like high school and college degrees, grades, and test scores—are often used to screen out many applicants for entry-level jobs before any consideration of their complete records. But all of these quality signifiers tend to screen out more minority applicants, and so are inevitably attacked as having disparate impacts. The EEOC, for example, recently issued a letter stating that requiring a high-school diploma for a position might be inherently discriminatory under the Americans with Disabilities Act.[33] Standardized tests have been legally attacked and removed as requirements as well. The "Ban the Box" campaign[34] is an effort to prohibit employers from inquiring about criminal histories, since some minorities are much more likely to have been convicted of a crime. The *reductio ad absurdum* where people convicted of sex crimes against children cannot be disqualified from jobs in child care is not far away; the unionist / government answer is that such people must be hired, paid, and promoted, but can be told to report to a room to serve their work days, since as with the bad teachers paid to sit in NYC's Rubber Room,[35] it's not that important that they actually be useful as long as equality is preserved —the task is not to produce, but to harvest the proceeds of political influence for clients of the political machine.

There is an argument for prohibiting employers from asking about college degrees for many positions—since minority applicants from failed urban schools fail to graduate from high school, or if they do, tend to drop out of college before they obtain a degree, using a college degree as a general requirement for jobs where the extra education is not required to do the job is discriminatory. With the dumbing-down of most colleges and universities, a degree requirement certifies mostly that the applicant can deal with arbitrary reward systems and complicated schedules of attendance with only long-term rewards, which bars most raised in the underclass cultures who have had little opportunity to learn self-discipline or other bourgeois values. Standards of learning for obtaining a soft-studies degree like psychology or political science from a low-end college are not much more rigorous than for high school, with many graduates not much more literate and knowledgeable after four more years of "education." Anyone who can navigate the bureaucracy and attend class is likely to be awarded a degree.

Scott Alexander in his Slate Star Codex piece "Against Tulip Subsidies"[36] wrote about a kingdom where marriage proposals customarily required a tulip, and what happened when tulips became expensive in a speculative market bubble (as they actually did in Holland around 1637):[37]

Suitors wishing to give a token of their love find themselves having to invest their entire life savings—with no guarantee that the woman will even say yes! Soon, some of the poorest people are locked out of marriage and family-raising entirely.

Some of the members of Parliament are outraged. Marriage is, they say, a human right, and to see it forcibly denied the poor by foreign speculators is nothing less than an abomination. They demand that the King provide every man enough money to guarantee he can buy a tulip. Some objections are raised: won't it deplete the Treasury? Are we obligated to buy everyone a beautiful flawless bulb, or just the sickliest, grungiest plant that will technically satisfy the requirements of the ritual? If some man continuously proposes to women who reject him, are we obligated to pay for a new bulb each time, thus subsidizing his stupidity?

The pro-subsidy faction declares that the people asking these questions are well-off, and can probably afford tulips of their own, and so from their place of privilege they are trying to raise pointless objections to other people being able to obtain the connubial happiness they themselves enjoy. After the doubters are tarred and feathered and thrown in the river, Parliament votes that the public purse pay for as many tulips as the poor need, whatever the price.

He makes the analogy to the Progressive movement for "free college," where everyone is viewed as entitled to a four-year degree at public expense, without much consideration of the cost or value of such degrees. Then he points out his own profession, medicine, as an example where arbitrarily costly educational requirements may have little benefit and high costs:

In America, aspiring doctors do four years of undergrad in whatever area they want (I did Philosophy), then four more years of medical school, for a total of eight years post-high school education. In Ireland, aspiring doctors go straight from high school to medical school and finish after five years.

I've done medicine in both America and Ireland. The doctors in both countries are about equally good. When Irish doctors take the American standardized tests, they usually do pretty well. Ireland is one of the approximately 100% of First World countries that gets better health outcomes than the United States. There's no evidence whatsoever that American doctors gain anything from those three extra years of undergrad. And why would they? Why is having a philosophy degree under my belt supposed to make me any better at medicine?...

I'll make another confession. Ireland's medical school is five years as opposed to America's four because the Irish spend their first year teaching the basic sciences—biology, organic chemistry, physics, calculus. When I applied to medical school in Ireland, they offered me an accelerated four year program on the grounds that I had surely gotten all of those in my American undergraduate work. I hadn't. I read some books about them over the summer and did just fine.

Americans take eight years to become doctors. Irishmen can do it in four, and achieve the same result. Each year of higher education at a good school—let's say an Ivy, doctors don't study at Podunk Community College—costs about $50,000. So American medical students are paying an extra $200,000 for...what?

Remember, a modest amount of the current health care crisis is caused by doctors' crippling level of debt. Socially responsible doctors often consider less lucrative careers helping the needy, right up until the bill comes due from their education and they realize they have to make a lot of money right now. We took one look at that problem and said "You know, let's make doctors pay an extra $200,000 for no reason."

And to paraphrase Dirkson, $200,000 here, $200,000 there, and pretty soon it adds up to real money. 20,000 doctors graduate in the United States each year; that means the total yearly cost of requiring doctors to have undergraduate degrees is $4 billion. That's most of the amount of money you'd need to house every homeless person in the country ($10,000 to house one homeless x 600,000 homeless).

Alexander goes on to cite more examples from his immediate family and friends of the use of degree and certification requirements to keep talented, motivated people out of professions and jobs:

But it's not just medicine. Let me tell you about my family.

There's my cousin. He wants to be a firefighter. He's wanted to be a firefighter ever since he was young, and he's done volunteer work for his local fire department, who have promised him a job. But in order to get it, he has to go do four years of college. You can't be a firefighter without a college degree. That would be ridiculous. Back in the old days, when people were allowed to become firefighters after getting only thirteen measly years of book learning, I have it on good authority that several major states burnt to the ground.

My mother is a Spanish teacher. After twenty years teaching, with excellent reviews by her students, she pursued a Masters' in Education because her school was going to pay her more money if she had it. She told me that her professors were incompetent, had never actually taught real students, and spent the entire course pushing whatever was the latest educational fad; however, after paying them thousands of dollars, she got the degree and her school dutifully increased her salary. She is lucky. In several states, teachers are required by law to pursue a Masters' degree to be allowed to continue teaching. Oddly enough, these states have no better student outcomes than states without this requirement, but this does not seem to affect their zeal for this requirement. Even though many rigorous well-controlled studies have found that presence of absence of a Masters' degree explains approximately zero percent of variance in teacher quality, many states continue to require it if you want to keep your license, and almost every state will pay you more for having it.

Before taking my current job, I taught English in Japan. I had no Japanese language experience and no teaching experience, but the company I interviewed with asked if I had an undergraduate degree in some subject or other, and that was good enough for them. Meanwhile, I knew people who were fluent in Japanese and who had high-level TOEFL certification. They did not have a college degree so they were not considered.

My ex-girlfriend majored in Gender Studies, but it turned out all of the high-paying gender factories had relocated to China. They solved this problem by going to App Academy, a three month long, $15,000 course that taught programming. App Academy graduates compete for the same jobs as people who have taken computer science in college, a four year long, $200,000 undertaking.

I see no reason to think my family and friends are unique. The overall picture seems to be one of people paying hundreds of thousands of dollars to get a degree in Art History to pursue a job in Sales, or a degree in Spanish Literature to get a job as a middle manager. Or not paying hundreds of thousands of dollars, if they happen to be poor, and so being permanently locked out of jobs as a firefighter or salesman.

This is a picture of a society where distant authorities control employment qualifications for political and bureaucratic reasons and thereby prevent many people who would be very good at a job from having any chance of getting it. The "free college" movement is just more of the same central-planning-style thinking: removing all obstacles so that everyone—no matter how poorly-motivated, ill-prepared, or congenitally stupid—goes to a college, no matter how dumbed-down. Which by magic will allow all of them to be placed in good professional jobs with high salaries and secure futures. Because college is good, everyone should go! And heaven help us when barely-competent professionals are running important institutions because they have been passed along through an education system where no one fails.

This faith in college education for all is the secular version of believing prayer in schools will somehow uplift the morality of children forced to pray. It is promoted not only by the "Baptists" who believe, but by the self-interested bootleggers who benefit from force-feeding students and tax dollars to academic bureaucracies that employ mostly Democrat-aligned voters, which is why more funding for college is always on that party's agenda.

This tax-supported credentialism has begun to erode standards in education, to the point where half or more students with A and B averages in high school still need remedial coursework[38] before even starting a college-level program. As the corrupting effect of government student loan financing took hold in colleges and universities, standards fell, and resources go to expensive facilities and administrators while teaching is often assigned to low-paid, abused gypsy adjunct instructors. The result is a pervasive decline in the quality of college graduates at all but the highest-level institutions and a heavy burden of debt on students who discover too late that a college degree is no guarantee of a career with salaries high enough to make payments on their student loans while also paying rent and eating. The suckers who "follow their dreams" as they have been told they should discover there are far too many humanities, film, and video game design graduates, and many end up working tables or bartending while their opportunity to start a family slips away.

The Party of Government continually promises to fix problems that don't exist to portray themselves as protectors of the weak. One of the most mainstream of these myths is the gender pay gap, which aggregates pay for all full-time workers to show women making about 78% of what men earn and implies that women are being paid less for the same jobs throughout the economy. Millions of diverse types of worker and employment are lumped together to come up with a simple number that is assumed to be the result of systemic discrimination.

No matter how many times this is debunked, government and partisan propagandists repeat the lie to justify more affirmative action and labor laws to raise women's pay and reduce job requirements. When it's pointed out the discrepancy comes largely from voluntary choices made by women—to take off years for childrearing, to work in clean and safe environments, to work with people rather than machines and physical tasks—labor partisans claim that there must be systematic discrimination holding down wages in female-dominated professions like childcare.

Ask anyone who manages people in a large corporation, and you'll discover that whatever minor pay discrepancies exist, corporate compensation schemes only allow limited differences. Men and women at a single company with the same jobs and performance are paid pretty much the same, with the minor differences related to preferences—men push harder for higher pay (and longer hours), while women on average value social relationships and shorter, more flexible hours. Some activists seem to imply that those who work too hard are implicitly making work life too competitive for women, and that all workers should be made to work less so that those with childcare and family responsibilities can be paid the same.

A free market in labor will always have discrepancies, with

competition and relative scarcity of experienced and driven workers in certain demanding fields compensated far more than those in low-skilled, pleasant jobs. It happens that more men end up in the dirty, difficult, demanding fields and sacrifice personal lives and family to outshine competitors; changing that would mean changing culture and human nature, forcing equality of outcome on a complex system that has rewards and sacrifices more important than mere financial compensation.

The pre-feminist world, say prior to 1960, tended to block women who wished to succeed in professional fields. It's good that this has changed—more women and more men who wanted to take roles not conforming to rigid gender stereotypes have been able to do so, and net welfare has increased as a result. Yet politicians seek to raise wishful thinking about "having it all" as a woman to a public policy goal—that labor regulation should force employers to hire set ratios of women and minorities regardless of fit and productivity, and pay the mother who works 30 hours a week the same as the driven young father who wants to rise to the top by working 60-hour weeks. This is part of the recipe for Euro-stagnation that is gradually damaging US growth, and forcing HR departments to act as the social engineering arms of the Federal EEOC and Dept. of Labor.

The EEOC intends to muscle private companies to comply, starting with their Jan. 29, 2016 announcement[39] that all companies with more than 100 employees would be required to report compensation broken down by race, gender, and ethnicity:

> "Too often, pay discrimination goes undetected because of a lack of accurate information about what people are paid," said Jenny Yang, the chairwoman of the Equal Employment Opportunity Commission, which will publish the proposed regulation jointly with the Department of Labor. "We will be using the information that we're collecting as one piece of information that can inform our investigations."
>
> …"Bridging the stubborn pay gap between men and women in the work force has proven to be very challenging," said Valerie Jarrett, a

senior adviser to Mr. Obama, noting that the median wage for women amounts to 79 percent of that for men. "We have seen progress, but it isn't enough."

And it will never be enough, since the Party of Government actually doesn't want their poll-tested issues to ever go away. While discrimination on a small scale still happens—individual managers and some small backwater companies still discriminate—on the whole women are given a fair shake and accommodated in today's corporate world. Pretending that millions of woman can get big raises for their current jobs by voting in Party of Government politicians is too valuable to give up as an election issue. The problem must be kept alive forever, even when all of its real aspects have been dealt with as much as a free market in labor—and an efficient economy with freedom of choice for companies and workers—allows.

Ashe Schow, a sharp feminist writer who doesn't buy the party line, says:

> I've written extensively on how the gender wage gap would be more accurately referred to as the "gender earnings gap," because the gap is due mostly to choices women make and not discrimination.

> But now you don't have to take my word for it, you can listen to Claudia Goldin, an economics professor at Harvard University. Goldin spoke to Stephen Dubner, the journalist behind the popular podcast "Freakanomics," in a segment about what really causes the gap. As one can imagine, Goldin comes to the same conclusion that I and many others have: That the gap is due mostly to choices men and women make in their careers and not discrimination.

> "Does that mean that women are receiving lower pay for equal work?" Goldin asked after listening to clips of President Obama and comedienne Sarah Silverman claim that women earn 77 cents to the dollar that men earn. "That is possibly the case in certain places, but by and large it's not that, it's something else."

That "something else," is choice—in the careers that women take, the hours they work and the time off they take. Dubner asked her about evidence that discrimination plays a role in the gap, to which Goldin responded that such a "smoking gun" no longer exists.[40]

Walter Olson of Overlawyered points out how the EEOC's collection of data might benefit law firms who can use it to back up lawsuits, with the inevitable costly settlements enriching the law firms and further reducing corporate freedom to work with individual employees to tailor working conditions, hours, and compensation:

> Aside from driving a high volume of litigation by the EEOC itself, the scheme will also greatly benefit private lawyers who sue employers, including class action lawyers. An employer might then weather the resulting litigation siege by showing that its numbers were good enough, or not. Would today's Labor Department and EEOC policies look much different if the Obama administration frankly acknowledged that it was devising them with an eye toward maximum liability and payouts?[41]

A study of recent graduates in STEM fields demonstrated how disparate pay could quickly be generated by different preferences in these supposedly objective fields:

> One year after they graduate, women with Ph.D.s in science and engineering fields earn 31 percent less than do men, according to a new study using previously unavailable data.

> The pay gap dropped to 11 percent when researchers took into account that women tended to graduate with degrees in fields that generally pay less than fields in which men got their degrees.

> The rest of the pay gap disappeared when the researchers controlled for whether women were married and had children.

> "There's a dramatic difference in how much early career men and women in the sciences are paid," said Bruce Weinberg, co-author of

the study and professor of economics at The Ohio State University. "We can get a sense of some of the reasons behind the pay gap, but our study can't speak to whether any of the gap is due to discrimination. Our results do suggest some lack of family-friendliness for women in these careers."[42]

"Family-friendly" means less focused, less demanding work. In science and engineering, focus is critical—a worker who is obsessed by the work and spends night and day thinking about a problem undistracted by children and social responsibilities is vastly more likely to achieve a breakthrough or a rigorous, clean, innovative design ahead of the competition. Multitasking and the interruption of concentration by family schedules and set break times[43] reduces productivity, especially in fields like programming where long and intense focus is required for the best work product. Not all jobs in these fields require this obsessive focus and many peripheral and support jobs can allow time for family life and other interests, but these jobs tend to pay less as well. To demand to be paid the same amount for them is to cheat the hard worker who is motivated to temporarily sacrifice much of the enjoyment of a well-rounded life for the sake of the task and who may be doing so to build the record of outstanding performance needed to build the base of a long career. And it should surprise no one that far fewer women are interested in that kind of unbalanced, unsocial, driven existence, even for short periods. The report goes on to say:

> The importance of helpful family policies is supported by the fact that single and childless women tended to have less of a pay gap than those who were married and those who had children. About equal percentages of men and women were married or partnered. And more men than women in the study (24 versus 19 percent) had children. But it was the married women with children who saw the lower pay.

> "Our results show a larger child-gap in salary among women Ph.D.s than among men," Weinberg said.

"We can't tell from our data what's going on there. There's probably a combination of factors. Some women may consciously choose to be primary caregivers and pull back from work. But there may also be some employers putting women on a 'mommy track' where they get paid less."

The researchers had data, not previously available to scientists, on 1,237 students who received Ph.D.s from four US universities from 2007 to 2010 and were supported on research projects while in school.

This data included federal funding support the Ph.D. graduates received as students, the dissertations they wrote (this told researchers what scientific field they studied) and U.S. Census data on where they worked and how much they earned one year after graduation, as well as their marital and childbearing status. Names and identifying characteristics were stripped from the data before the scientists had access to it.

Results showed clear differences in what men and women studied, with women clustered in the lower-paying fields. Overall, 59 percent of women completed dissertations in biology, chemistry and health, compared to only 27 percent of men.

Meanwhile, men were more than twice as likely to complete dissertations in more financially lucrative fields like engineering (45 versus 21 percent), and were 1.5 times more likely to study computer science, math or physics (28 versus 19 percent).

....Once they graduate, the differences between men and women with Ph.D.s continue. While industry tends to pay the largest salaries, women are more likely than men to work in government and academic settings. In fact, women in the study were 13 percentage points less likely than men to work outside of academia and government.

Women tend to choose more sociable, more supportive work

environments, in fields that pay somewhat less. It is likely this is in part not only their conscious preference, but a kind of luxury afforded by the remnants of traditional gender roles—while free not to follow those roles, most men and women still have them embedded in their plans and goals, and the goal of family and a male primary earner and female caretaker and secondary earner is now the norm. In that context, a woman's choice of lower-compensation jobs and fields makes perfect sense as part of her strategy. Attempts to force choices that would absolutely equalize the sexes in compensation and representation in all fields are not only doomed to fail but increasingly harmful to productivity.

The original feminist demand for "equal pay for equal work" was aimed at releasing women from the labor laws that restricted their freedom to negotiate pay and work hours for themselves. These laws were intended to "protect" women from working long hours, at night, or under "unwomanly" conditions, under the paternalistic theory that women needed to be discouraged from occupations that might interfere with their duties as wives and mothers. What we see today is similar paternalism, unconsciously assuming that women need government help to negotiate good salaries and working conditions that suit their goals.

Jeffrey Tucker of FEE wrote:

> The phrase "equal pay for equal work" is in play again, with an intended meaning we all know. The idea is that government should force (really force, this time) private employers to boost the pay of women to match the rate of men in the same positions.

> Almost every state had laws that specifically limited when women could work. It's a bad idea; more than that, the policy actually betrays the original meaning of the phrase, circa 1920; more about this in a bit.

> Such a law, heavily enforced (after all, equal pay has been the law for

half a century), would actually handicap women in the marketplace, taking away their ability to price compete. It would require an army of bureaucrats to enforce by overriding business control over wages and salaries. And because you can comply by either raising wages or by lowering the professional status of women, it would install a new glass ceiling for women, outpricing their labor in the market for professional advancement.

There is a mighty social cost too. It would do very cruel things to the reputation of all women of accomplishment. It would signal to the world that they only achieved through government power, the use of which is much like putting a gun to people's heads. Anyone can do that. Nothing to brag about, nothing to feel proud about, nothing for which to take credit.

Maybe you detect a patronizing hint to the demand. It's as if women can't really cut it in the professional workforce. They can't manage their own careers or make their own deals. They can't cut it. They need the help of the state.

There's more than a hint of misogyny here. And indeed, if you look at the history of labor legislation as it pertains to women, that is exactly what you find.

...In the early part of the 20th century, restrictions on women's work and the regulatory imposition of lower wages were put in place for eugenic reasons. The life goal of women is not to make money but to further the race. Their place is not in the factory but in the home bearing and raising children. Hence, regulations should punish their commercial ambitions.

Feminists in those days were savvy: they saw exactly what was going on. They used the phrase "equal pay for equal work" to call for an end to these regulatory restrictions on women's work. It was a clarion call not for government but to allow the market to work! It was: let the market be permitted to pay women equal to man, because the law wouldn't allow it.

What kinds of laws? Almost every state had laws that specifically limited when women could work: not before 6am and not after 10pm. And there were maximum working hours too: not more than 50. (That might sound like more than a full-time job, but 100 years ago, this workload was seen as less than serious.)

Such laws were typical. Also, states and even the federal government offered payments to mothers not to work. It was the earliest form of what we call the welfare state, and the motivation was, again, certainly eugenic. How can the best women breed the best offspring if they are hanging around the factories instead of using their reproductive talents to lift the quality of the human population?"

The Progressives believed in "scientifically" regulating everything in life to create better and healthier people. They disregarded individual freedom and Constitutional rights, and have memory-holed their support for eugenics and the anti-black motivations of the minimum wage laws they created. Cleansed of what are now seen as racist and sexist motivations, the same Progressive program of micro-management of labor laws and private choices is back to win votes from people foolish enough to believe them this time.

Part Two

HR and Labor Regulation

A hundred years ago, employment and recruiting were handled by individual managers—both private-sector workers and government employees were recruited, and served at the pleasure of those managers above them. Arbitrary, abusive, or corrupt practices were common, and managers were relatively free to use their position to benefit themselves or indulge their prejudices at the expense of the enterprise.

Industrial and labor relations as a field got its start around 1900. Frederick Winslow Taylor (1856-1915) explored what he termed "scientific management," which others later referred to "Taylorism." He strove to improve economic efficiency in manufacturing jobs by breaking down manufacturing processes into discrete steps, timing them and splitting them up in an assembly line to quantify and speed up each worker's part of the process. This is the doctrine that gave us "mindless" factory work—the same small step done over and over by one worker, then the work moving on to the next worker for an additional step, before finally arriving completed at the end of the line, as perfected by Henry Ford in the assembly line for the Model T. The assembly line relied on the availability of standardized parts, and standardized the labor steps to assemble them so that no overall skill was required and employees could also be viewed as largely interchangeable cogs.

As organizations grew and labor laws and unions as countervailing forces became important, companies developed personnel departments specializing in recruiting new employees and deciding pay and benefits questions. The "human resources management" field grew up as a specialization of the knowledge required to manage large numbers of employees under the many new legal and political constraints, and protection of the company or organization from lawsuits, union troubles, or government punishment became critical. The abbreviation HR for Human Resources was the new name for the Personnel Department on steroids, responsible for keeping lower-level managers out of trouble when making hiring, firing, and pay decisions. While team managers still had considerable input in deciding who to hire and fire and how much to pay them, they were required to work within guidelines provided by law, regulations, and an increasingly remote HR department. The immediate concerns of managers about team fit and competence were then subject to new constraints of state and federal regulation, overriding hiring managers' prejudices but also overriding their local knowledge.

There had always been good and bad employers, and depending on the competitive environment and level of skill (and rarity) of a class of employees, they could be either well-treated and secure, or poorly-treated and arbitrarily harassed and fired for reasons we would now consider improper, like race or sex. Recourse was reputational—in a many-employer city, larger employers who treated workers poorly would discover only desperate or naive people would apply for their jobs. Newcomers would take jobs with bad employers but transition to better ones as they gained experience, if business was growing.

The new framework of unions, labor laws, and internal HR worked to establish a minimum standard for worker treatment. Bigoted or abusive managers could find their own jobs endangered as bad behavior was brought to the attention of upper management and resulted in negative consequences for the organization. But it also drove obviously improper behavior and motivations for hiring and firing decisions underground—a sophisticated bigot or sexual harasser in a hiring manager's role could still get away with hidden discrimination.

It can be hard to determine how much credit to assign new labor laws and unions for the improvement in labor conditions in the era from 1900 to the 1970s, when today's HR came into prominence. As in most social movements, the laws and organizations evolved together, and enlightened businesses were often reforming their own behavior in advance of the law and union pressure, recognizing that a stable and happy labor force made them more profitable and productive. As a recent example, private companies led the way to providing partner benefits for gay employees, far in advance of any legal requirements to do so. By the time of the Supreme Court's ruling establishing same-sex marriage as a civil right throughout the country (Obergefell v. Hodges, 2015),[45] most major corporations provided such benefits.

Today the legal landscape for employers is so complex and regulations so easy to violate unknowingly that even the smallest companies have an HR department or outsource the function to a specialized contractor (though there are exceptions, and a recent movement toward eliminating them.[46]) The HR department is tasked with reducing the risk to the organization of leaving hiring, firing, and compensation policies in the hands of local managers, and as a risk-avoiding function they typically are overly cautious and reliant on metrics like credentials, performance evaluations, and written applications to make decisions. Since HR is not intimately familiar with the makeup of specific teams and the complex skills required for maximum effectiveness in some positions, prescreened applicant pools provided by HR will typically have some excellent potential employees disqualified by their crude filters, and overall organizational goals like presenting good diversity numbers for regulators may lead to neglect of local goals like hiring the best performer for a particular position.

HR departments are intended to project corporate goals into team personnel decisions, but are more usefully viewed as internalized guards against hazards to the enterprise from lawsuits and regulatory punishments. Big corporations now spend heavily on lobbying, political contributions, and legal assistance, but most HR spending is also "protection money," a cost of doing business in a highly-regulated environment. And upper-level management attention to HR functions tends to be an afterthought, with many HR departments staffed by people unfamiliar with the company's business and with little incentive to increase productivity. When ass-covering is your primary activity, product or service innovation and quality have a lower priority. HR functionaries are roughly analogous to the commissars or political officers of Communist regimes, a separate hierarchy of spies to report on and control internal units. The interests of managers and HR can diverge drastically, with HR coming to be viewed as the enemy within, to be avoided and routed around. One high-tech team manager wrote, "How can you tell HR is lying? Their lips are moving."[47]

There is widespread dissatisfaction with HR departments. Companies have outsourced some of their functions—for a small company, it can be far cheaper to outsource back-office functions like accounting and payroll, and many routine HR functions can similarly be done by low-cost contractors.

But most large companies still have a full-fledged and costly HR department, and despite cutbacks in noncritical personnel, the HR department protects itself by pointing to all the government punishments that might rain down on the company foolish enough to defy the bureaucrats by neglecting diversity training or failing to at least appear to be spending on recruiting more minorities and women. But as part of a protection racket, HR comes to have a hostile relationship with some of the more productive parts of the enterprise.

Discontent has been simmering for years despite HR "thought leaders" promoting their visions. One 2005 article in *Fast Company* starts this way:

> Well, here's a rockin' party: a gathering of several hundred midlevel human-resources executives in Las Vegas... They are here, ensconced for two days at faux-glam Caesars Palace, to confer on "strategic HR leadership," a conceit that sounds, to the lay observer, at once frightening and self-contradictory. If not plain laughable.
>
> Because let's face it: After close to 20 years of hopeful rhetoric about becoming "strategic partners" with a "seat at the table" where the business decisions that matter are made, most human-resources professionals aren't nearly there. They have no seat, and the table is locked inside a conference room to which they have no key. HR people are, for most practical purposes, neither strategic nor leaders.
>
> I don't care for Las Vegas. And if it's not clear already, I don't like HR, either, which is why I'm here. The human-resources trade long

ago proved itself, at best, a necessary evil—and at worst, a dark bureaucratic force that blindly enforces nonsensical rules, resists creativity, and impedes constructive change. HR is the corporate function with the greatest potential—the key driver, in theory, of business performance—and also the one that most consistently underdelivers. And I am here to find out why.

Why are annual performance appraisals so time-consuming—and so routinely useless? Why is HR so often a henchman for the chief financial officer, finding ever-more ingenious ways to cut benefits and hack at payroll? Why do its communications—when we can understand them at all—so often flout reality? Why are so many people processes duplicative and wasteful, creating a forest of paperwork for every minor transaction? And why does HR insist on sameness as a proxy for equity?

It's no wonder that we hate HR. In a 2005 survey by consultancy Hay Group, just 40% of employees commended their companies for retaining high-quality workers. Just 41% agreed that performance evaluations were fair. Only 58% rated their job training as favorable. Most said they had few opportunities for advancement—and that they didn't know, in any case, what was required to move up. Most telling, only about half of workers below the manager level believed their companies took a genuine interest in their well-being.[48]

Many HR staff are well aware of their company's goals and work hard to promote them. But many others are buried in a web of bureaucratic process mandates and spend their time fighting daily fires without any thought to improving those processes to make them more efficient and less frustrating for company managers and employees.

HR staff are insular and widely distrusted by managers. While they take matters of compensation, fringe benefits, and recordkeeping out of the hands of managers, they tend not to understand the jobs of the employees they are supposed to recruit and retain. Where an enlightened HR might work at nurturing the company's workers to make them more productive and more loyal, in practice HR's time is spent responding to government and legal concerns, with managers' productivity and employee knowledge devalued.

We'll look at who staffs HR departments these days, where they're trained, and what they know when they get their first job in HR. Much as happened with public school teachers, the establishment of specialized degree programs in HR did not produce a better class of HR employees—it did the reverse, as the field attracted less motivated, less intelligent students looking for a sociable job with less pressure and lower pay than most business professions. As the *Fast Company* article continued:

> HR people aren't the sharpest tacks in the box. We'll be blunt: If you are an ambitious young thing newly graduated from a top college or B-school with your eye on a rewarding career in business, your first instinct is not to join the human-resources dance. (At the University of Michigan's Ross School of Business, which arguably boasts the nation's top faculty for organizational issues, just 1.2% of 2004 grads did so.) Says a management professor at one leading school: "The best and the brightest don't go into HR."

> Who does? Intelligent people, sometimes—but not businesspeople. "HR doesn't tend to hire a lot of independent thinkers or people who stand up as moral compasses," says Garold L. Markle, a longtime human-resources executive at Exxon and Shell Offshore who now runs his own consultancy. Some are exiles from the corporate mainstream: They've fared poorly in meatier roles—but not poorly enough to be fired. For them, and for their employers, HR represents a relatively low-risk parking spot.

> Others enter the field by choice and with the best of intentions, but for the wrong reasons. They like working with people, and they want to be helpful—noble motives that thoroughly tick off some HR thinkers. "When people have come to me and said, 'I want to work with people,' I say, 'Good, go be a social worker,'" says Arnold Kanarick, who has headed human resources at the Limited and, until recently, at Bear Stearns. "HR isn't about being a do-gooder. It's about how do you get the best and brightest people and raise the

value of the firm."

So HR is a ghetto, and HR staff in industries like high tech tend to be culturally very different—and look down on—the engineering staff that creates the products that give the company an edge in the market. As we'll see in the next chapter, HR staff are mostly women, and favor the fashionable progressive goals of diversity and equality of outcome. The marketplace for products, though, is not interested in "participation trophies" and punishes companies that lose sight of competitive realities. If your product falls behind, the company is dead, and all those diversity programs die with it.

> Most human-resources managers aren't particularly interested in, or equipped for, doing business. And in a business, that's sort of a problem. As guardians of a company's talent, HR has to understand how people serve corporate objectives. Instead, "business acumen is the single biggest factor that HR professionals in the U.S. lack today," says Anthony J. Rucci, executive vice president at Cardinal Health Inc., a big health-care supply distributor.
>
> Rucci is consistently mentioned by academics, consultants, and other HR leaders as an executive who actually does know business. At Baxter International, he ran both HR and corporate strategy. Before that, at Sears, he led a study of results at 800 stores over five years to assess the connection between employee commitment, customer loyalty, and profitability.
>
> As far as Rucci is concerned, there are three questions that any decent HR person in the world should be able to answer. First, who is your company's core customer? "Have you talked to one lately? Do you know what challenges they face?" Second, who is the competition? "What do they do well and not well?" And most important, who are we? "What is a realistic assessment of what we do well and not so well vis a vis the customer and the competition?"

HR at its worst pursues bureaucratic goals unrelated to final output because HR staff don't understand the productive process. Like bureaucrats everywhere, they respond to their local environment by producing programs, reports, and paperwork that have little bearing on productivity. All that activity—training programs, recruiting outreach, special events and team-building consultants—is pursued without much measurement of the results of those efforts:

> HR pursues efficiency in lieu of value. Why? Because it's easier—and easier to measure. Dave Ulrich, a professor at the University of Michigan, recalls meeting with the chairman and top HR people from a big bank. "The training person said that 80% of employees have done at least 40 hours in classes. The chairman said, 'Congratulations.' I said, 'You're talking about the activities you're doing. The question is, What are you delivering?'" But human-resources managers, [Ulrich] acknowledges, typically undermine that effort by investing more importance in activities than in outcomes. "You're only effective if you add value," Ulrich says. "That means you're not measured by what you do but by what you deliver." By that, he refers not just to the value delivered to employees and line managers, but the benefits that accrue to investors and customers, as well.

The metrics HR uses to justify its cost, both directly in terms of its own spend but indirectly in imposing time-consuming programs and processes on managers and employees, tend not to measure effectiveness in increasing quality, production efficiency, or staff morale. And the CEO and board see HR as a necessary cost of doing business and don't examine alternatives, allowing HR to slowly grow more powerful and less accountable to the managers it supposedly serves.

HR often reports to the CFO, and thereby becomes a cost-saving arm. Public companies can fall into the managed-earnings trap, where every hiccup in revenues and earnings is smoothed by carefully-timed layoffs. Many mature Silicon Valley companies now go through layoffs every few quarters, usually justified as responding to poor prospects in one business line or other, but really aimed at keeping investors soothed and the stock price up. Upper-level management bonuses and stock options depend on a high and stable stock price; HR becomes the earnings-management handmaiden of the CFO, allowing short-term gains for top employees and investors at the expense of long-term development of a productive, stable workforce.

Further, HR departments grow to resemble the government bureaucracies whose regulations they interpret and apply. They are isolated and shielded by their protection function, imagining themselves more critical to the organization than they are, while actually having no real understanding of business:

> "As HR leaders we feel ourselves to be near the pinnacle of the organization," wrote one HR exec. "The organization reports to us. It must meet our demands for information, documents, numbers." Leaders? As is often the case with bureaucrats, servants are mistaking themselves for masters. They're also clueless about the subject they pride themselves in knowing best, which is people. Eighty-three percent of HR folk believe their employees intend to stay on for another year, double the percentage of employees who said that. A similar number, 81 percent, of HR workers believe their employees would recommend the company to a friend. Only 38 percent of the employees agreed. These failures matter: Employee turnover costs businesses an estimated $11 billion a year, with recruiting costs standing at roughly 150 percent of the employee's annual salary....
>
> HR places a disturbingly high premium on what it calls "communication skills" and what you and I call "talking." A survey found that 83 percent of HR professionals cited training in communication skills as important to getting a job in the field, while only two percent cited the importance of classes in finance. Actually knowing how the business runs doesn't much register with HR. Using HR as talent spotters makes about as much sense as asking the florist for help filling out the roster on your basketball team.[49]

A few companies are experimenting with eliminating their HR departments entirely, with many routine personnel functions outsourced and a return to hiring manager control over the hiring process and performance management—promotions, training, and teambuilding. The WSJ reports mixed results:

> When LRN Corp., which helps companies develop ethics and compliance programs, restructured a few years ago, the 250-employee business abolished most job titles and department names. It also did away with its human-resources department, which had dealt with recruiting and compensation issues, among other things.
>
> "We wanted to force the people issues into the middle of the business," said David Greenberg, Los Angeles-based LRN's executive vice president.
>
> Companies seeking flat management structures and more accountability for employees are frequently taking aim at human resources. Executives say the traditional HR department—which claims dominion over everything from hiring and firing to maintaining workplace diversity—stifles innovation and bogs down businesses with inefficient policies and processes. At the same time, a booming HR software industry has made it easier than ever to automate or outsource personnel-related functions such as payroll and benefits administration.
>
> Some workers say they feel the absence of an in-house HR staff acutely, especially when it comes to bread-and-butter HR responsibilities such as mediating employee disputes and resolving pay problems. LRN and other companies that are going it alone say they are working out the glitches as they go.
>
> Ruppert Landscape Inc., an 11-year-old landscaping company with 900 employees, has never had a traditional HR department. Instead, managers must balance renewing contracts and ensuring that a client's grass is cut to the proper height with hunting down talent at college recruiting sessions and teaching employees about the company's 401(k) plan.
>
> CEO Craig Ruppert said the decentralized structure fosters autonomy and accountability among leaders across the company,

which is based in Laytonsville, Md., and covers markets from Philadelphia to Atlanta. He estimates that its managers spend 5% of their time on matters related to human resources.

"I just have a hard time understanding how somebody in an office two or four states away can do a better job of solving an employee problem than someone who has a vested interest in the employee," Mr. Ruppert said.[50]

Naturally HR academics and specialists warn that eliminating the HR department opens the business up to legal and regulatory hazards. The article continues:

"Whenever you consider eliminating portions of HR you have to think of the financial risk, the strategic risk," said Steve Miranda, the managing director of Cornell University's Center for Advanced Human Resource Studies and a former HR executive at Lucent Technologies, now part of Alcatel-Lucent.

Managers often lack specialized knowledge that is crucial for keeping a company competitive and on the right side of the law, he said. If they don't understand the latest rules under the Family and Medical Leave Act, for example, they can open their company up to lawsuits; if they don't know where to find qualified engineers, they can end up behind in the battle for talent.

But as we will see, there's ample evidence that one current HR practice—screening applications using ATS (Applicant Tracking Systems) that filter resumes and applications for skill keywords—does a terrible job of identifying and attracting engineering talent. Most hiring still comes through personal and industry contacts. HR departments may be worse than useless as recruiters—they sometimes actively repel the best applicants.

Looking at the services provided, HR staff are often now just intermediaries between software systems like ATSs and the managers and employees needing their help. There's not a lot of functional difference between the HR staff person who comes by in person but has next to no knowledge of the business activity and some online video counseling service who understands the employment law and regulation just as thoroughly but costs half as much as full-time on-site staff. Companies that have tried to push all HR work back to managers have found themselves in legal trouble:

> Outback Steakhouse, a unit of Bloomin' Brands Inc., had no HR department before 2008 but created one not long after the Equal Employment Opportunity Commission sued the restaurant chain for sex discrimination. In 2009, Outback paid $19 million to settle the case and agreed to add an executive-level HR position.

> Interpersonal issues must be handled differently when HR isn't around to mediate. Klick Health, a Toronto-based marketing agency focused on health care, has forgone a human-resources department partly in favor of two "concierges," employees with customer-service backgrounds whose job is to create what CEO Leerom Segal calls a "frictionless" work experience for employees.

> For the concierges, that means chores ranging from setting up mentoring sessions and career-development paths to picking up a birthday gift for a worker's spouse.

> When co-workers can't stand each other or employees aren't clicking with their managers, Mr. Segal expects them to work it out themselves. "We ask senior leaders to recognize any potential chemistry issues" early on, he said, and move people to different teams if those issues can't be resolved quickly.

> Former Klick employees applaud the creative thinking that drives its culture, but say they sometimes felt like they were on their own there. Neville Thomas, a program director at Klick until 2013, occasionally had to discipline or terminate his direct reports. Without an HR team, he said, he worried about liability.

> "There's no HR department to coach you," he said. "When you have an HR person, you have a point of contact that's confidential."

Clearly, when HR departments are eliminated managers need more help and guidance. But in the future, companies will retain outside firms and find other innovative ways to keep their HR departments small and focused on higher-level workforce planning. We'll return to the subject of downsizing and streamlining the HR function in the chapter on Future HR.

Information on the staffing of HR departments themselves is not easy to come by. HR-focused writings tend toward academic Social Justice gobbledygook, and commonly-observed dominance of HR staffing by women and academics is hard to confirm with hard data from individual companies, though there are some statistics collected at the national level in the US. Historically, Personnel departments were staffed by the same type of people one would find in accounting or finance—clerks and paperwork handlers—but the managers tended to be male (as they were for other corporate functions.) As Personnel became HR and HR-specific degree programs began to appear, hiring shifted to people who had studied HR as a field—with simple organizational psychology, benefits law, and concepts of social equity and diversity baked in to new graduates. What did not get studied so thoroughly was economics, technology, specific types of business knowledge, or statistics. HR graduates today are trained in a party line Social Justice ideology which sets them up as enforcers of government edicts on diversity, with less emphasis on ideals of merit and productivity that would promote the competitiveness of the business they are supposedly helping to direct.

Business advisor Ram Charan noted that typical HR managers had little perspective on the overall business, as he wrote in the Harvard Business Review:

> But it's a rare CHRO [Chief Human Resources Officer] who can serve in such an active role. Most of them are process-oriented generalists who have expertise in personnel benefits, compensation, and labor relations. They are focused on internal matters such as engagement, empowerment, and managing cultural issues. What they can't do very well is relate HR to real-world business needs. They don't know how key decisions are made, and they have great difficulty analyzing why people—or whole parts of the organization

—aren't meeting the business's performance goals.

Among the few CHROs who do know, I almost always find a
common distinguishing quality: they have worked in line operations
—such as sales, services, or manufacturing—or in finance. The
celebrated former CHRO of GE, Bill Conaty, was a plant manager
before Jack Welch brought him into HR. Conaty weighed in on key
promotions and succession planning, working hand in glove with
Welch in a sweeping overhaul of the company. Mary Anne Elliott,
the CHRO of Marsh, had had several managerial roles outside HR.
She is overhauling the HR pipeline to bring in other people with
business experience. Santrupt Misra, who left Hindustan Unilever to
join Aditya Birla Group in 1996, became a close partner of the
chairman, Kumar Mangalam Birla, working on organization and
restructuring and developing P&L managers. He runs a $2 billion
business as well as heading HR at the $45 billion conglomerate.[51]

Charan's observation is that effective HR heads came out of business
operations, not from academic programs with a social sciences and
labor-influenced background. But new HR hires are now low-paid
(relative to engineers and sales) and inexperienced recent graduates
who have limited understanding of the business, its products, and
competitive markets. Such people will likely have no difficulty
believing in the gender "pay gap" because they themselves have jobs
in a kind of feminine and minority ghetto within the company, where
most of their fellow HR staff believe in affirmative action and social
justice efforts as a moral crusade. One lesson from this tendency: if
you are staffing up your own company's HR department, start at the
top with someone who is deeply experienced in your business and
will hire HR staff who demonstrate a commitment to making the best
products with the best people to survive and profit in a competitive
marketplace. "Activist" HR staff who see your business as a platform
for doing social work—who want to mold your employees to promote
social welfare and support social justice causes—will gradually dull
your company's competitive edge and in the long run destroy it.
Overseas competitors, especially Asian companies, will not be as

hampered by hiring policies designed to right social wrongs.

We'll look later at how the Federal Equal Employment Opportunity Commission (EEOC) is top-heavy with blacks and women, showing that the EEOC itself is not achieving statistical representation or diversity. The same is true of their internal enforcers, the HR departments. The Bureau of Labor Statistics (BLS) collects statistics on occupations and shows this data for 2015:[52]

HOUSEHOLD DATA
ANNUAL AVERAGES
11. **Employed persons by detailed occupation, sex, race, and Hispanic or Latino ethnicity**
[Numbers in thousands]

		2015			
			Percent of total employed		
Occupation	Total employed	Women	Black or African American	Asian	Hispanic or Latino
Total, 16 years and over	148,834	46.8	11.7	5.8	16.4
Management, professional, and related occupations	57,060	51.5	9.2	7.7	9.1
Management, business, and financial operations occupations	24,108	43.6	8.2	6.3	9.4
Management occupations	16,094	39.2	7.3	5.8	9.7
Chief executives	1,517	27.9	3.6	4.7	5.5
General and operations managers	899	27.6	6.9	4.7	10.8
Legislators	13	...	...	...	...
Advertising and promotions managers	87	53.5	0.0	5.0	6.6
Marketing and sales managers	1,006	43.2	6.2	6.6	9.7
Public relations and fundraising managers	81	59.2	10.6	5.2	5.6
Administrative services managers	195	47.7	9.9	3.0	7.2
Computer and information systems managers	652	27.2	5.6	14.2	4.8
Financial managers	1,197	49.6	7.2	7.9	9.4
Compensation and benefits managers	23	...	...	...	...
Human resources managers	290	73.3	11.9	2.2	10.8
Training and development managers	41	...	...	...	...
⋮					
Claims adjusters, appraisers, examiners, and investigators	321	65.3	14.6	3.1	10.4
Compliance officers	248	49.0	11.4	4.2	9.5
Cost estimators	112	17.8	0.4	3.2	8.1
Human resources workers	682	74.0	15.4	4.9	10.7
Compensation, benefits, and job analysis specialists	58	73.0	14.1	6.9	8.4
Training and development specialists	118	62.1	19.7	2.0	7.0
Logisticians	117	40.9	14.4	4.2	20.2
Management analysts	848	39.7	9.3	10.1	5.9
Meeting, convention, and event planners	159	78.6	11.1	5.5	12.3
Fundraisers	77	73.4	7.2	1.1	1.9
Market research analysts and marketing specialists	251	58.8	4.8	6.9	9.7
Business operations specialists, all other	213	56.7	9.2	7.0	9.0
Accountants and auditors	1,732	59.7	9.5	11.3	7.4
Appraisers and assessors of real estate	76	33.3	5.9	0.9	3.9
Budget analysts	44	...	...	...	...
Credit analysts	21	...	...	...	...
Financial analysts	322	43.0	11.1	16.2	8.4
Personal financial advisors	438	37.9	7.6	7.4	9.4
Insurance underwriters	107	55.6	8.9	5.6	5.3
Financial examiners	15	...	...	...	...

Notice that women dominate the HR profession—with above-70% representation in both management and staff of HR. Blacks, meanwhile, don't do quite as well in HR management—but are overrepresented by 30-40% at lower levels.

This is US-economy-wide, of course, and individual companies and industries may diverge from these averages further. It is a common observation, for example, that Silicon Valley companies have even more female-centric HR staffs. And as at the EEOC, Latinos remain underrepresented in both HR management and staff.

When your HR rep comes to tell your team that you have to give preference to minority and female hires, ask them when HR staffs will recruit enough men, Asians, and Latinos to achieve true equity and diversity.

Some HR professionals decry the female ghettoization of HR. James R. Landrith, a male HR professional, wrote of his experience as a male in a female-dominated role:

> For years, men did rule the HR world as most companies could not see a female employee outside of the administrative ranks, food service or cleaning help. As the profession transitioned from "personnel" to "human resources" the gender mix tilted out of balance. I don't particularly view this imbalance as negative or positive. It simply is the reality....

> As a man working in a field heavily dominated by women, it can be both a challenge and an advantage. I've been dismissed or treated as a nuisance as the sole male in a given group by a female supervisor who was quite happy to develop her female subordinates, while doing her best to alienate or ignore me....

> The reactions from employees outside of HR departments have been the most dramatic. Quite often, they are surprised when the "new HR" is a man or they wonder if I am "from corporate." I work hard to win the trust and respect of the people who depend on me to assist them with their concerns or interpret policy and ensure it is enforced fairly. My gender is not key to my success in human resources work, but it is obvious to employees that I am different. After over a decade of HR experience, I am still contacted periodically by employees from prior locations and even former employers. Often, they just need a friendly ear to listen to them vent or they want to pick my brain regarding an issue that is bugging them. That is about building trust and confidence—not gender.

> ... The assumption that women are naturally more compassionate and maternal when in positions of power or authority is quickly dispatched when dealing with an authoritarian type in a human

resources role. There are plenty of women who operate under that philosophy while performing their duties. I've encountered them in supervisory roles or as peers.[53]

Stereotypes and generalizations about female-dominated organizations would suggest that they are more emotional, less logical; more safety-oriented and less willing to take risks to accomplish higher goals; more likely to talk out feelings than to act; and more cliquish and petty, and less likely to focus on the larger goals of the organization.[54] Of course these generalizations are untrue of many specific women in HR roles, but Ben Eubanks writing as a young male HR professional comments:

> I can still remember the first time I walked into a NASHRM event and looked around. There were about a hundred people in the room. Of that number the six guys (including me) stuck out like sore thumbs. It kind of made me laugh, because I've never worked in a job where the men outnumbered the women. It doesn't really bother me, but I've always been a little curious about why the imbalance occurs.
>
> I don't want to lay any blanket statements on the ladies out there, but my little experience seems to point to most of them focusing on compliance and how to keep things "safe." More of the males, however, seem to be focused on how to keep the goals moving forward and holding onto the strategic focus.
>
> Like I said, I don't like blanket statements and generalities, because I've certainly met dozens of female HR pros with a high strategic focus. However, due to the high percentage of women overall, there certainly are a lot of them who are doing that compliance work...[55]

Some HR professionals are quite happy with female dominance and see it as a natural result of stereotypically feminine strengths in nurturing and empathy. Male writer John Sumser hyperventilates at HR Examiner:

HR is the only predominantly female function in the contemporary organization. It is the beach head of accomplishment in the generational move of women from home to the executive suite. While the oft-repeated stereotype is that men are HR's decision makers, the truth is that women occupy two-thirds of the HR executive seats.

It's useful to imagine that the people who populate the HR Department are heroes. The function provides work, upward mobility and access to the heart of organizational culture for a class of people with little organizational history.

Being a fundamentally female function, HR behaves differently than other parts of the organization. It's more networky and can be nurturing. It's natural that development is housed here.

The essence of HR might be its ability to make clear judgments about really intangible things like personality, potential and match-making. These are stereotypical female things.[56]

Some men feel discriminated against when their initial interviews for a position are with mostly white HR women who aren't knowledgeable about the work:

The job I have now—I was interviewed by a white male, a white female, and a black female all at once and I was obviously hired, but 95% of the time its just a pure wall of white women whom I am apparently unable to please. It is just awful—men are screwed in this society, even with education. I have a 4yr degree, but they hire white girls at my job right out of high school and they pay them more than me—despite my education and seniority.

I try to leave my job and look for other ones because it's so unfair—yet [at] every job I apply to [there is] an army of white women who think, "you're not a good fit." I feel that I am being judged on criteria that I don't understand. I am a good employee, I have worked at my current job for over a year, you would think an employer would see that and say, "hey, he's dedicated," but nope. It's awful—men need employment but we try and try and try and get nowhere.[57]

Another dark side of female HR dominance is increasing discrimination against some female applicants. It turns out women who screen applications have a tendency to forward handsome men for further interviews and reject beautiful women (who might compete too successfully with them in the workplace-as-hunting-ground):

> In an experiment that involved sending out more than 2,500 resumes either with or without photos of the applicant, economics researchers Bradley Ruffle at Ben-Gurion University and Ze'ev Shtudiner at Ariel University Centre sought to answer the question of whether being good looking could help you find a job. The answer surprised them: Not if you're a woman. Pretty women faced an uphill struggle to get a chance at a job.

> The economists hadn't reckoned on the fact that 93 percent of the HR staffers deciding whether to call in someone for an interview were female. It turns out that HR women (who also tend to be young and single and hence still in the dating market for men) are eager to meet with handsome men. But they're jealous of beautiful women. So your business is losing out on talented people (and wasting time with untalented ones) based on their looks.[58]

Some feminists suggest high-performing women have been slotted in HR roles as a means of shunting them off the CEO track.[59] It has become a self-fulfilling prophecy—as women came to dominate HR departments, HR has come to be viewed as a pink-collar ghetto, a feminized and lower-status department from which few would graduate into the highest levels of management. As managers from the rest of the company rise, they see HR as a nuisance that does more to impair their work than assist, and so when they become CEOs and members of the board, they continue to see HR as a necessary evil and not a source of competent and effective executives.

The reasons for the disparity and the gender imbalances [in HR] remain open for debate, as does the impact created by the imbalances. For some, it is a taboo subject that stretches the limits of political correctness and therefore is only marginally discussed. For others, the imbalance is profoundly important and demands further discussion and research.... Willock (2007) states that "75% entry of women into HR is too high, and you get the sense that something is wrong here." Other comments from HR executives interviewed for Willock's article ranged between moderate concerns with the high percentages, to an alarming concern that this should be a burning issue that needs to be addressed... there are varying opinions as to whether or not the high numbers even matter. Some believe that the imbalance may hurt the profession in ways that cannot be clearly validated, and might be speculative at best. Are women, for example, hiring their own into the profession because of a certain comfort level within the majority? Or is it simply because men see the profession as a matriarchal stronghold designed to nurture and administrate, while offering little in the way of power and advancement?[60]

HR departments in many companies have been "captured" by the political forces outside the company that regulate labor, punish violations with fines and public shaming, and pressure companies into paying off diversity activists looking for support for their causes and sinecures for their political allies. The increasing complexity of regulations and government enforcement has, as in academia and hospitals, increased the number of deadweight HR employees needed to handle administration. Like the commissars and parallel political officers of the old USSR, HR functionaries are unconsciously acting not only for managements wanting managers to avoid legal and ethical trouble, but also for governments reaching into the organization to achieve political goals and promote government control of private businesses. Smart managements will neutralize these tendencies by paying close attention to attitudes and activities of HR managers and staff. While companies need to avoid trouble with governments, they need the best employees and competitive products and services to survive and thrive.

In the Gender Pay Gap chapter we argued that the "women make only 77 cents on the dollar" aggregate statistic is due to women's choices of field, type of work, and desire to take time off for raising children. One of the counter-arguments is that female-dominated fields are paid less because of some sort of systemic discrimination. The Patriarchy has decided to pay less in those fields because they are dominated by women...!

Aside from the impracticality of such a conspiracy—implying the free market in labor somehow fails, forcing workers in those fields to accept lower pay instead of moving on to more lucrative opportunities—there's some truth hiding in the claim. Fields dominated by women do tend to pay less. And there are a few examples where fields once male-oriented or at least balanced became female-dominated, and the average pay level dropped. Cause and effect? Or did the declining pay and improving security of these jobs lead them to become relatively more attractive to women looking for flexibility and more social workplaces?

Some examples of the phenomenon: 1) Public elementary school teaching, 2) Non-tenured higher education teaching, 3) Medical administrators, 4) HR administrators and staff (as we have seen).

The female dominance of elementary school teaching in the US was complete by 1900. Women were paid much less than men for the same teaching jobs—a result of real discrimination, and the sense that women would leave to marry and raise a family so their commitment was temporary. As a result, employing mostly young women as teachers became a cost-saving mechanism, and males left the field as salaries dropped and better opportunities with higher status and possibilities for advancement became available:

> The drive for universal education increased the demand for teachers and the associated costs of instruction, giving an advantage to

schools that hired female teachers. Female teachers were paid about half as much as their male counterparts in standardized schools (Grumet, p. 39). In fact, some scholars attest that "feminization occurred because school districts were unwilling or unable to pay the rising costs of retaining male teachers as school terms became longer and teaching became less attractive to men" (Rury, p. 27). The wage gap between the genders was smaller in rural schools, possibly because there were fewer qualified candidates to fill teaching positions. Rural and southern areas tended to have more informal teaching with less discrepancy between the salaries of male and female teachers, and had mostly male teachers or an equal balance of men and women (Strober and Lanford). In the 1800s, male teachers tended to remain in their positions longer than female teachers, which may explain some of the wage gap. Women often used teaching as a way to earn an income between their own adolescence and motherhood. Teaching began as a job that was expected to cover living expenses for a young, single person or to supplement other sources of income. As teaching became a women's career, the salary remained low even though a good number of female teachers never married and continued to teach.[61]

The era of young women teaching for a few years before marrying and leaving the job market ended when mothers generally began to work outside the home. For some period during that transition, female teachers were expected to leave teaching when they married even when they wanted to continue, which led some to hide their marital status. Primary-school teachers were never of high status, but their status dropped further when men almost entirely abandoned public school teaching (many male teachers continued to teach at private schools, where their autonomy and status were greater.)

By 1850, the feminization of teaching had taken hold, especially in urban areas. Feminization was not a preference of schools at first. "School committees often searched in vain for men teachers before finally hiring women.... One major concern was discipline," but separating classes by age in larger urban schools made discipline easier. The cost savings of female teachers may have been a result of feminization, rather than its cause. It was difficult for schools to find enough male teachers to fill all positions. "Teaching paid poorly compared with other jobs that men could get in urban areas, and the demands of teaching in big-city school systems--with eight months or more of school each year—precluded men teaching as a part-time job. Simultaneously, the nineteenth-century ideology of 'domestic feminism' limited the range of occupations to which young middle-class women could aspire." There was a dearth of willing men and a plethora of educated, young white women qualified to teach for low salaries....

Teaching became formalized, and the percentage of women increased from 1850 to 1900. Schooling in the more urban North was more formalized, with more female teachers and sharp pay differences between men and women. When schooling became formalized, female teachers were seen as very desirable because they were seen as cheap, as better teachers of young children, and as more willing to conform to the bureaucratization of schooling. Male principals were employed to deal with disciplinary problems that their female teachers were unable to handle....

The feminized state of teaching has been both a boon and a burden to the women who teach. Female teachers historically postponed or hid marriages to maintain their careers. It was not until the mid-1900s that married women were allowed to continue teaching, but when they did, it was a career that integrated relatively well with childrearing. The teaching schedule has excellent "mommy hours," with afternoons and evenings free, plus summer and winter vacations that correspond with children's vacations. Since there is less of a hierarchy among teachers, it is easier to take time off and then re-enter the workforce than it is with other careers. Unfortunately, the salary and prestige of teaching are very low, and the mother-friendly benefits of teaching may contribute to maintaining it as a low-prestige career. The teaching hours and part-year schedule are well suited to women with children, making the profession fit easily into traditional women's lives, but this has contributed to the feminization of the profession, leading to lower salaries and prestige. Teaching also has a relatively low retention rate compared to other occupations, especially for women. "Those who defected were mainly wealthier, smarter, and more often married than those who continued to teach."[62]

The bureaucratization of a profession—with limited autonomy but greater security and reduced and more flexible hours, plus the ease of taking time off and moving between positions allowed by certification requirements and uncompetitive salaries—encourages female dominance. Highly-competitive, high-paying, performance-oriented occupations remained more difficult both to enter and succeed in, so the path of least resistance for a woman wanting a family-friendly career remained entry to one of the regulated fields where cooperative skills and consensus were more important than measurable productivity, and the pay reflected that.

Publishing is another field where women have come to dominate an industry—as in teaching, by the 1960s "There was a dearth of willing men and a plethora of educated, young white women qualified to [do editorial work] for low salaries."[63] Publishing had always employed large numbers of women in clerical and lower-level positions though men dominated editorial, managerial, and sales jobs. This began to change rapidly in the 1960s, and by the 1990s publishing was dominated by women, until today every part of the industry is female-dominated, from agents to editors to even authors. It's often noted that the reading of books also became a primarily female-associated activity during that period, with women buying and reading far more books than men to the point where female-favored genres like romance outsell all other fiction.

Job Queues, Gender Queues: Explaining Women's Inroads Into Male Occupations by Barbara F. Reskin and Patricia A. Roos has a detailed history of the rapid evolution of publishing from a male-dominated to a female-dominated industry, tracing it to factors including the increasing size and commercialization of the consolidating publishing companies and the historically low pay in the industry which discouraged men from entry while allowing upper-class educated white women to take it over from below:

Caplette observed that "the gradual increase of women editors in the last decade [the 1970s] has, within the last few years, become an upsurge—nearly half of trade and mass-market paperback editors are now women." Confirming her impressions are those of more than forty industry informants who agreed that the 1970s brought dramatic progress for women in editing and other publishing jobs.

Although women advanced in many occupations in the 1970s, their gains in editing outstripped those in most other occupations.... I found that changes in the publishing industry and the editorial role set the stage for women's gains by altering both the supply of male would-be editors and the demand for women....

For most of this century, publishing's glamour and its image as a "gentlemen's profession' were sufficient to attract more than enough qualified recruits. Then, although industrial expansion heightened the demand for editorial workers, the concomitants of that growth reduced the industry's attractiveness to its traditional workforce: talented young men from high socioeconomic backgrounds.

Dwindling attraction for men. Publishing's primary draw for such men had been entree into the world of culture without the taint of commerce. But commerce is exactly what outside ownership meant. At the same time, as we have seen, editorial work lost many of the features that had compensated nonwealthy workers for low wages. To make matters worse, commerce was supplanting culture without conferring the usual economic incentives of commercial careers. Although editorial wages had always been low, there were other compensations. One editor said, "I consider the right to publish books which don't make money a part of my salary." Just as some editors lost that right, wages may have actually declined. In 1982, entry-level pay for editorial assistants was as low as an $9,000 a year, and several people I interviewed noted that it is increasingly difficult, perhaps impossible, to survive—much less support a family—in Manhattan on editorial wages. An industry expert said, only partly in jest: "Only college graduates with rich parents willing to subsidize them can afford to work in editorial jobs any more." In the face of society's growing emphasis on a fashionable life-style and the increasing tendency to use income as "the measure of a man," publishing's low wages further deterred men from pursuing editorial jobs. Better-paying media jobs (technical writing for high-tech companies, corporate public relations, advertising) and graduate school lured away talented men interested in communications.

With declining opportunities for mobility and challenges to the traditional promotion practices that had given men a fast track to the top, little remained to draw men to editorial work. A woman editor...in 1978 remarked, "The average man thinks that he has a God-given right to start in as an editor." To the extent that this was true, entry-level jobs as editorial assistants (often a euphemism for secretary when these were women's jobs) attracted few men, and the industry increasingly relied on women as editorial assistants.

Increasing supply of women. The gentility that had rendered publishing jobs appropriate for upper-status men did so too for "respectable" women whom traditional values encouraged to pursue cultural and aesthetic pursuits. As a long-time assistant at Harper & Brothers said, "Young women getting out of college were so anxious to get a job in something they could be proud of that they would go into publishing and work for practically nothing." Gender-role socialization further enhanced women's qualifications for publishing by schooling them in verbal and communications skills that equipped them with the facility and inclination to work with words and predisposed them toward the interpersonal work that editing often involved. One female holder of a master's degree said of her secretarial job in the mid-1950s, "I thought it was an honor to read books and write... flap copy." Working in an intellectual and cultural industry situated in one of the metropolitan publishing "capitals" offered an added incentive to women graduating from prestigious eastern colleges, particularly before the 1970s, when few alternatives presented themselves to career-minded women.

The massive influx of women into the labor force during the 1970s expanded the pool of women available for editorial jobs, and the women's liberation movement encouraged women to consider occupations customarily reserved for men. Publishing attracted women also because it reputedly presented fewer obstacles than many other industries. Moreover, male occupations in predominantly female industries—particularly growing industries— tend to be more hospitable and hence more attractive to women. Thus, although women knew they faced discrimination in publishing, they probably realized that other commercial fields were worse. Publishing's low wages were less likely to deter women than men because their socialization had not encouraged them to maximize income. Because women lacked access to many better-paying jobs, they did not have to forgo more lucrative opportunities for jobs as assistants or editors, and their limited alternatives presumably also explained their willingness to accept the changes that were making editorial work less desirable to men. As a result, the supply of female applicants remained unabated or grew, while that of males declined. Moreover, several interviewees contended that because publishing could no longer attract the most qualified men, female applicants often had better credentials than the males who did apply. If publishers chose the best applicant (as the new emphasis on profits dictated), it would probably be a woman....

In other words, women became attractive to publishers because of their literary and interpersonal skills, their presumed ability to read for a largely female readership, and their expertise in growing segments of the industry—and because they would work cheap. These factors, combined with their availability as a surplus labor pool that could be readily drawn into the workforce, made women an acceptable solution to publishing's economic fluctuations.[64]

As publishing grew to be dominated by upper-class white women, it also came to be dominated by progressive feminists—of both sexes. Not all women in publishing are third-wave feminists, but many are, and like the Ivy League males they replaced, they view their power to get politically-progressive but uncommercial books published as a partial compensation for their low-paid and otherwise low-autonomy jobs. The industry relies on a cheap labor pool of new graduates hoping for an entry into more stable, higher-paying tenured editorial jobs, much as academia now relies on low-paid, abused adjunct teachers. The last of the older generation of editors and managers is leaving now, which leaves the legacy publishing industry with few editorial workers who understand more typical American families and blue-collar or male values. Those small and contrarian publishers who put out books of more interest to mainstream readers and men, like the Hollywood producers that made a bundle on the movie *American Sniper*—which respectfully told the morally-complex story of a Texas-based sniper in Iraq and the aftermath of his service—have discovered that big publishing's neglect of this large audience makes it much more profitable to serve it.

Jason Pinter, bestselling thriller writer, discovered this downside when, working as an editor, he could get no support for a male-attracting book:

> In an essay from late April, Pinter describes how (during his days in publishing) he attempted to acquire a book by professional wrestler Chris Jericho. His efforts almost failed for lack of men in the acquisitions meeting, he says—if one colleague's 15-year-old nephew hadn't been a wrestling fan, the book wouldn't have made it through. It was "the fault of a system in which in a room of 15-20 people, not one of them knew what I was talking about…"[65]

The same type of less-competitive, bureaucracy-tolerant, socially-oriented person has gone into HR as a field, studying sociology, psychology, and diversity, while employing personal relationships to make their way up in a field where results are very hard to quantify. The lower salaries in HR keep more effective thought-leaders from entering, yet companies continue to increase HR staff without realizing that they are bringing in people who don't highly value excellence or competitive success. And the result has been emphasis on diversity and harmony over long-term growth and profit. Companies that carefully screen their HR staff and keep the focus on necessary business activity will have a competitive advantage and avoid the long-term decline a politicized HR department will cause.

So modern HR departments are risk-averse, feminized, and tend to know little about the technical requirements of jobs they are recruiting for while screening out promising candidates liberal arts majors don't like. Perhaps the degree programs feeding industry new "HR professionals" are at fault? Let's investigate...

Here's a typical outline of what an HR degree program should include :

General Education and Business Courses—In the first and second years of the program... HR majors will usually need to take at least three credits of coursework in mathematics, statistics, English, writing, communications, history, political science, psychology, and social science... Since human resources professionals are given the responsibility of motivating employees, adhering to federal regulations, and developing successful workplaces, having sound business knowledge is a must. HR majors will likely have to complete introductory courses in business administration, finance, management, accounting, marketing, and business law.

Major Human Resources Coursework—... According to the SHRM curriculum guidebook, required content areas will include labor relations, employment law, ethics, globalization, job analysis, workplace diversity, organizational behavior, performance management, staffing, recruitment, strategic HR, compensation and benefits, training development, talent management, and workforce planning. In some cases, undergraduate programs will also deal with secondary content areas like career planning, human resource information systems, mergers and acquisitions, corporate social responsibility, outscoring, and workplace health....[66]

One clue is that HR degree programs necessarily train students on compliance with labor laws and government mandates on diversity and equal opportunity, since a primary function of HR departments is to direct managers to avoid triggering punishments and lawsuits for violating those directives. But this means many HR program faculty come out of labor law and have picked up the tendency[67] of labor lawyers and economists to favor union and anti-free-market ideals.

Democratic and union-supported political machines further this bias by funding anti-business academic centers like the Labor Center at UC Berkeley:[68]

> One of the ongoing stains on the integrity of the University of California system is its publicly funded labor institutes. They are union-controlled "think tanks" that are about engaging in left-wing political activism rather than balanced thinking. They churn out one-sided studies that provide fodder for union political objectives. Their most recent efforts gave cover to California's decision to boost the minimum wage to $15 an hour by 2022....

> Universities are rightly home to varying ideologies and research. But it's wrong to publicly fund a think tank that engages in bald-faced advocacy for one particular group. ... it's really disturbing to suggest these think tanks provide "various ideas" about anything. They provide ideas with the union stamp of approval.

> "Far from what should be expected from academia, the institute doesn't even hint at a non-partisan agenda and regularly not only trains union organizers (presumably for political purposes) but also authors biased studies," wrote the Howard Jarvis Taxpayers Association's legislative director... Note the people behind this effort: labor leaders, community activists, a labor-allied former legislator, state labor lobbyists. Check out the advisory board at the UC Berkeley Labor Center. Virtually every member has a union affiliation. As Harper rightly notes, they are "partisan operations."

> State funding has been controversial, but the institute still receives direct public funding. It's also dismaying seeing UC's reputation sullied by such priorities. But the real problem is the nature of the

research—and the effect it has on political debates across California.

"A new study found that a quarter of the region's workforce would see a 20 percent pay bump if Santa Clara County upped the minimum hourly wage to $15 by 2019," according to a report last week in a San Jose business publication. The county paid $100,000 to —you guessed it—a labor institute to provide such a rosy prediction. The study gave like-minded elected officials political cover.

I first came across the [labor] institutes in 2010 when the Berkeley institute produced a study suggesting that public-sector workers receive lower overall compensation than private-sector workers, despite their exceedingly generous pensions. I consulted experts and was astounded by its shortcomings. Take a look at the titles of institute studies. They drip with union bias.

California unions have myriad financial privileges. The state automatically deducts dues payments from public members. Workers must join the union to keep their jobs. Unions are the most powerful lobbies in Sacramento. If they want to produce research that backs their point of view, good for them. But why should taxpayers fund it? [69]

Labor law and economics departments and researchers are primarily funded by governments and labor unions that are biased toward increasing labor regulations, which in turn builds a larger empire for compliance staff—both in government and HR, where HR staffers act as their enforcement arm. This means academic HR training is also heavily biased toward regulation, and it's rare for a new HR hire trained by such a program to wholeheartedly embrace the values of management for profit in a free market. It's no surprise that people in charge of training others for a field believe their field is important and tend to want it to enlarge its scope of authority—which increases the status and power of those already high in its ranks.

But this means hiring a new HR staffer graduated from an HR degree program is more than likely hiring someone more committed to "social justice" than to your organization's success, with an inherent conflict of interest—they will identify with the regulators more than the organization that pays their salary, and cooperate with likeminded careerists both in government and in your own organization to neglect goals of competitive efficiency. HR staffers will often support each other's politicized progressive views and bias their decisions toward hiring mediocre employees they favor for cultural and diversity reasons while making life difficult for ornery but productive workers who don't do as well sucking up to them. Management neglect—"it's not important, it's just HR"—lets HR progressives have a free hand, and they can slowly sink your company, then move on to the next with their credentials intact to repeat the process.

Not only do HR staff tend to have internalized progressive and labor values, they also have little subject area knowledge when screening potential hires, recommending people who don't have deep understanding and screening out those who do using superficial degree and certification requirements.

This problem is quietly recognized in many companies, where candidates are theoretically brought to a hiring manager's attention by HR after advertising and outreach, but where in practice hiring managers wisely ignore HR's candidate lists to bring in people they have found themselves through industry contacts and their own more knowledgeable searches. If it were not for that, HR's hiring screens would have crippled many corporations long ago, and this internal battle continues as HR responds to political pressure to reach diversity goals by trying to limit hiring managers' ability to select the best hires. Resistance to these mandates continues as companies issue press releases on their success at improving diversity while pragmatic managers route around HR. A FEE article by Harrison Burge sums it up:

> While HR employees may be equipped to attract talent, this is only one-half of their economic problem. The other half, the one in which HR is ill-equipped, is the process to secure (hire) these resources-specialized labor across a multitude of job functions—despite not

understanding specific skills and relative importance of these skills to respective hiring managers.

In this respect, HR and their algorithms serve as central planning commissars, devoid of the feedback and knowledge needed to approve or disapprove candidate hiring for the company's departments. As technical innovation and the development of required skillsets to fill these openings inevitably continues, the service provided by the traditional, centralized HR hiring department to their coworkers in specialized, technical departments may suffer.

The contrast between HR departments, whose foremost objective is compliance with government regulations and whose structure reflects the bureaucracy that they enshrine, and companies' other lean, innovative departments could not be more stark. Government interventions in HR have the unintended consequences of burdening companies' other departments, which operate not according to government dictates, but solely based upon profit and loss.[70]

These pressures increase the dead weight of bureaucracy inside the company while distracting management from the focus necessary for survival and competitive success. We would think it intolerable to be saddled with a Chinese Communist Party political officer who made sure the party songs were sung and banners displayed in the office—but we see the wall of labor law disclosures and politically-driven slogans and decrees foisted on us by the Party of Government as normal. The cynical management view—that it's just a cost of doing business, to be ignored and avoided—has allowed a gradual increase in these directives until they are seriously compromising productivity.

It's true that many HR professionals are working hard to support their organization's business strategy—these would be the very best of HR who look beyond compliance toward a more complete view of the business goals. These HR managers are valuable, tend to have come from operations and not out of an explicit HR degree program, and have some insight into the business and technical staff concerns. They are worth the higher salaries they tend to command. CEOs and boards make their worst mistake in hiring lower-cost degreed-but-mediocre drones for HR, thinking this important function—which in the long run determines the productivity of the teams that make up the engineering and production staff—is just a cost center to be minimized. This book is not directed at the many dedicated, business-oriented HR professionals, but the tide of drones replacing them in less alert businesses.

Until the bursting of the dotcom bubble in 2000, Silicon Valley firms, at least, were able to call on specialized recruiters who had themselves been engineers and could recognize quality candidates. That business dried up after the bubble burst, and almost all of those knowledgeable veteran recruiters retired, to be replaced as the tech industry recovered by low-cost but incompetent recruiters who scanned resumes and cold-called working prospects to try to drum up business. Being unwilling to pay for quality in a critical function—recruiting—also costs more in the long run.

I'll quote directly from one anonymous veteran of corporate HR:

> ... the induced bias you discuss is recognized by quite a few HR managers as well as line managers. The 64-dollar question is what to do about it. In the Fortune 500 company where I worked in HR we called it "antiquing the rookie". Most made it; a few did not. However, my point is that it took consciousness of the problem and specific actions to overcome it.

> It is interesting to me that you mention the UCB Labor Center. I actually found their various papers useful in training staff about the unspoken (and unsound) assumptions contained therein, appeals to emotion rather than objective analysis, statistical legerdemain, etc. That and the reading of cases (particularly EO matters). Particularly with new staff, the request to "tell me how that (oil/gas/chemical) unit works (I found, by the way, that not a few engineers were stumped by those questions, and I found they were generally gone in a year or two).[71]

This points again to the malign influence of academic labor-progressive ideas which teach students in HR degree programs to see their role as doing good for society, with doing the best job for the business employing them as an afterthought. That new HR staff have to be disabused of these notions and re-educated to start to contribute means the degree programs are not training for the realities of corporate life, and smart employers might avoid HR degree program graduates in favor of more general business degrees. The prejudices HR program graduates have absorbed are actively harmful to your business.

Academic training in HR assumes that business revenue streams are secure and that HR's job is to distribute the wealth fairly. Federal and state labor regulation is assumed to be reasonable, though an occasional particularly damaging new regulation will be fought; one correspondent pointed to the SHRM's (Society of Human Resource Managers') opposition to the Labor Department's new FLSA salary threshold regs (viewed as damaging business by greatly increasing the number of employees subject to overtime rules) as evidence that HR managers do recognize the negative effects of excess regulations. But they do on the whole accept the regulations already in place, which are well beyond anything imagined by the Founders as a power of the Federal government authorized in the Constitution. The era of progressive command-and-control regulation, which has gradually sapped the growth of the economy, will continue so long as companies continue to hire HR staff who believe in such regulations.

Part Three

Affirmative Action

Affirmative Action (AA) was an outgrowth of the Civil Rights movement in the United States (1954-68), which culminated in the passage of the Civil Rights Act of 1968. The term was first used in US law in President John F. Kennedy's Executive Order 10925 signed in 1961,

> ...which included a provision that government contractors "take affirmative action to ensure that applicants are employed, and employees are treated during employment, without regard to their race, creed, color, or national origin." In 1967, gender was added to the anti-discrimination list. In 1989, the International Convention on the Elimination of All Forms of Racial Discrimination stipulated (in Article 2.2) that affirmative action programs may be required of countries that ratified the convention, in order to rectify systematic discrimination. It also states that such programs "shall in no case entail as a consequence the maintenance of unequal or separate rights for different racial groups after the objectives for which they were taken have been achieved."[72]

As originally envisioned, affirmative action was intended to reform the previous institutional discrimination against blacks and other disfavored minorities by making special efforts to recruit them and increasing their representation in higher education, company workforces, and government employment. The ultimate goal was colorblind treatment—to establish equality of opportunity for all. At that time, the end of such "temporary" policies was foreseen as a generation or two away, when the need for such special treatment would have faded away as systemic racism and sexism would have been overcome and equal opportunity restored.

In the United States, affirmative action was first applied to racial discrimination in part to redress the wrong of slavery and Jim Crow laws in the South, but then extended to other minorities and women.

India attempted to reduce the unfairness of the caste system there by implementing quotas and set-asides. Malaysian policy reserves special benefits for ethnic Malays,[73] in an effort to reduce the dominance of ethnic Chinese and Indians in the economy.

In each of these cases, affirmative action had damaging side-effects. Beneficiary groups were often poorly-defined, with racial preferences in the US often assisting relatively privileged people whose families in many cases had recently immigrated and who had never suffered from the cultural and economic oppression of slavery. Cynics started to assume all new hires who might have benefitted from AA were less qualified (as indeed, on average, they were), a stigma which prevented even the beneficiaries from feeling totally responsible for their own successes. As AA programs aged and became institutional sacred cows, some minorities (like Asians) were dropped from the classes being favored, AA became more controversial, and a backlash began.

In 1978, the Supreme Court ruled in University of California v. Bakke that racial quotas were impermissible as a violation of the Equal Protection Clause of the Fourteenth Amendment, but that a candidate's race could be considered as one factor in achieving a more diverse student body. In 2003, the Supreme Court ruled again that race could be considered as a factor, though narrowing its use further. Race preferences in admission became a political football, with public institutions trying to hide the extent to which they discriminated against Asian and white candidates in favor of blacks and Latinos because they knew the programs were political poison. In the meantime, sex discrimination had more than disappeared in college admissions, with the majority of admitted and graduating students at most universities now female; some have called for affirmative action programs to benefit males since they now are well below 50% of enrollments.

Once entrenched, affirmative action policies become business as usual, with any change to them threatening the status quo. Once seen as temporary, AA is used to justify a Progressive activist push to equalize the numbers of women and 'approved' minorities in any business or occupation that is considered desirable, while ignoring disparities elsewhere.

We'll start our survey of affirmative action around the world with a look at the EEOC, where women and blacks are overrepresented, but legal competence is a lower priority.

In the US, the Equal Employment Opportunities Commission (EEOC) is the executive agency which enforces the employment antidiscrimination laws:

> The EEOC was established on July 2, 1965; its mandate is specified under Title VII of the Civil Rights Act of 1964, the Age Discrimination in Employment Act of 1967 (ADEA), the Rehabilitation Act of 1973, the Americans with Disabilities Act (ADA) of 1990, and the ADA Amendments Act of 2008. The EEOC's first complainants were female flight attendants. However, the EEOC at first ignored sex discrimination complaints, and the prohibition against sex discrimination in employment went unenforced for the next few years.[74]

Any individual who feels they have been discriminated against can file a complaint with the EEOC.[75] If the case when investigated appears to be a violation of the law, the EEOC will try to negotiate a settlement with the employer, and if that fails, may file suit to enforce the law. If there appears to have been no outright violation of law, the EEOC will issue a Notice of Right to Sue, which allows the complainant to file suit privately—this appears to put the EEOC in a position to forestall a rush of groundless lawsuits in the courts, since they may also find the complaint so worthless that it doesn't require investigation and they won't give the complainant their imprimatur for a private lawsuit.

The EEOC requires employers to report the racial and ethnic categories of their employees. These categories are defined by the Office of Management and Budget periodically; currently they are the same classifications used by the US Census. The overlapping category "Hispanic or Latino" covers an immensely varied population of multiple races, ethnicities, and languages; the Asian category includes an even more varied collection of peoples. The absurd complexities are laid out in an official EEOC document.[76] Employers are expected to "encourage" employees to declare themselves in the appropriate category, and there is no standard other than self-declaration.

These reports can be used to allege discrimination without any other evidence when the composition of a workforce diverges from the local population under the "disparate impact" theory—the variation is assumed to be evidence that some discrimination must have occurred. The EEOC only acts on this when there is political hay to be made; the disparate makeup of elementary school teachers (primarily female), garbagemen (primarily male), and other obvious examples of disparities resulting from group preferences are never acknowledged.

An example of politicized abuse of the disparate impact theory occurred under President Carter in 1980:

> The EEOC has been criticized for alleged heavy-handed tactics in their 1980 lawsuit against retailer Sears, Roebuck & Co. Based on a statistical analysis of personnel and promotions, EEOC argued that Sears was systematically excluding women from high-earning positions in commission sales, and was paying female management lower wages than male management. Sears counter-argued that the company had in fact encouraged female applicants for sales and management, but that women preferred lower-paying positions with more stable daytime working hours, as compared to commission sales which demanded evening and weekend shifts and featured drastically varying pay. In 1986, the court ruled in favor of Sears on all counts, noting that the EEOC had not produced a single witness who alleged discrimination, nor had the EEOC identified any Sears policy that discriminated against women.[77]

The EEOC can be viewed as an agency to arbitrate claims of discrimination against individuals by employers (normally private businesses, but also government agencies and nonprofits), where the employer has access to more information and can bring to bear greater resources on any dispute, which would normally make it hard to fight them in a court of law where big pockets can win simply by delaying and imposing costs on the plaintiff. While seen as fighting for individuals who have been discriminated against, it also intercepts complaints and investigates them at low cost compared to class-action lawsuits, union strikes, and other mechanisms that might be employed by those seeking relief. The EEOC often negotiates settlements by informally adjudicating disputes and making it clear to the parties involved how an actual lawsuit might fare. After a complaint is filed, the EEOC investigates and either certifies it as justified—in which case either the aggrieved party or the EEOC may sue if a settlement is not reached—or dismisses it. If complaints are found to be unwarranted, a civil suit is less likely to be brought since attorneys working on a contingency fee basis will see the case as likely to fail, making it an unprofitable use of their time.

Agencies like the EEOC are rarely created solely to protect their supposed clients. Generally the business community prefers arbitration over the courts to save money, and jury awards are notoriously unpredictable, with some juries punishing what they view as bullying by awarding damages far beyond what the individuals involved could reasonably be said to have suffered. Thus this kind of agency is supported by both voters (who believe it protects individuals from unfairness) and businesses (who see its operations as more predictable and cheaper than the cost of court cases which might otherwise be filed against them.)

The downside of this, from the point of view of businesses, is that there is a very low barrier to filing a complaint—anyone can do so easily and cheaply, and complaints are often undocumented or on their face unsupported, but still must be investigated and dealt with by both the EEOC and the business. Complainants typically don't understand the law and require assistance to either amend their original complaint to capture actionable offenses or limit their allegation to the pattern of behavior they can document.[78] Many complainants give up during this process as their ability to respond and satisfy the agency is tested.

The EEOC takes into account known abusers of its process and can deny complaints based on a record of such abuse:

Abuse of Process-§ 1614.107(a)(9)Section 1614.l07(a)(9) is the appropriate provision under which an agency may dismiss a complaint on the extraordinary grounds of abuse of process.

(a) Abuse of process is defined as **a clear pattern of misuse of the process for ends other than that which it was designed to accomplish.** ...

(1) For example, in reviewing a complainant's prior complaints, the Commission has found abuse of process where the complainant presented similar or identical allegations, evidencing a pattern of initiating the complaint process whenever the agency did anything that dissatisfied the complainant. ... The Commission has stressed in such cases that a party cannot be permitted to utilize the EEO process to circumvent other administrative processes; nor can individuals be permitted to overburden the EEO system, which is designed to protect individuals from discriminatory practices.

Example:

The complainant originally filed a complaint of discrimination in non-selection for promotion. Subsequently, he repeatedly files complaints of reprisal, alleging that the agency was denying him official time to prepare EEO complaints, denying him the use of facilities and storage space for his EEO materials, providing improper EEO counseling, and unfairly keeping tabs on the amount of official time he is spending on his EEO complaints. Many of the allegations in these complaints are vague, and raise allegations previously raised in earlier complaints. In fact, he had on several occasions copied a previous complaint on which he would write a new date in order to file new complaint. Over the course of several months, he filed a total of 25 complaints in this manner. The agency could consolidate the subsequent complaints and dismiss them under § 1614.107(a) for abuse of process. The complainant had demonstrated a pattern of abuse of the process, involving multiple complaints containing identical or similar allegations. (See, e.g., Kessinger v. U.S. Postal

Service, EEOC Appeal No. 0197639 (June 8, 1999); Story v. U.S. Postal Service, EEOC Request No. 05970083 (May 22, 1998)).[79]

If the complaint is found by the EEOC to be reasonable and settlement isn't reached, the resulting court case can cost an employer far more than a year's wages for several employees. Business disruption costs and expenses for attorneys, discovery, and court time can easily reach hundreds of thousands of dollars, which is why small cases involving one or a few employees will typically be settled. When the case alleges mistreatment of a larger number of people or far-reaching changes in an employer's practices would be required to settle it, going to court can be the lower-cost solution.

Cases reaching court have declined in recent years, from 465 in 1999 to 174 in 2015. So the vast majority of the 90,000 cases filed annually are resolved before reaching court. As with criminal plea bargains, settlements often occur regardless of guilt, since the cost of a business going through a court process to reach dismissal or a finding in their favor is so high. Justice is rough at best, and it's fair to say that many people who have been discriminated against are never aware of it or able to prove it, much less go through a complicated and damaging process for relief. It is almost always wiser to move on to a new employer or transfer within a company to avoid the reputational downside of becoming a complainant. Defenders of the EEOC and the law would say that despite the uneven and inequitable enforcement, it has achieved greater sensitivity to the issue in businesses that might otherwise not have reformed their processes or taken note of low-level management prejudices. It is an unanswerable question whether the costs outweigh the benefits, or whether competition for good employees would have tended to lead to the same reforms without the overhead.

There is a complicated interplay between agencies like the EEOC and the NLRB and labor advocates and plaintiff attorneys. In recent decades, Democratic administrations have tended to support labor union and attorney plaintiff interests, while in Republican administrations, business concerns tend to be heard more clearly by the appointed administrators. Some decisions by the agencies under the Obama administration appear to have been aimed at increasing revenues for the plaintiff attorneys and giving unions more power to organize and negotiate with employers. Since both unions and plaintiff attorneys are major Democratic donors, this has the appearance of payoffs to donor classes.

From the LinkedIn Pulse article dated 2-24-2016, "Employers Deserve ANSWERS about EEOC's Position Statement Policy":[80]

> Last week, EEOC Commissioner Chai Feldblum reissued the EEOC's press release, "EEOC Implements Nationwide Procedure for Releasing Respondent Position Statements and Obtaining Responses from Charging Parties," claiming that this new procedure "will help make for better investigations." As a former EEOC Trial Attorney, this statement so perplexed me that I could not help but attribute it to absolute ignorance about Field operations or outright mendacity.

> Under the EEOC's longstanding Priority Charge Handling Procedures (PCHP, adopted in 1995), the EEOC's "investigations" are so perfunctory for the majority of charges (i.e., "B" charges) that they hardly resemble "investigations" at all: "B" charges are "handled," not "investigated," and according to the EEOC's own data, nearly two-thirds of them are dismissed with No Reasonable Cause determinations. Notably, the EEOC's budget has not grown commensurately with its more recent administrative power expansions, which means that the overwhelming majority of its investigations will remain as superficial and cursory as ever, while the EEOC devotes its limited resources to the 3.5% of charges (i.e., "A" charges) that may have merit.

> So, who profits from this EEOC policy? For Plaintiff-side attorneys like EEOC Chair Jenny Yang and her ilk in the National Employment Lawyers Association (NELA) and the National Trial Lawyers Association (NTLA), this policy is a gift. Employers lose, as usual, in the EEOC's and Plaintiff bar's irrational "Victim/Villain" view of employment disputes.

[A]n EEOC Charge (Form 5) need only be "minimally sufficient," simply consisting of "a written statement sufficiently precise to identify the parties, and to describe generally the action or practices complained of." 29 C.F.R. 1601.12(d). As both an EEOC Trial Attorney and longtime EEO defense attorney, I have seen many, many "minimally sufficient" charges like the example below:

"I am a disabled woman over 40 years old, and believe I was discriminated against because of my disability, gender, and age in that: I performed my position reasonably well; The employer terminated my employment despite my adequate performance; Other employees not belonging to protected groups with similar infractions or performance deficiencies were not terminated."

According to the EEOC, Respondents are entitled to no additional information to conduct their investigations, evaluate the merits of the allegations, or assess their litigation risk, leaving them to wonder: What disability? Who does she consider "comparators"? What is she talking about? We fired her for poor performance!

Instead, from these scraps of information, Respondents must literally guess about the precise nature of the allegations and then effectively disprove them in a carefully drafted Position Statement supported by documents. Under the EEOC's nationwide policy, an EEOC investigator will then provide this Position Statement and documents to the Charging Party and her attorney for rebuttal—i.e., the Charging Party's first written statement and supporting documents that discrimination actually occurred. The EEOC will NOT provide this rebuttal information to Respondents and their defense counsel, even though the EEOC regularly issues determinations and makes conciliation demands based only on that limited information. Likewise, the EEOC routinely refuses to disclose investigative information to Respondents in the conciliation process, thereby allowing EEOC personnel to bluff about the quantum and quality of evidence in settlement negotiations.

From a strategic perspective, therefore, the EEOC has provided an informational windfall (i.e., "free discovery") for trial lawyers: trial lawyers get full access to information to bolster their lawsuits against employers, while employers remain clueless about the precise nature of the allegations.

After the EEOC lost a number of high-profile court cases like the Sears case of 1980, where EEOC allegations of "disparate impact" of Sears practices on women in sales employment were unaccompanied by evidence or complaints, settlements have predominated. The staff at the EEOC has evolved over the decades since; new recruits tend to have been beneficiaries of AA themselves, and the Obama administration has encouraged agency activism throughout government, but especially in the Office of Civil Rights and the EEOC. But courts remain unpersuaded by their cases, slapping them down for lack of evidence and overreach. Walter Olson commented:

> ...it's not easy to think of an agency to whose views federal courts nowadays give less deference than the EEOC. As I've noted in a series of posts, judges appointed by Presidents of both political parties have lately made a habit of smacking down the commission's positions, often in cases where it has tried to get away with a stretchy interpretation of existing law. See, for example, the Fourth Circuit's rebuke of "pervasive errors and utterly unreliable analysis" in EEOC expert testimony, Justice Stephen Breyer's scathing majority opinion in Young v. U.P.S. on the shortcomings of the EEOC's legal stance (in a case the plaintiff won), or these stinging defeats dealt out to the commission in three other cases.[81]

The EEOC is a prime example of the extremes of incompetence that are reached when AA hiring is the highest priority. Unlike many government agencies and private companies, mediocre or worse AA hires are not just scattered through the organization where they can be routed around, but make up most of the staff and management. The result is a look at the Idiocracy of the future, where lawyers can't law, analysts can't analyze, and investigators make s**t up for their reports. Where political affiliation is more important than competence, the result is an ethnic and political spoils system no more productive than Andrew Jackson's patronage appointments.

In the most recent high-profile case, the EEOC's settlement demands were so unjust the accused company spent a lot of money to take their case all the way to the Supreme Court, resulting in another embarrassing slapdown and award of as much as $4 million in attorney's fees to the company:[82]

> ...In last week's Supreme Court decision in CRST Van Expedited, Inc. v. EEOC, it was back to the dunking booth for the much-disrespected commission. The ruling, written by Justice Anthony Kennedy, was unanimous. It laid out in detail a long tale of shoddy EEOC litigation waged against the Iowa-based trucking company CRST, in which the commission took a female driver's complaint of sexual harassment during training and attempted to expand it into a giant "pattern and practice" lawsuit that might have been settled for millions. Rather than settling, the trucking company decided to fight. The ensuing litigation did not, to understate things, show the EEOC at its best.

> It eventually became clear that the federal anti-bias agency had failed to investigate or otherwise adequately advance more than 150 of the claims it had tried to add, which were accordingly dismissed, leaving only two intact. A federal judge granted CRST attorneys' fees on the prevailing Supreme Court standard of Christiansburg Garment, which permits defendants to recover fees when an employment discrimination claim is "frivolous, unreasonable, or groundless." The EEOC, however, resisted the fee order on the grounds that, under a quirky Eighth Circuit interpretation, even a frivolous claim does not generate a fee entitlement unless decided "on the merits." And the 150 claims it had bungled had not been dismissed "on the merits" – they hadn't gotten even that far.[83]

While there's no way to tell exactly which EEOC staff would qualify as "diversity hires" (people who would not have been the best candidates for the job if their race, sex, or ethnicity had not been given special preference), we can guess from the extreme overrepresentation of those classes. Here are the numbers from OPM for EEOC's 2010-2014 staff:

Diversity Categories	2010	2011	2012	2013	2014
Native Hawaiian / Pacific Islander	0.1 %	0.1 %	0.1 %	0.1 %	0.1 %
American Indian / Alaskan Native	0.7 %	0.6 %	0.6 %	0.5 %	0.7 %
Asian	3.8 %	3.6 %	3.7 %	3.8 %	4.2 %
White	38.8 %	39.6 %	39.1 %	38.7 %	38.9 %
Hispanic	13.8 %	13.5 %	13.7 %	14.0 %	14.5 %
Black	41.7 %	41.1 %	41.4 %	41.3 %	40.2 %
More Than One Race	1.1 %	1.4 %	1.4 %	1.5 %	1.4 %
Female	64.4 %	63.6 %	63.9 %	63.9 %	62.5 %
Male	35.6 %	36.4 %	36.1 %	36.1 %	37.5 %

From: Equal Employment Opportunity Commission: Diversity and Inclusion: Overview[1]

The most obvious overrepresentation: Black staffers are at 40% of the EEOC staff, while only 12% of the US population, a factor of more than three. Female staff are at 62.5% vs. 50%, and self-designated Hispanics at 14.5% vs 17% in the general population. White staffers, at 39%, are two-thirds as numerous as would be expected from their 62.2% of the general population. Another part of the report has Disabled staff at 18%, much more than the 11.7% of the total population considered disabled.[84]

What do we make of this? It is certainly reasonable for those most interested in the issues addressed by an agency to preferentially apply for jobs there; it is natural to want to work on issues you believe are meaningful and important. But the irony is that the EEOC does not accept such reasoning when a private company argues that its imbalances are due to employee preferences. We can imagine the EEOC leaning on itself to hire more whites, males, and able workers to make up for the imbalance, and filing a court case alleging "disproportionate impact" of the EEOC's hiring process—since their numbers are so skewed, the EEOC must ipso facto be discriminating in employment!

The US is not the only country where affirmative action remedies for historical grievance or racial and ethnic discrimination have been counterproductive. Countries like Lebanon, where religious and ethnic differences have resulted in civil war and decline, even go so far as to reserve posts in government for representatives from particular religions and tribes. We'll examine three countries closely:

India, where multiple religions and castes left from waves of conquest and local tribal history were at first tolerated by the imperial British rulers, then opposed. The new government of independent India then began a thorough program of caste preferences designed to ameliorate centuries of discrimination, with limited success and additional social turmoil as preferences became another political football in a fractious society. India's modernization and freed economy has done more for lower castes than preferences ever did;

Malaysia, where native Malays established preference programs to reduce Chinese-ethnic dominance, but ethnic and cultural isolation continue as both Chinese- and Indian-origin citizens feel discriminated against and are emigrating;

And **Nigeria,** where preferences designed to spread government jobs and business amongst tribes helped lead to civil war and increased tensions. The preferences are often ignored and corrupt favoritism continues, while tribal strife increases as the government has lost control of some territories.

For those in the US who have grown up with affirmative action programs in place, familiarity can lead to blindness—one can't see the hypocrisies and damages of institutionalized racial preferences in your own land when they are so familiar. Examining similar policies in very different countries and cultures makes you wonder why their people can't see the obvious unfairness and damage. And then you remember we have the same flaw...

India's waves of conquest and settlement left thousands of tribes intermingled, and with a prevailing ideology of patronage and spoils; tribal and caste ties determined social roles, down to the details of what kinds of jobs people could have. British conquest at first recognized existing arrangements, then began the process of liberalization, and after independence, the new Indian governments made further efforts to reduce the hold of caste discrimination.

The Indian caste system is vastly more complex than most outsiders realize, and efforts to catalog and define what caste is often fail. There are at least 3,000 recognized castes, and the recognition of caste as a factor in employment probably dates back thousands of years in the form of reservation of high positions for Brahmins. Reservation of voting strength and employment in the affirmative action sense of uplifting those who had been discriminated against began in the early 1900s. The "Communal Award," a system of representation apportioned by ethnicity and religion, was introduced by the British administration in 1933. Voting and representation was separated for Muslims, Sikhs, Indian Christians, Anglo-Indians, Europeans, and the "untouchable" Dalit caste. This guaranteed some voice in the government to previously powerless classes. After Independence, this system continued after the Poona Pact between supporters of reservation and Gandhi, who had fasted to protest against the British practice of separate voting and representation for Dalits.

The Indian Constitution of 1949 recognized Scheduled Castes (SCs), Scheduled Tribes (STs), and Other Backward Classes (OBCs) as needing assistance to make up for historic discrimination. Reservation schemes have since carved out minimum proportions of each of these for new government jobs, university admissions, and other purposes. The total percent of the population eligible for special consideration is around 50%.

Reservation percentages vary greatly by state, and actual discrimination faced by some castes varies as well—a caste can be seen as untouchable in one geographic area, while accepted in another. And in recent decades, many members of the "backward" classes and oppressed castes have migrated to urban centers and jobs unrelated to their historic categories. You would expect that as India grows more cosmopolitan and historic prejudices have begun to fade, at least in professional and urban settings, that the reservation system would gradually dissolve also. But like affirmative action in the US, it remains a contentious issue, with tribal pride and prejudices continuing to create contention over these set-asides.

Political turmoil, riots, and a mounting number of deaths show that the stresses created by the reservations system are increasing. In their long and detailed story "Caste Quotas in India Come Under Attack", *The New York Times* of 8-30-2015 covered one of the recent riots as middle castes began to demand to be allowed into the reservation system:

> The resentment built slowly in Hardik Patel. It took root when he watched his younger sister lose out on a college scholarship because of India's version of affirmative action, a system of strict quotas that reserves nearly half of government jobs and public college slots for those who come from disadvantaged castes or tribes.
>
> It deepened as he talked to other young Patels from his farming village, where it seemed as if everyone had a story of a job lost, a door closed, or a dream thwarted all because the Patel clan is considered too well off to qualify for inclusion in India's quota system.
>
> This spring, with help from a loose network of friends, Hardik Patel began organizing Patels all over Gujarat, a western state of 63 million people, including roughly 10 million Patels. Meeting at farmhouses and restaurants, connecting on Facebook and WhatsApp, they quickly turned their shared resentment into an audacious plan that culminated on Tuesday when Hardik Patel, a baby-faced 22-year-old,

stood on a stage here before 500,000 wildly cheering people, almost all of them young Patel men, and took dead aim at an entrenched quota system that India's leading politicians have spent decades defending and expanding as a means to win votes from one caste or another.

In an act of political jujitsu, Mr. Patel demanded that the Patels, who belong to the Patidar caste, be included in the very quota system they despise—knowing that if the wealthy and politically powerful Patels of Gujarat can qualify for special quotas, then so must every other caste in India.

"We are not begging," he defiantly told the crowd. The roar of a half-million Patels chanting "Hardik! Hardik!" echoed off nearby apartment buildings, where still thousands more Patels lined rooftops and balconies. The adoration was all the more remarkable since almost no one had ever heard of Hardik Patel before last month.

It was not just the enormous size of the Patel rally, or the underground swiftness with which it came together, that left India's political and media elites universally stunned. It was also the depth of the rebuke it represented to Prime Minister Narendra Modi. Mr. Modi came to national prominence because strong support from the Patels helped elect him chief minister of Gujarat in 2001.

When he ran for prime minister in 2014, Mr. Modi extolled the success of what he called "the Gujarat model"—a set of business-friendly policies he claimed had led to widely shared prosperity for the people of Gujarat. Those claims have now been called into question by 500,000 of his most faithful supporters, many of whom, in dozens of interviews last week, described a Gujarat where a young, educated work force is finding it increasingly difficult to find good private-sector jobs.... The point of the protest, he explained in an interview, was to confront [Prime Minister Modi and his government] with a brutally difficult choice—either side with the Patels who had brought them to power, or else earn the Patels' political wrath by siding with the castes and tribes that currently benefit from the quota system.

"It's a vicious cycle," he said, mopping sweat from his face with a rag. "The more they demand, the more the political masters give them; the more they get, the more the political masters answer to them."

...That night, and over the next two days, police officers were repeatedly caught on camera smashing cars and beating unarmed civilians, even some with hands raised. "Police Unleash Terror," read the headline in one Ahmedabad newspaper.

Across Gujarat, mobs responded with equal fury, burning buses and police stations and targeting the homes of Gujarat's ministers. Rajanikant Patel's home was burned. By Thursday, 10 people were dead, including a police officer, the army had been called in, and Mr. Modi had gone on television to appeal for peace....

Not five miles away, across the Sabarmati River that bisects this city, the fear was palpable in an impoverished, hopelessly overcrowded neighborhood ... Almost everyone in this neighborhood comes from a caste that benefits from the quota system, including Narayan Parmar, 51, who said he felt profoundly threatened by the demands of the Patidars. Thanks to the quota system, Mr. Parmar landed a job 28 years ago at the city's sewage plant.[85]

The Economist of 2-27-2016 covered the latest rioting, "Backward ho! —Higher castes demanding lower status make a mockery of positive discrimination":[86]

A city under siege can resist many things, but not thirst. On February 22nd both the national government and that of Haryana, a state that rings Delhi, the Indian capital, on three sides, crumpled after rioters sabotaged a canal that supplies nearly half the water to the sprawling metropolis. Some 28 people died as police backed by soldiers struggled to control arsonists and looters, as well as more peaceable protesters, who blocked roads and railways into Delhi. But with taps running dry it was easier to capitulate to the rioters' main demand, which is to allow the Jats, a caste-like community that is powerful in Haryana, to gain "reservations"—that is, a share of state favours formally reserved for the supposedly poor and downtrodden.

It is not the first time that a relatively privileged group among India's 3,000-odd castes has resorted to threats and blackmail to win inclusion in an official category known as "other backward classes", or OBCs. Such protests have become alarmingly frequent. Last August in Gujarat a protest by the Patidars, a caste which, like the Jats, is traditionally composed of yeomen farmers but has increasingly joined the urban middle class, brought a crowd of perhaps 500,000 people on to the streets of Ahmedabad, the state's main city. Ensuing riots left a dozen people dead. In late January the Kapus of Andhra Pradesh set railway carriages ablaze. The Gujjars of Rajasthan are another ethnic group, many of whose members, no longer wholly rural, are prospering. Accounting for 6-7% of the state's people, they staged protests in 2008, 2010 and again last May.

These people are demanding to be "downgraded" to the category of OBC (Other Backward Classes) to gain from the reservation schemes already in place:

In 1990 the federal government set national criteria for defining OBCs, fixing their quota at 27% and capping the overall reservations for all three groups at 50%. Further tinkering has created an increasingly elaborate structure of reservations. Some states certify hundreds of caste groupings as OBCs, while others have pushed their quota closer to 70%. Government commissions that vet applications for OBC status have grown increasingly imaginative, uncovering such subcategories as "backward-forward" castes, parts of a caste group that have fallen behind the rising status of other parts, or the so-called "creamy layer", ie, members of an OBC who are denied benefit because their family income is above a defined maximum (about $10,000).

As in all such schemes, what started as a temporary boost to make up for past wrongs has become a political football. By treating people as members of a class rather than as individuals, these schemes actually increase social tensions and racial animosity:

...the preamble to India's constitution included a call for fraternity along with justice, liberty and equality. Its framers envisioned reservations primarily as a weapon to target social exclusion, and saw it as a temporary measure. Their long-term goal was to do away with the iniquity of caste barriers altogether. Instead, by appealing to one category or another for votes, India's politicians have perpetuated and entrenched a system that fragments the country into jealous islands of class privilege.

As in the US, the pressure to admit more students from affirmative action-favored classes results in wealthier and relatively privileged members of those classes being admitted while poorer, less privileged students with greater academic promise are pushed out:

> In Tamil Nadu, for instance, 69 percent of university admissions are now set aside for what the state has determined to be "backward castes." Many of those favored with these set-asides have controlled Tamil Nadu's government and much of its resources for generations, but they claim special status by pointing to a caste survey done in 1931....
>
> Five prominent university officials in Tamil Nadu said in interviews that those given set-asides at their institutions were generally the children of doctors, lawyers and high-level bureaucrats. The result is that rich students routinely get preference over more accomplished poor ones who do not happen to belong to the favored castes.[87]

One hopeful sign: the gradual freeing of the Indian economy has allowed lower-caste members to become successful entrepreneurs, which would have been unthinkable under the previous "License Raj"[88] system of corrupt thickets of regulation:

> Karl Marx was wrong about many things but right about one thing: the revolutionary way capitalism attacks and destroys feudalism. As I explain in a new study,[89] in India, the rise of capitalism since the economic reforms of 1991 has also attacked and eroded casteism, a

social hierarchy that placed four castes on top with a fifth caste—dalits—like dirt beneath the feet of others. Dalits, once called untouchables, were traditionally denied any livelihood save virtual serfdom to landowners and the filthiest, most disease-ridden tasks, such as cleaning toilets and handling dead humans and animals. Remarkably, the opening up of the Indian economy has enabled dalits to break out of their traditional low occupations and start businesses. The Dalit Indian Chamber of Commerce and Industry (DICCI) now boasts over 3,000 millionaire members. This revolution is still in its early stages, but is now unstoppable.

Milind Kamble, head of DICCI, says capitalism has been the key to breaking down the old caste system. During the socialist days of India's command economy, the lucky few with industrial licenses ran virtual monopolies and placed orders for supplies and logistics entirely with members of their own caste. But after the 1991 reforms opened the floodgates of competition, businesses soon discovered that to survive, they had to find the most competitive inputs. What mattered was the price of your supplier, not his caste.

Many tasks earlier done in-house were contracted out for efficiency, and this opened new spaces that could be filled by new entrepreneurs, including dalits. DIOCCI members had a turnover of half a billion dollars in 2014 and aim to double it within five years. Kamble says dalits have ceased to be objects of pity and are becoming objects of envy. They are no longer just job-seekers, they are now job creators.

Even in rural areas, dalits have increasingly moved up the income and social ladders in the last two decades. One survey in the state of Uttar Pradesh shows the proportion of dalits owning brick houses is up from 38 percent to 94 percent, the proportion running their own businesses is up from 6 percent to 36.7 percent, and the proportion owning cell phones is up from zero to one-third. Some former serfs have now become bosses. A rising proportion have become land-owners, and sometimes hire upper-caste workers. Even more revolutionary, say dalits, is the change in their social status. Once they were virtually bonded laborers, and could not eat or drink with the upper castes. Today the bonded labor system is almost gone, and dalits operate restaurants at which upper castes eat and drink. They remain relatively poor and discriminated against, but economic reform since 1991 has revolutionized their social and economic status.[90]

The combination of increased geographic and social mobility and a more cosmopolitan middle class is making the cast preference system look like the anachronism it is. There are still major stresses between Muslims and Hindus and a tumultuous democratic process, but the outlook is hopeful as more economic reforms decrease contention over status and jobs, which leads to even more liberalization.

Malaysia is another country where attempts to reserve places in education and jobs for certain ethnicities have led to strife and ongoing political problems. The Malays arrived on their peninsula thousands of years ago via Indonesia, and while originating in the same broad migration to Asia as the Chinese, are noticeably different in appearance and culture. British rule beginning in the 1870s brought new mines and rubber plantations which imported Chinese and Indian laborers, as well as a Chinese cosmopolitan business and commercial population in the cities. The Chinese population of today is still split between a wealthier city population and the poor, largely rural descendants of miners.

About half of today's Malaysian population are ethnic Malays, while 30% are of Chinese descent and 8% are of Indian origin. Japanese occupation in WW2 was welcomed by some Malays, and with negotiated independence from Britain in 1957, the new Malaysian constitution reserved special status for Malays. Race riots between Chinese and Malays occurred frequently through the 1950s and 60s, and Singapore was expelled to become a separate country in 1965 since its largely Chinese population resented rule by the Malay-dominated Malaysia. Thus Malaysia eliminated from its polity the population of Chinese who dominated Singapore and were the source of much of the opposition to those Malay-preference policies.

A deeper dive into the history of the Chinese in Malaysia:

The situation of the 7 million ethnic Chinese in Malaysia is tentative at best, mainly due to the dichotomous and contradictory social roles played by two divergent elements within the Chinese community: the rural-poor and the urban-commercial sector. The urban-commercial sector of the ethnic-Chinese community, in conjunction with foreign (mainly British) interests, completely controlled the country's economy. The ethnic-Malays countered Chinese economic clout by institutionalizing Malay dominance in the newly independent (1957) Malayan state.

Communal tensions had become pronounced following the Japanese occupation during World War II. The Malays at first sided with the Japanese against the British colonial administration but became increasingly disillusioned with Japanese dominance. The Chinese, on the other hand, were badly mistreated by the Japanese authorities (and their Malay collaborators) and many joined an armed resistance group, the Malayan People's Anti-Japanese Army (MPAJA). After the Japanese defeat, the MPAJA attempted to establish political control in the Malayan peninsula and engaged in a violent retaliation against suspected Malay collaborators. Ethnic violence flared throughout the peninsula....

Malay distrust of the Chinese (and Indian, see separate entry) "foreign element", stimulated by the MCP insurgency and exacerbated by the ethnic tensions displayed during the aborted incorporation of the Chinese-dominated island of Singapore (1963-1965), erupted into serious communal rioting in the summer of 1969 following a successful Chinese and Indian electoral challenge to the Malays' political hegemony. The legal imposition in 1970 of the New Economic Policy (NEP), designed to redress "bumiputra" (all groups indigenous to Malaysian territory) economic disadvantages, was the important result of the 1969 disturbances. The NEP, however, tended to assign remedial advantages only to ethnic-Malays. It thereby buttressed Malay political and military dominance with economic power, mainly to the disadvantage of the aboriginal peoples and Indian groups.[91]

Malay, Chinese, and Indian communities tended to remain separated by language and culture, educated in separate schools and socially isolated. Resentment between the groups has built up over generations, and the continuing preferences for bumiputra breed more resentment, while Malay politicians continue to scapegoat the Chinese. An anecdote from a review of Thomas Sowell's book *Affirmative Action Around the World:*

In 2004 while on cruise (I was active duty in the Navy at the time), our ship arrived in Port Kelang, Malaysia, not too far from the capital of Kuala Lumpur. A bus took us sailors into the city and cabs were lined up calling for Americans to get into their taxi's despite a group of al-Qaeda sympathizers threatening to attack Americans (that problem was taken care of). Me and few friends hop into the cab and the guy seemed so nice but suddenly he went into a racist rant about Chinese people. He also hinted that some cabs refused service to the Chinese. I was shocked. If people of Chinese heritage were born in Malaysia, was it lawful for this man or any other ethnic Malay to refuse service? ... I realize that affirmative action in that country may have played a part in it. I don't want this for our country.[92]

From "A Never-Ending Policy," a story in *The Economist* of 4-27-2013:

The policies which favour ethnic Malays and other indigenes at the expense of Malaysia's ethnic Chinese and Indian citizens are an oddity in the realm of state discrimination. It is not unusual that they favour a majority, the two-thirds of the population known as the bumiputra, or sons of the soil. But it is peculiar that their Chinese and Indian targets have never ruled Malaysia.

Their presence in the country, though, was encouraged under British colonial rule without the consent of native Malays. After independence this became a source of grievance, one exacerbated by the minorities' wealth. In 1969 mobs burned Chinese shops, killing hundreds. The government responded with a "New Economic Policy" (NEP) aimed at improving the lot of the bumiputra with preferences in university admissions and for civil-service jobs. Billed in 1971 as a temporary measure, the NEP has become central to a system of corrupt patronage....

Provisions that require a certain proportion of the shares of any publicly quoted company to be in bumiputra hands, and that favour bumiputra-owned firms for various government contracts, undoubtedly enrich a few well-connected Malays. And the policies seem good for bumiputra civil servants: the civil service is now 85%

Malay, if one excludes teachers. But they do little for the rest. "There has been little or no trickle-down effect, and I think more bumiputra know this today," says Wong Chen of Pakatan Rakyat, the main opposition party. The increasing wealth of ethnic Malays in past decades echoes rising fortunes across South-East Asia, casting doubt on the idea that affirmative action has been a particular help.

Malaysia's Chinese and Indian citizens chafe at being second-class citizens. Quotas in university admissions are particularly resented. Most universities in Malaysia reserve 70% or more of their places for bumiputras. Chinese and Indian students flock instead to private and foreign ones. Those who leave often stay away. A World Bank study in 2011 found that about 1m Malaysians had by that stage left the country, which has a total population of 29m. Most were ethnic Chinese, and many were highly educated. Some 60% of skilled emigrants cited "social injustice" as an important reason for leaving Malaysia. This exodus makes it a less attractive place to invest in.

Supporters of the NEP argue that, without such assistance, Malays will not catch up economically or academically. Critics worry that it dulls their incentives to excel. There is evidence of a skills gap. Nearly half the managers at Malaysian manufacturing firms surveyed by the World Bank said that the ability of local skilled workers to handle information technology was either "poor" or "very poor". Mahathir Mohamad, a former prime minister who in his time extended the reach of the NEP, lamented in 2002 that bumiputras too often treat university places as "a matter of right", neglecting their studies.

A survey in 2008 found that 71% of Malaysians agreed that "race-based affirmative action" was "obsolete" and should be replaced with a "merit-based policy". The ruling coalition pays lip service to such ideas and has tinkered with the racial preferences—lowering, for example, the fraction of a company's shares that has to be in bumiputra hands when a service company goes public. The opposition argues for "colour-blind" affirmative action—that is, policies that favour the poor in general, rather than the bumiputra specifically. But are enough of the sons of the soil ready to make the change?"

So the ethnic preferences are pushing highly-educated citizens to leave the country and are seen by most thoughtful observers to badly need reforming, yet nothing is changed.

Another feature of the Malaysian preferences also seen elsewhere is their continuation and expansion long after imbalances have been corrected. The Malay population has become an even larger majority in the years since the policies were implemented, and Malays now dominate the country's government and most of the wealth and jobs. Asia-Pacific regional magazine *The Diplomat* goes into more depth in its story of 11-10-2015 by Han Bochen, "Malaysia's Chinese Diaspora: The Other Side of the Story: Conventional narratives overlook the marginalization of ethnic Chinese in Malaysia— especially the Chinese poor.":

> While the Chinese do hold political power as part of the ruling coalition, it is their success in the economic realm that has been the main source of dissatisfaction for ethnic Malays. Right-wing groups often complain about a Chinese take-over of the country's economy, and encourage ethnic Malays to unite under the idea of "ketuanan Melayu", or Malay pre-eminence, against the Chinese domination of the economy. Ordinary Malays have adopted the rhetoric as their own, using social media as a tool to speak out against any indication that the Chinese are second-class or disadvantaged.
>
> Looking purely at numbers, it does seem that the Chinese have it much better. Census data from 2014 show that the average monthly gross income for the Chinese is much higher than that of any other ethnic group in the country. Adding to this narrative are lists like the Forbes' 50 Richest, which consistently reveal that the majority of Malaysia's richest are of Chinese descent (in 2015, eight of the top 10 Malaysian nationals on the Forbes list were Chinese).
>
> Under this banner, two intertwined narratives have been consistently marginalized: that of the mirage of Chinese dominance in Malaysian society, and that of the Chinese poor.

First of all, despite the lack of indication in the Malaysian constitution, there's no debate over the fact that the prime minister must be of Malay origin, meaning that Chinese political power will always hit a brick wall. Furthermore, there is little support from the Chinese community for the Malaysian Chinese Association (MCA), the voice for the ethnic-Chinese population in government. Political observers agree that, that while they are vocal in the opposition, the Chinese have a largely insignificant voice in Malaysian parliament.

Secondly, it is the Malays, not the Chinese, that actually control most of the economy. Since the enactment of the New Economic Policy (NEP) in the 1970s—a set of affirmative action policies for ethnic Malays aimed to reduce inequality between them and their ethnic-Chinese counterparts—the Malays have monumentally improved their situation. They control most of the major banks, including the central bank, the government linked companies (GLCs), as well as constitute the majority of the top professional and highest-paying occupations in the private sector.

What the impressive statistics touting Chinese success obscure is that while there is a sizable ethnic Chinese middle class, income inequality is also most rampant within the Chinese population. All the wealth is concentrated within a few, and there is a large number of Chinese who are either below the urban poverty line or slightly above the poverty line. Furthermore, while many of the NEP measures are still in force protecting the ethnic-Malays, there is relatively little government support for non-Malays in poverty. Correspondingly, there is a dire lack of academic study and census focus on the Chinese poor.

Meanwhile the government certainly isn't helping matters with its rhetoric. The "Bangsa Malaysia" policy introduced in the 1990s, aimed to create an inclusive national identity for all Malaysian residents, has evolved into a nebulous concept. Over the years the government hasn't ceased to refer to the ethnic Chinese as "pendatang," which means "immigrant" in Malay. Such language confirms, and often exacerbates, the distinctions that exist between Malaysian nationals. In early February Rural and Regional

Development Minister Datuk Seri Ismail Sabri Yaakob used racial language to encourage Malay consumers to boycott Chinese-owned businesses that have been raising their prices.[94]

For a look at the Indian-origin Malaysians who are also chafing under ethnic set-asides, the *New York Times* story of 2-10-2008 has some revealing anecdotes:

KUALA LUMPUR, Malaysia—Malaysian Indian Casket, a shop on the outskirts of this modern and cosmopolitan city, sells coffins in all sizes: standard coffins clutter the entrance, child-size boxes are stacked high on the shelves and extra-large models, those for the tallest of the deceased, are stored in the back.

But there is no variety in the ethnic background of the clientele. "All the customers are Indian," said Aru Maniam, a shop salesman.

In death as in life, Malaysians are divided by ethnicity. The country's main ethnic groups—Malays, Chinese and Indians—have their own political parties, schools, newspapers and, in the case of Malays, a separate Islamic legal system.

For years this segregation was promoted as the best formula for social harmony in a country that advertises itself as "Truly Asia" because of its diversity, but where the memory of ethnic riots in 1969 is invoked as proof of the fragility of cross-cultural relations. Nearly 200 people died in that spasm of violence.

Now, ethnic tensions are again rising, driven in large part by dissatisfaction among the country's Indians, who have mainly lost out in the long battle of all three ethnic groups over power, privilege and religion....

Some Indians in Malaysia are very rich, but a majority have not been able to move up from the lowest rungs of society. The children and grandchildren of rubber tappers, they remain poor, poorly educated and overrepresented in menial jobs....

Chinese Malaysians, who form the core of the merchant class, are angry about quotas that keep many of them out of local universities and about the government's preference for hiring Malay companies, among other issues.

Malaysia's ethnic tensions were born during the 19th and early 20th centuries, when Chinese and Indian workers came to what was then called Malaya and helped drive the colonial economy of tin and rubber. But this influx created resentment among Malays, who lost control of the economy to British plantation owners and Chinese businesses. The Malay sultans later struck a deal with the British: Malays would retain political supremacy in Malaysia after independence in exchange for citizenship for the Chinese and Indians....

Today, bumiputra make up 60 percent of the population but have 87 percent of government jobs. They receive discounts of 5 to 10 percent on new homes and are allotted 30 percent of stock shares in initial public offerings. Newspapers are filled with notices of government construction contracts exclusively reserved for companies controlled by bumiputra.

"It's completely unacceptable that you cannot get awarded a contract just because of the color of your skin," said Lim Guan Eng, an ethnic Chinese Malaysian who is secretary general of the Democratic Action Party, the leading opposition party in Parliament. "That grates tremendously. We are treated as though we are third- or fourth-class citizens."[95]

In the United States, the preference system got started as a remedy for the evil of slavery and Jim Crow segregation and has never been as extreme as the Malaysian preferences, which were motivated by a colonial history. But similar resentment is building among those who are pushed out by the preferences for politically-favored groups. The US is fortunate in having less extreme ethnic and religious differences to deal with, as well as an ideal of equal treatment under the law, but the political rewards of setting groups against each other and stoking resentment are similar.

The modern state of Nigeria emerged from British colonial rule in 1960. A polyglot confederation of tribes that had never been a state in pre-colonial times, it soon was wracked by the civil war of 1967-70, with military rule alternating with democratically-elected governments until some stability was achieved starting in 1999. The election of 2011 was the first to be internationally recognized as free and fair.

With a population approaching 200 million and a growing economy with oil resources, trouble arises from the tribal and ethnic divisions of such an artificial state. There are over 500 ethnic groups speaking over 500 languages, with three primary tribes: Yoruba, Hausa, and Igbo. With the official language of English and the British colonial heritage, many students from Nigeria have been educated at British and US universities. Conflict between the Anglo-American culture of law and fairness and the older tribal systems of favoritism and graft is ongoing.

The northern part of the country is primarily Islamic, and the Boko Haram movement has challenged the central government's control in the Northeast. Meanwhile, the oil production in the Niger Delta region has been fought over by rebels and government. Until recently the government was highly corrupt and insider deals and direct theft siphoned off most of the country's wealth.

Nigeria's constitution of 1999 established equal rights for all citizens. To counteract tendencies to favor ethnic and tribal associates, a "Federal Character Principle requires that there is no predominance of persons from a few states or... ethnic groups in the government or any of its agencies," and "The Federal Character Commission... establishes, monitors and enforces an equitable formula for the distribution of employment in the public services across the 36 states in the country."[96]

These principles are widely flouted in Nigerian governments, both federal and local. There is limited political will to enforce affirmative action rules in government employment, and women in particular are marginalized, with little cultural support for the ideal of equality, especially in less developed areas. A sort of hybrid system which awards government positions to connected candidates by ethnic affiliation gives Nigeria the worst of both worlds.

The stresses of conflict between the preference law and standard practices boil over frequently. Local editorial writers point out the need to scrap both old corrupt practices and the supposedly corrective preferences to emphasize merit:

> The senator representing Bayelsa-East Senatorial District in the upper chamber of the National Assembly, Mr. Ben Murray-Bruce, appeared to be bristling with rage when he recently commented on the 'Federal Character' and 'Quota' principles. Like the contentious Quota System applied when processing admission into federal educational institutions, the Federal Character principle amplifies the diverse configuration of Nigeria as a nation along ethnic (majority or minority), religious (Christian-Muslim mainly) and other lines, such as the educationally advantaged and disadvantaged...
>
> While the quota system came into being before the country's independence in 1960, according to reports, the Federal Character principle became officially recognised in the 1979 Constitution as a vehicle for ethnic representation in the public sector. Today, the Federal Character Commission (FCC) is in place... to implement and enforce the Federal Character principles of fairness and equity in the distribution of public posts and socio-economic infrastructures among the various federating units.... The commission now deploys its officials to physically monitor all federal recruitment exercises and ensure that they substantially comply with approved guidelines.
>
> The controversy over the years, however, has been that with Federal Character and Quota System taking the centre stages in admission, recruitment, promotion and appointment processes, the advancement of the country's public institutions, which ought to be

the drivers of development, is neither based on merit nor competence. It is against this backdrop that critics insist that the nation urgently needs a review of her educational policies and an extensive educational infrastructural development to accommodate its growing student population, for example.

This seemed the point Bruce reiterated when he said Federal Character was drawing the country back. The senator said: "Nigeria must make progress though tribe and tongue may differ. **The only way to do that is by saying goodbye to ethnicity and hello to merit.** Compare the progress that Nigeria made before the quota system (1960-66) and the retrogression we have made since 1966 till date. The difference is clear. Federal Character cannot make an electrical power station work. It can't make refineries work. Only merit can ensure this. As a result of Federal Character, Nigeria Airways went from 30 aircraft to bankruptcy and a debt of over $60m by the year 2000. Quota System and Federal Character lead to a sense of entitlement in beneficiaries and resentment in others. Merit is a better way of life…".

Such has been the nature of contempt many harbour for the two retrogressive systems which, in any case, have their roots in the national political games that predated the nation's independence from Britain in 1960…. what is obvious is the uneven educational, infrastructural, industrial, political and socio-economic development of Nigeria's constituent parts since 1960… The setbacks were compounded by the selfish, carefree, manipulative, exploitative and dishonest attitudes of subsequent leaders. A fraction of the dilemma presently would include the 10.5 million children reported to be out-of-school in the North alone, as well as the insurgency in the North East that has compounded the problem. This may take decades if not centuries to overcome. How ready are Nigerian leaders to enthrone an educational system that would produce competent drivers of development nationwide in the foreseeable future? How ready are leaders to depart from rendering insincere, unpatriotic, corrupt, and self-serving leadership; and help Nigeria conquer the pangs of illiteracy, mass poverty and joblessness, avoidable diseases and death? Federal Character and Quota System are merely cosmetic solution to a chronic cancer.[97]

But the quota system in place has created a constituency which blocks
its reform. 'Globalisation' of Nigeria is leading to local agitation by
the most educated and advanced Nigerians for an end to the
preferences. They yearn for merit—and utilities that work, water
supplies that are clean, public revenues safe from looting, better
education for all, and a freer, safer society:

> There has been so much concern about how the Federal Character
> principle has since its introduction in 1979, promoted mediocrity
> within the public service, and retarded national growth and progress.
> Introduced after the civil war to promote national integration, and to
> address the fears of sections of the country which felt marginalized,
> the Federal Character principle was meant to ensure that public
> service appointments reflect the country's diversity: religious, ethnic,
> geographical and linguistic, and by extension, that resource
> allocation reflects the fact that this is a federal system and not a clan.

> It is thus an ethnic balancing mechanism. The assumption is that if
> the public service is truly representative, this will promote a sense of
> national loyalty and inclusion.... But today, the general impression is
> that Federal Character as applied has resulted in an erosion of merit,
> and that the observed inefficiency in the state bureaucracy is
> traceable to it, and in other areas of national life, it has not
> necessarily brought better spread of opportunities. The oft-
> recommended solution as was again reportedly argued at a recent
> colloquium in Lagos, in honour of Professor Anya Anya, is to
> **abolish the Federal Character principle and replace it with a merit-
> based system.**

> ...The quality of human resource in any organization determines the
> quality of inputs and outputs. That is why organizations look for the
> best and the brightest. And if the public service in Nigeria can be
> taken as an organization, the kind of people who run, lead and
> manage it have not necessarily been the best and the brightest that
> the country should have. But I am tempted to argue that the problem

is not the Federal Character principle or quota system....

Where the problem lies is when people hide under the Federal Character principle to lower standards so that their kinsmen can have opportunities, or when in the name of Federal Character, **needless cost is incurred and room is created for the incompetent to rise....** The story is often told about how the Joint Admissions and Matriculation Board and some universities, for example, have different cut off points for students from different parts of the country. It is this kind of story, if it is true, that raises questions about how the Federal Character principle is an assault on merit. If the required score for any prospective student of Medicine is 290, then all applicants must score 290 in the qualifying examination before they can gain admission....

To rise gradually above it all, we must grow an enlightened society. We must develop a sense of Nigerian-ness, **build a nation, such that people will be given opportunities, and promoted, not on the basis of affiliations, but their ability and the content of their character.**[98]

The ideal of merit-based advancement—and the painful losses for all of society if positions are awarded based on tribal ties, race, or sex—is something that many Nigerians understand. It's a shame that political correctness and progressive control in the US keeps the incompetent and mediocre in critical jobs in government and regulated businesses.

We've only touched on a few examples here. For a longer cross-cultural, multinational look at affirmative action policies and their harmful effects, see Thomas Sowell's *Affirmative Action Around the World: An Empirical Study:*

> ...there really is a serious shortage of empirical studies of the results of affirmative action everywhere in the world even as available evidence casts doubt on the efficacy of such programs. This is truly astonishing in the USA, where program evaluation requirements are written into virtually every federal program enacted into law.

One review of the book was particularly trenchant:

> The overriding conclusion of every study is that AA does not work, almost universally hampers the progress of racial minorities instead of helping, and creates racial tension so severe it has resulted in the deaths of over a million people in Nigeria and India (the two worst cases). The severity of these consequences is directly proportional to the stringency of the AA rules. The US version of AA for instance is really quite weak when compared internationally, with its broad racial classes and use of normalizing quotas. Policies in other countries were far more severe and therefore damaging. For instance in Malaysia, the government literally forced Chinese business owners to give interests in their own private businesses to the ethnic Malays in order to promote their equality in commerce. Malaysia's policies eventually resulted in an unusual historic event, the first ever instance of a country voluntarily disowning part of its own territory, Singapore in this case, in order to separate the two now violently opposed racial groups. The case of Nigeria is the saddest of all, where there was formerly racial harmony of this multiethnic state, once the strict AA policies were imposed the country fell into one of the worst civil wars in history, breaking the country into separate territories [with] an enormous death toll.[99]

...almost universally AA policies were intended for narrow use, and temporary in nature. Yet as with all government programs, they inevitably take on a life of their own, instead of lasting only a few decades they live forever, and grow in scope as in the US from helping blacks, to eventually helping every group that can lobby their way in from hispanics to native americans to white women. It is at this point that the real purpose of AA becomes all too clear, both in the US as in countries around the world—the wholesale purchase of minority votes at the expense of the entire country.[100]

As in all efforts to redress grievances long after their occurrence, the costs are borne by many who had no hand in and did not benefit from the wrongs done, and the reparative benefits are not well-targeted to the actual victims of injustice. "Social justice" is justice between groups or tribes—like group punishment, remedial actions can be inherently unjust to individuals involved, and become more so as time goes on and the original victims and victimizers have long since died.

Affirmative action policies in college admissions are closely watched, and illustrate the problems of any such effort. When all colleges try to increase their minority enrollments, they end up admitting minority students who are as a group dramatically less well-prepared for the academic programs and rigors of competitive fields, which tends to make those students change majors to less competitive "soft" fields or ethnic studies as a refuge, which ultimately limits their success outside of a ghetto of affirmative action-friendly government, HR, and nonprofit fields. Black students who would have happily studied and been successful in STEM programs at lower-pressure, less-selective colleges find themselves falling behind, dropping out, or changing to softer studies.

Formation of cultural enclaves within schools, and self-segregation by race and ability, tends to prevent those admitted because of affirmative action from successfully adopting the dominant culture of their chosen field of study, which reduces their chance of successfully completing a degree program and going on to a productive career.

These damaging consequences are referred to as *mismatch*, and *Mismatch: How Affirmative Action Hurts Students It's Intended to Help, and Why Universities Won't Admit It*[101] by Richard Sander covers it well.

Secondary negative effects include resentment from those who feel they have lost out because others got preferences, and a pervasive sense of inauthenticity among those who may have benefitted. The casual assumption that minorities in highly-competitive colleges are only there because of special preferences harms those students further, especially if they themselves suspect it may be true. While some overcome all of these negatives to go on to success in fields like investment banking they might have found hard to enter without the elite college imprimatur, most do not. The worst-case scenario for a promising young student is to succumb to the academic and social pressure and drop out, which if they have taken on heavy student loan debt is far worse for them than having gone to a lesser school where their abilities would have been better matched to the program. The second-worst scenario is change of major and field to enter a less-competitive ghetto like gender or ethnic studies, where competition is reduced and support is based on class characteristics and not excellence; by settling for ghettoization, these students end up in low-paying jobs and have few prospects outside of government and nonprofit political organizations, which reinforces their commitment to grievance politics and the spoil system.

Being able to overcome difficulties and succeed on your own merit and effort is key to building self-esteem and confidence. Both legacy admits (students who get admissions preference because family members are alumni and donated money) and affirmative action admits struggle, but the wealthy scions have their way prepared already and can afford to scrape by (at, say, Yale) while partying their way through. Affirmative action admits don't have that luxury.

Another phenomenon seen in highly-selective schools: affirmative action for well-off, upper-class students who happen to have dark skin. Students whose parents are diplomats or immigrated in recent years and therefore never suffered from slavery or Jim Crow discrimination get the same preferences as those whose families did. Barack Obama is a prime example, with a middle-class white mother and a Kenyan father who only visited the US in adulthood. Neither branch of his family could have suffered from past racial discrimination or the lingering effects of slavery and he grew up in relative affluence, attending an elite private school in Hawaii, yet received admission preferences to Columbia and Harvard Law School because of his skin color and racial background.[102] The desire to prove that "racism is over in America" smoothed the way for his election as "the first black President" while truly disadvantaged students who happened to be white or Asian got no boost from preferences.

Affirmative action by government was accomplished by law, with supportive court rulings that allowed race and sex discrimination in the name of redressing prior discrimination. Courts and voters have been trying to walk back this mistake for decades, with many jurists and ultimately Chief Justice John Roberts writing, "The way to end racial discrimination is to stop discriminating by race."[103]

The EEOC and antidiscrimination laws encouraged private business and all levels of government and larger nonprofits to establish affirmative action programs for employment, ranging from outright quota systems to recruitment outreach. Quota systems created ill will and were overturned when legally challenged, and so the watchword became diversity—striving for an ideal of inclusion. The double standard that allowed lesser-qualified persons of the desired race or sex to be chosen over more-qualified candidates of deprecated classes became less blatant, but is still a strong component of many government and some private hiring decisions.

In the decades since affirmative action was begun, employee turnover has replaced nearly all of the old-line managers (who were indeed seat-of-the-pants deciders and in many cases discriminated on the basis of race and sex, as well as other heuristics now deemed inappropriate) with a new crop of more-correct managers, many of them beneficiaries of affirmative action themselves. This has enshrined diversity as a nebulous good, with academic efforts to justify it as increasing productivity, as in a paper from MIT: "Diversity, Social Goods Provision, and Performance in the Firm":

> The study used eight years of revenue data and survey results, covering 1995 to 2002, from a professional-services firm with more than 60 offices in the United States and abroad. The data included some all-male and all-female offices—both of which are unusual, the

researchers note—in addition to mixed-gender offices. The survey data allowed Ellison and Mullin to study the employees' ratings of office satisfaction, cooperation, and morale, not just one generalized measure of workplace happiness.

Among other results, the economists found that shifting from an all-male or all-female office to one split evenly along gender lines could increase revenue by roughly 41 percent. To see how this could happen, Ellison suggests an analogy with a baseball team. "A baseball team entirely composed of catchers could have high esprit de corps," Ellison says, noting that a band of catchers could share experiences, equipment, or tips for handling knuckleballs. "But it would not perform very well on the field."

Similarly, greater social diversity implies a greater spread of experience, which could add to the collective knowledge of a group of office workers and make the unit perform more effectively. Another wrinkle Ellison and Mullin found is that just the perception that firms are diverse was sufficient to produce satisfaction among employees—but this perception did not necessarily occur in the places where more extensive gender diversity accompanied better bottom-line results. "In offices where people thought the firm was accepting of diversity, they were happier and more cooperative," Ellison says. "But that didn't translate into any effect on office performance. People may like the idea of a diverse workplace more than they like actual diversity in the workplace."

Ellison acknowledges that in focusing on a single firm that was willing to provide data, the study was necessarily limited in scope, and says she would welcome further research. Management studies on social capital, she says, do not necessarily link the matter to objective financial results; economics studies of social capital have generally focused on issues such as public finance or even soldier behavior, and not job issues.

"There have been a number of studies looking at things like diversity and performance, but they don't always use the [bottom-line] measures of performance that economists might prefer," Ellison says.

At the same time, she adds, "Highlighting the workplace setting, as a place for economists to study social capital, is also useful."[104]

These "studies" rarely prove anything, though one consistent result is that teams with *some* cultural norms in common make for happier workplaces—not something we needed a study to discover. Ideologically-driven social scientists have set out again and again to demonstrate that "diversity" increases creativity or productivity, but find evidence either weak or nonexistent. For example, many studies attempting to demonstrate corporate boards with more women are better simply don't, yet are publicized as if they do because it's a narrative the media want to promote. Northwestern Professor Alice Eagly wrote :

In an ideal world, social science research would provide a strong basis for advocacy and social policy. However, advocates sometimes misunderstand or even ignore scientific research in pursuit of their goals, especially when research pertains to controversial questions of social inequality. To illustrate the chasm that can develop between research findings and advocates' claims, this article addresses two areas: (a) the effects of the gender diversity of corporate boards of directors on firms' financial performance and (b) the effects of the gender and racial diversity of workgroups on group performance. Despite advocates' insistence that women on boards enhance corporate performance and that diversity of task groups enhances their performance, research findings are mixed, and repeated meta-analyses have yielded average correlational findings that are null or extremely small.

On politically charged issues, science and policy are not linked by a smooth highway but by a more treacherous route where issue advocates hold sway. Advocates are often ideologically polarized players who eagerly invoke social scientific data that support their objectives but whose use of science can be selective and thus unrepresentative of the available scientific knowledge. Researchers, in turn, may fail to communicate effectively to advocates and policy makers, at least in part because research can yield findings that are more complex and less affirming of advocates' goals than what they desire and expect. Under such circumstances, is it possible for social scientists to serve as honest brokers who communicate research findings to invite creative thinking about evidence-based policy? Is it more common that researchers are shunted to the sidelines, with their findings exploited and often inaccurately portrayed by ideologically polarized advocates?[105]

Professor Eagly continues with an examination of mass media reports claiming diverse corporate boards are associated with more profitable companies, and finds the underlying studies less than convincing:

Advocacy to include more women on boards of directors is extensive in the United States and many other Western nations. This advocacy makes sense given the low representation of women as directors, currently 19% in the Fortune 500 (Catalyst, 2015) but only 9% if smaller firms are included (Adams & Kirchmaier, 2015). Although social justice arguments could be deployed to favor increasing women's share of board memberships, advocates have typically focused on the so-called "business case," by indicating that companies with more women on their boards perform better—that is, they have better financial outcomes (e.g., Ernst & Young, 2014). This attention to the economic value of diversity reflects the capitalist societal context in which shareholder value and profits are the measures of corporate success.

The business-case claim that adding women increases corporate success appears often in daily newspapers. In one example, Claire Cain Miller (2014) wrote in the New York Times, "Several studies have shown that diversity on boards improves decision making and profits." Also, Jena McGregor (2014) offered in the Washington Post, "Researchers have long found ties between having women on a company's board of directors and better financial performance." And Tiffany Hsu (2012) added in the Los Angeles Times, "Need a balance sheet boost? Try adding some women to the board of directors."

What is the source of these claims? The advocacy organization Catalyst (2004) produced a study showing that among Fortune 500 firms, those in the top quartile of female representation on their boards of directors performed better than those in the bottom quartile. The reported performance data consisted of the financial outcomes of returns on equity, sales, and invested capital. This initial report and its replications (Catalyst, 2007, 2011) claimed "a link" between women on boards and corporate performance. Also, the management consulting company McKinsey produced a related study of large European publicly traded corporations that demonstrated better financial outcomes for the 89 firms with the highest level of gender diversity in their top management (including on boards), compared with the average of European listed firms (Desvaux, Devillard-Hoellinger, & Baumgarten, 2007; see also Desvaux, Devillard, & Sancier-Sultan, 2010). Similar data came from the 2020 Women on Boards advocacy organization (Kurth, 2015) and the Credit Suisse financial services organization (Dawson, Kersley, & Satella, 2014). These reports were further disseminated in the business press (e.g., Taylor, 2012; Wittenberg-Cox, 2014) and by consulting firms (e.g., International Finance Corporation, 2014).

The reports from advocacy and consulting organizations offered comparisons of groups of firms that differed in the gender diversity of their corporate boards—for example, between the top and bottom quartiles in the Catalyst (2004) research. These studies would certainly not be publishable in academic journals because of the elementary form of their data presentations. Such group comparisons do not reveal the strength of the relation between the participation of women and financial success. The analyses lacked even correlations relating the percentages of women on corporate boards to corporate outcomes or simple scatter plots of these relationships. Such studies do not meet the standards of the relevant academic disciplines, which are economics and management. Does it matter that the studies are academically substandard? The answer to this question is an emphatic yes.

Statistically trained investigators, and perhaps even students who have had one or two statistics courses, would recommend at least the presentation of correlation coefficients and furthermore would raise questions about two matters: (a) possible reverse causation from financial success to the inclusion of women and (b) possible confounding of the percentage of women on boards with omitted variables that may influence corporate success. On the first point of reverse causation, which advocacy and consulting organizations have acknowledged (e.g., Catalyst, 2004; Desvaux et al., 2007), firms that are more profitable may have the resources to seek out and attract women with the requisite corporate executive experience. On the second point, omitted variables might include, for example, firm size, given that women directors are more common on the boards of larger firms (Adams, 2015; Hillman, Shropshire, & Cannella, 2007). Any positive correlation between board gender diversity and financial outcomes might not survive controls for firm size and many other variables potentially correlated with the percentage of women directors.

Social scientists routinely analyze such correlational data using statistical techniques designed to rule out such ambiguities, which economists refer to as endogeneity (Antonakis, Bendaham, Jacquart, & Lalive, 2014). For example, given data over time, researchers can exploit these repeated observations while controlling for the stable differences between firms (in so-called "firm fixed effects" analyses). In addition, to address omitted variables, they also may introduce instrumental variables that are correlated with the predictor of interest (gender diversity) and with the outcome variables (financial success) only through their relation with gender diversity. Using such methods, investigators can eliminate many confounds and thus discern causal relations with some certainty, whereas investigators have little basis for inferring causality from correlations or comparisons of firms grouped by their level of diversity.

An exemplary study that invoked statistically appropriate techniques examined 1,939 firms from the United States for the period 1996–2003 (Adams & Ferreira, 2009). The observed positive relation between the percentage of female directors and financial outcomes became negative when statistical controls for endogeneity were introduced—that is, greater gender diversity was associated with poorer firm outcomes. The findings also showed that women had better attendance at board meetings and were more likely to sit on monitoring committees; their presence was associated with more CEO resignations after poor company performance. The increased monitoring associated with the increase in the presence of women on boards appeared to have positive effects on firms with weak governance but negative effects otherwise. In the aggregated data, these negative effects outweighed the positive ones. Consistent with these findings, effects of gender diversity on financial outcomes can be causally related to the behavior of female versus male directors and their placement on board committees. Other causal possibilities include a negative effect of female directors on stock prices because of investor gender bias, especially by institutional investors, who are especially attentive to corporate governance (Dobbin & Jung, 2011).

This is another example of the junk science, particularly social science, produced when ideological advocates take over both research funding and execution. The desired outcome is found whether supported or not by the data, and statistics are massaged as needed to provide a headline-worthy conclusion to bring the researchers more publicity and thereby improve their chances for further funding. Entire academic careers are now based on politically-correct government funding.

Yet despite a lack of hard evidence, diversity as a goal has become a sacred cow designed to allow racial and sexual preferences to continue under the guise of enhancing productivity. The standard Silicon Valley coder team now consists of one white, one Asian, and one Indian, all male, with a female QA or UX engineer taking part at critical times; this works out well because they are all geeks, selected because they can cooperate and code based on shared geek culture. Race and sex are not relevant. When, as in marketing and sales of consumer products, outreach to a broad range of consumers is required, smart management sets up teams who have members of all the important cultural groups, since inside knowledge of what will work on each is important. Imposing affirmative action goals on top of management hiring decisions can only harm the best companies.

Asians, as "model minorities" widely seen as out-achieving whites, were quickly dropped from most affirmative action programs despite the presence of truly disadvantaged subgroups like the immigrant Vietnamese Hmong. The education-oriented Asian population in the US on the whole now opposes affirmative action, correctly sensing that their children's chances for gaining admission to elite schools are significantly decreased by admissions preferences. At schools like Harvard, it is widely assumed the admissions office actively caps Asian enrollment, as they once discriminated against Jews who would have been overrepresented in the first half of the twentieth century had objective qualifications been used. Genteel discrimination to deny hardworking students and their parents the rewards of diligence and sacrifice is producing a backlash, as when Asian-American parents organized to block the California legislature's attempt to re-authorize racial preferences in state university admissions:

> California has prohibited affirmative action at public institutions for two decades, and the ban certainly hasn't hurt Asian Americans, who today account for a plurality—about a third—of the students at University of California schools despite making up just 15 percent of the state's population. But when the state senate introduced a Democrat-backed amendment that would've asked voters whether to lift the ban, Asian Americans staged public demonstrations and wrote blistering editorials; they hosted a Republican-registration drive ("to scare the Democratic Party") and gathered on TV talk shows to warn viewers of the proposal's implications.

> "This is the most racist bill ever," said a participant on one such show. "We come from a faraway land, China, and [we came] here to pursue fairness, equal education opportunities. Education is an essence and a core value of our culture, and we pass it along to generations and generations ... In the future, when [our kids] grow up, it doesn't matter how much we devote to their education, it doesn't matter how much effort they put into their own education— years of work will be gone, only because of their skin color."

> Much of the wrath has been targeted at Ivy League schools, which consider a range of academic and non-academic factors in the

admissions process. Students for Fair Admissions (SFFA)—a group representing primarily Asian American students and parents—contends in a lawsuit that Harvard College uses implicit racial quotas even though they're illegal. (It accuses the University of North Carolina at Chapel Hill of similar allegations in a separate lawsuit.) Despite being the country's fastest-growing minority group, and despite applying to college in greater and greater numbers, the percentage of Asians admitted at elite schools has, according to SFFA, essentially flatlined over the last two decades. "That suggests that Harvard and the other Ivies have a hard-fast, intractable quota limiting the number of Asians that they will [accept]," said Edward Blum, a scholar at the American Enterprise Institute and the president of SFFA.

Whereas Asian American enrollment at the California Institute of Technology, which bases admission strictly on academics, grew from 25 percent in 1992 to 43 percent in 2013, it slightly decreased at Harvard—from 19 percent to 18 percent. SFFA also points to a widely cited Princeton study, which in 2005 found that an Asian American applicant must score 140 points more than her white counterpart on the 1600-point SAT.

The Asian American Coalition for Education (AACE) uses similar logic in a separate civil-rights complaint, which requests that the Education and Justice departments investigate the admissions processes at Yale University, Brown University, and Dartmouth College. The AACE, which represents more than 130 organizations, contends that the schools, in relying on de facto racial quotas and stereotypes, deny admission to highly qualified Asian American applicants while admitting non-Asian students of equal caliber.

Asians have been victimized by race-based policies throughout the country's history pointing to the 1882 Chinese Exclusion Act and the WWII-era Japanese internment camps, among other injustices. The Asian race, critics argue, includes countless ethnicities that are sorely underrepresented in higher education yet all clumped together in a single category on application forms: Cambodians, Laotians, and Hmong, for example. According to the AACE, the complaint

represents the largest joint action ever taken by Asian Americans
against the Ivy League.[106]

Efforts to reform affirmative action admissions policies are aimed at
identifying individuals who have been disadvantaged but
demonstrate the potential to overcome that through grit and
determined effort already demonstrated in lower-quality schools. But
this flavor of diversity-seeking, which would be more just to all than
race or sex preferences, has not actually been implemented in most
institutions on anything more than an informal level. The great
meritocratic experiment—using standardized tests as a key
component of admissions decisions—was begun by the Ivy League
schools starting with Harvard's use of the new SAT to award
scholarships beginning in 1933, and then taken up by most colleges
by the 1960s. It allowed students from faraway places and schools
with unknown or low quality standards to demonstrate their ability to
work with more challenging material, and universities began to give
preferences to geographic and culturally diverse students who did
well on the tests.

The Ivies and other elite schools discovered the downside of this
strategy: students from less wealthy and connected families were less
likely to enter elite business and political classes, where they could
support their alma maters through influence, connections, and large
donations. Tests also did not identify the students with the best
emotional intelligence or political skills, and some brilliant admitted
students turned out to be social basket cases unable to succeed in
social systems. Institutional imperatives prevented admissions from
being a completely neutral, meritocratic process then, and the
pendulum has now swung away from merit to the point where many
universities are removing test requirements to allow students to be
admitted who objectively could not qualify by tests and grades. An
"affirmative action mafia" has been created, and objective tests are
now viewed as discriminatory. A "diversity student" admitted for
racial balance usually ends up as a diversity hire in a government job,
perhaps at the EEOC or Justice Department, where the power of their

position can be used to reinforce the punishment of going against the political tide by scrapping preferences. Their pathway smoothed into government roles, they now are heavily overrepresented in the Dept. Of Education, where they promote punitive measures aimed at colleges that don't toe the line. As a result, the elite institutions quietly choose to admit the most politically savvy and upper-class minority candidates, who will enter the elite ruling class and continue feeding back influence and cash to their alma maters as the old WASP elite did. The original goal of giving the disadvantaged a boost to make up for past discrimination is lost, replaced by the superficial appearance of diversity—diversity of skin colors and ethnic origins disguising the fact that most students are still from relatively privileged backgrounds.

Harvard professor Steven Pinker committed academic heresy when he wrote in support of restoring standardized tests to a central place in admissions:

> Like many observers of American universities, I used to believe the following story. Once upon a time Harvard was a finishing school for the plutocracy, where preppies and Kennedy scions earned gentleman's Cs while playing football, singing in choral groups, and male-bonding at final clubs, while the blackballed Jews at CCNY founded left-wing magazines and slogged away in labs that prepared them for their Nobel prizes in science. Then came Sputnik, the '60s, and the decline of genteel racism and anti-Semitism, and Harvard had to retool itself as a meritocracy....

> At the admissions end, it's common knowledge that Harvard selects at most 10 percent (some say 5 percent) of its students on the basis of academic merit. At an orientation session for new faculty, we were told that Harvard "wants to train the future leaders of the world, not the future academics of the world," and that "We want to read about our student in Newsweek 20 years hence" (prompting the woman next to me to mutter, "Like the Unabomber"). The rest are selected "holistically," based also on participation in athletics, the arts, charity, activism, travel, and, we inferred (Not in front of the children!), race,

donations, and legacy status (since anything can be hidden behind the holistic fig leaf). ...

[Admissions officers fear] selecting a class of zombies, sheep, and grinds. But as with much in the Ivies' admission policies, little thought was given to the consequences of acting on this assumption. Jerome Karabel has unearthed a damning paper trail showing that in the first half of the twentieth century, holistic admissions were explicitly engineered to cap the number of Jewish students. Ron Unz... has assembled impressive circumstantial evidence that the same thing is happening today with Asians....

What would it take to fix this wasteful and unjust system? Let's daydream for a moment. If only we had some way to divine the suitability of a student for an elite education, without ethnic bias, undeserved advantages to the wealthy, or pointless gaming of the system. If only we had some way to match jobs with candidates that was not distorted by the halo of prestige. A sample of behavior that could be gathered quickly and cheaply, assessed objectively, and double-checked for its ability to predict the qualities we value....

We do have this magic measuring stick, of course: it's called standardized testing. I suspect that a major reason we slid into this madness and can't seem to figure out how to get out of it is that the American intelligentsia has lost the ability to think straight about objective tests. After all, if the Ivies admitted the highest scoring kids at one end, and companies hired the highest scoring graduates across all universities at the other (with tests that tap knowledge and skill as well as aptitude), many of the perversities of the current system would vanish overnight. Other industrialized countries, lacking our squeamishness about testing, pick their elite students this way, as do our firms in high technology. And as Adrian Wooldridge pointed out in these pages two decades ago, test-based selection used to be the enlightened policy among liberals and progressives, since it can level a hereditary caste system by favoring the Jenny Cavilleris (poor and smart) over the Oliver Barretts (rich and stupid).

If, for various reasons, a university didn't want a freshman class composed solely of scary-smart kids, there are simple ways to shake up the mixture. Unz suggests that Ivies fill a certain fraction of the incoming class with the highest-scoring applicants, and select the remainder from among the qualified applicant pool by lottery. One can imagine various numerical tweaks, including ones that pull up the number of minorities or legacies to the extent that those goals can be publicly justified. Grades or class rank could also be folded into the calculation. Details aside, it's hard to see how a simple, transparent, and objective formula would be worse than the eye-of-newt-wing-of-bat mysticism that jerks teenagers and their moms around and conceals unknown mischief.

So why aren't creative alternatives like this even on the table? A major reason is that popular writers like Stephen Jay Gould and Malcolm Gladwell, pushing a leftist or heart-above-head egalitarianism, have poisoned their readers against aptitude testing. They have insisted that the tests don't predict anything, or that they do but only up to a limited point on the scale, or that they do but only because affluent parents can goose their children's scores by buying them test-prep courses.

But all of these hypotheses have been empirically refuted. We have already seen that test scores, as far up the upper tail as you can go, predict a vast range of intellectual, practical, and artistic accomplishments. They're not perfect, but intuitive judgments based on interviews and other subjective impressions have been shown to be far worse. Test preparation courses, notwithstanding their hard-sell ads, increase scores by a trifling seventh of a standard deviation (with most of the gains in the math component).... SAT correlates with parental income (more relevantly, socioeconomic status or SES), but that doesn't mean it measures it; the correlation could simply mean that smarter parents have smarter kids who get higher SAT scores, and that smarter parents have more intellectually demanding and thus higher-paying jobs. Fortunately, SAT doesn't track SES all that closely (only about 0.25 on a scale from -1 to 1), and this opens the statistical door to see what it really does measure. The answer is: aptitude. Paul Sackett and his collaborators have shown that SAT scores predict future university grades, holding all else constant, whereas parental SES does not. Matt McGue has shown, moreover, that adolescents' test scores track the SES only of their biological parents, not (for adopted kids) of their adoptive parents, suggesting that the tracking reflects shared genes, not economic privilege.

Regardless of the role that you think aptitude testing should play in the admissions process, any discussion of meritocracy that pretends that aptitude does not exist or cannot be measured is not playing with a full deck....[107]

Knee-jerk "equality of outcomes" thinking has led to a partial abandonment of the aptitude tests that played a key role in opening the Ivies to the culturally and economically disadvantaged. Identity-group politics has led to government pressure (enforced by control of research and student-loan funding) to dole out admissions and jobs to members of politically-protected classes even though it erodes the excellence of the institutions and ultimately harms the nation as a whole by spreading the virus of racial and gender consciousness.

But there is hope. More common Americans are resisting the government's efforts to divide and classify them as anything other than Americans. Glenn Reynolds points out Prof. James Scott's book *Two Cheers for Anarchism:*

One need not have an actual conspiracy to achieve the practical effects of a conspiracy. More regimes have been brought, piecemeal, to their knees by what was once called '**Irish Democracy,**' the silent, dogged resistance, withdrawal, and truculence of millions of ordinary people, than by revolutionary vanguards or rioting mobs.[108]

More and more Americans, like Barack Obama, have complicated multiracial and multiethnic origins. The broad classifications invented by the census and EEOC tend to lump together proud individual peoples, with the worst examples being "Hispanic" and "Latino,"[109] obscuring enormous differences between origins in Spain, Cuba, Puerto Rico, Mexico, central America, and South America, and "Asian," covering peoples from Iran/Persia (sometimes—the bureaucrats can't decide[110]) to India to China and Vietnam. It has always been difficult to get people to categorize themselves when the categories were designed by bureaucrats ignorant of their culture, but the melting pot that is the US now contains multitudes of mixtures defying such simple binning.

Add that to the American values, which see origin, race, religion, and ethnicity properly subsumed by allegiance to the ideals of the Constitution, and large numbers of citizens are passively resisting by not answering or writing in "American" when asked such questions. It is illegal to ask for such information in employment applications, but employers are legally required to report the numbers to the EEOC. So far, at least, all such categories except official Native American tribal membership are legally undefined and there is no way to dispute anyone's self-reported classification.

This means anyone who wants to can report themselves as any race, religion, or gender (now that the political establishment is enforcing gender self-choice for everyone.) It is inherently ridiculous to set up a system offering special rewards for racial characteristics when there can be no legal definition of race; only the willingness to report honestly and thereby volunteer to be harmed by preferences keeps everyone from declaring themselves or their children members of favored classes.

Americans view the Indian caste system as vile, and the Indian caste preference scheme as an ugly bandage on a festering wound, but have tolerated affirmative action in the US for too long out of guilt over the stain of slavery. But unless a person can demonstrate slave ancestry and continuing discrimination not due solely to cultural factors, it cannot be fair to all the new Americans and citizens whose ancestors never benefitted from slavery to harm them to favor those of a slightly darker skin color.

As a result, "Some Other Race" is growing rapidly as a preferred answer to intrusive questionnaires. From "The Rise of the American 'Others'" by Sowmiya Ashok in the August 27,2016, *Atlantic:*[111]

Something unusual has been taking place with the United States

Census: A minor category that has existed for more than 100 years is elbowing its way forward. "Some Other Race," a category that first entered the form as simply "Other" in 1910, was the third-largest category after "White" and "Black" in 2010, alarming officials, who are concerned that if nothing is done ahead of the 2020 census, this non-categorizable category of people could become the second-largest racial group in the United States.

Oh no! "Officials" are alarmed! How dreadful it would be if racially-divisive political appeals stopped working to guarantee votes and continuing power for the Party of Government!

Among those officials is Roberto Ramirez, the assistant division chief of the Census Bureau's special population statistics branch. Ramirez is familiar with the complexities of filling out the census form: He checks "White" and "Some Other Race" to reflect his Hispanic ethnicity. Ramirez joins a growing share of respondents who are selecting "Some Other Race." "People are increasingly not answering the race question. They are not identifying with the current categories, so we are trying to come up with a (better) question," Ramirez told me. Ramirez and his colleague, Nicholas Jones, the director of race and ethnic research and outreach at the Census Bureau, have been working on fine-tuning the form to extract detailed race and ethnic reporting, and subsequently drive down the number of people selecting "Some Other Race."

The American solution: stop asking about race. It's none of your business.

The U.S. census form has evolved over 226 years. "Race is the oldest question we have in this country," Ramirez said. "We asked it in our first census in 1790, and we have been asking it ever since, every 10 years in a different way and different shape, but consistently throughout." "White" has been the only consistent racial term since August 1790, when marshals knocked on doors in the original 13 states and in the districts of Kentucky, Maine, Vermont, and the Southwest territory (Tennessee) to classify people as a "Free White Males" or "Free White Females," "Slave," or "All Other Free

Persons." The civil-rights era was a pivotal moment for how census data was used, Jones said. "Prior to that, the measurement of race and ethnicity in the census was often used, not for helping people, but to show how people can be differentiated," he told me. "But from the 1960s onwards, the measurement was really used to address problems and concerns." Today, it also serves to reapportion congressional seats and Electoral College votes.

The end of slavery should have meant the end of this question on the census. There is no proper governmental use for this information, since there is no proper governmental action that should depend on the race or religion of the citizen. France has the right policy: "The French Republic prohibits performing census by making distinction between its citizens regarding their race or their beliefs."[112] And every effort to categorize people fails in a true melting pot:

> A number of factors affect census results. Take, for example, an increase in ethno-racially mixed families. Among marriages in the United States, 15 percent are between people of different racial and ethnic origins, according to Richard Alba, a sociology professor at the City University of New York's Graduate Center. Alba's research also found that one in seven infants are born into an ethno-racially mixed family. "This is a really new and possibly important development because these are individuals who grow up in families that involve whites and minorities. They are truly straddling the dividing lines in American society," he said. "We don't really know enough about them to be able to say how they will identify themselves, how they will locate themselves within American society."

We need to help them decide to categorize themselves as part of groups needing preferences and programs!

> In 1977, the Office of Management and Budget, which supervises the U.S. Census Bureau, issued a directive on racial and ethnic classification for federal statistics. Ethnicity—such as "Hispanic" and "not Hispanic"—was separate and distinct from the concept of race. As a result, the "Some Other Race" category captured a lot of

Hispanics. Twenty years later, the OMB issued a fresh directive, allowing respondents to report more than one race on the 2000 census form. The racial categories available were: "White," "Black, African-American or Negro," "American Indian or Alaska Native," "Asian," and "Native Hawaiian or other Pacific Islander." The "Latino" classification was also introduced as an alternative phrasing for the "Hispanic" ethnic category. But the "Some Other Race" category, long part of the census, was not mentioned in the OMB directive. Instead, the Census Bureau decided to keep it to capture respondents who didn't identify with any of the other categories provided.

The race classifiers keep trying to find a scheme to get people to bin themselves, trying out a series of test questionnaires designed to increase self-declaration. The effort succeeded at reducing the Some Other Race responses, but not without raising questions from participants:

> [F]ocus-group participants… raised a series of questions: What was the census form really asking? Some felt "race" and "origin" were the same. Others believed "race" was defined as skin color, ancestry, or culture, while "origin" referred to where they or their parents were born. The takeaway: The terms were confusing and needed to be defined or eliminated altogether.

> The bureau's focus-group moderators went a step further, asking questions to try to understand participants' "situational identity," too, recognizing that respondents discussed and reported on their race differently depending on the context in which questions were asked. They explored themes of awareness and fluidity with questions such as, "When did you first become aware of your race?" to understand if and how racial identity changed over time. Jones noted that "the categories are not an attempt to define race biologically, anthropologically, or genetically, but we know that some people interpret it that way."

Census officials also found that people were more likely to report their race as long as they had a way to express their self-identification. "If you look at the current way we ask the race and ethnicity questions, one of the issues you will see here is that we don't have a write-in line for 'White' or 'Black,' so many groups went down to the 'Some Other Race' category," Jones told me. When space was offered for people to write in their choices, respondents seldom checked the box that said "White" or "Black" and instead wrote in "Irish" or "Jamaican" or similar. "The proportions were very different, too. It went from 3 to 5 percent of the white or black population giving the bureau detailed responses, to over 50 percent of whites and 75 percent of blacks using the write-in lines," he said.

Tweaks and additions to the form continue today. A new category dubbed "MENA" was tested during the 2015 NCT in an attempt to allow respondents who may have Middle Eastern, North African, or Arab roots to identify themselves. In the combined question format of the experiment sample, the "MENA" category was included as the seventh race, after "Hispanics." "What we observed in the AQE and the focus groups were that the Middle Eastern and North African population saying that they didn't see themselves in the current categories," Jones said. Last year, the Census Bureau met with the Arab American Institute and leading Middle Eastern and Arab American scholars, activists, and organizations to discuss including it to the form in 2020.

Or you could just stop asking. Identity is now seen as set of fluid, self-declared characteristics even for gender, much less race, culture, religion, and ethnicity. No lawful program should discriminate based on any of these factors, and when antiquated special privileges exist in law favoring women, men, racial groups, Native Americans, Native Hawaiians, etc., these should be seen as un-American and removed as quickly as possible.

One example of the problem: redistricting required by court orders under the Voting Rights Act designed to promote the election of black representatives by creating majority black districts is now devaluing black votes, as these districts vote so heavily for Democrats that they result in a few safe D reps ("wasting" the excess D votes) and more R reps from rural and suburban districts than might occur under a less race-motivated redistricting scheme.[113] This concentration explains why Republicans tend to control the US House of Representatives, not the widely-cited gerrymandering of districts, which is a less important factor.

Part Four

HR Hiring and AA

We reviewed Affirmative Action (AA) in the US and elsewhere and its negative effects, both on those who were intended to benefit from it and on the organizations that have implemented it. As time has passed, the original AA programs—meant to give a temporary boost to the prospects of black people damaged by slavery and a century of Jim Crow and racial discrimination—have broadened to include other protected classes like Latinos and women, and narrowed to exclude most Asians and other minorities that have succeeded without assistance despite past discrimination. AA programs in college admissions have been legally attacked and reformed in some places, but AA continues to influence hiring in many workplaces, especially in those subject to intensive government regulation like banks, schools, and hospitals. By continuing to put diversity goals above competence and efficiency, organizations have damaged their effectiveness and decreased accountability—protected classes are less likely to be disciplined or fired, and as a result every employee senses that merit is less important and the best are rewarded less while the worst performers are retained and promoted if required to meet diversity goals.

As a result, the least-efficient sectors of the economy are either government-funded or regulated. But corporations have copied the Civil Service-style job categories and hiring mechanisms, especially those larger corporations which have adopted the Federal government's General Schedule (GS)-style level system specifying job responsibilities and pay levels. Workers below top management are hired under the organization's general contract provisions as written in both labor law and specific policies documented in company handbooks, while higher executives may have specially-tailored contracts with provisions like golden parachutes (contract-cancellation bonuses), noncompete agreements, and custom deferred-compensation and stock option plans. We won't look at executive hiring, which is rarely influenced by HR screening and qualifications.

Until recently, private employers were relatively safe in choosing objective criteria for judging job applicants so long as no protected class members were being discriminated against—judged improperly based on skin color, national origin, sex, religion, or other irrelevant factors. That changed in the government sector when courts began to outlaw examinations and other requirements that they said had a disparate impact on protected classes—in other words, if the supposedly objective criteria did not pass the same percentage of protected classes as other applicants, it was deemed improper even if evidence pointed to its validity as a measure of future job performance. Most private industries ignored this and continued to hire on a combination of merit and personal recommendations, knowing that evaluations of job candidates from previous managers and industry contacts were likely to be more trustworthy and end up adding value to the company. Lawsuits made giving a negative recommendation hazardous, though, so many companies changed their policy to prohibit managers and HR from giving out any opinion on performance records of past employees—which led to today's kabuki dance where a troublesome employee is either damned with faint praise or blackballed in informal tone of voice phone calls, but never in writing.

As companies have grown and HR departments gained influence over hiring processes, most companies have tried to find ways to screen outside candidates that reduced the time-consuming and distracting work of resume evaluation and interviewing by hiring managers and team members. Recessions and slowing growth made hiring less frequent and many hiring staff and outside recruiters were eliminated as cost-saving measures. Personal recruiting was replaced by Internet sites and recruiting boiler rooms where low-paid recruiters cold-called prospects to almost accidentally match them with openings. That was a waste of everyone's time, so now companies are trying out services that purport to automate resume screening and interviewing, presenting hiring managers with supposedly qualified candidates and prepackaged video interviews for quick evaluation.

But any centralized scheme for pre-screening new hires is subject to political influence—HR can bias the screening to boost AA candidates and blackball competent candidates of undesired classes, like whites, Asians, and older people. When a non-technical 30-year-old female HR screener sees a resume from a 58-year-old white male engineer, she can dismiss it based on her bias against a man she would probably have trouble controlling—and this bias in hiring is every bit as bad for the organization as a previous era's bias against competent women and homosexuals. And no one is keeping statistics which might demonstrate how she is preventing some highly-competent candidates from being reviewed by the hiring manager and team.

There are several negative consequences. First, hiring managers may be unhappy with all of the candidates presented, unaware that some likely good fits were never allowed into the process. As a result, positions may stay open for long periods and much time is wasted rejecting inappropriate candidates who pass AA and HR screenings but can't convince the team they'd be right for the role. Another negative is a tendency to stick with internal candidates, who are known quantities from internal word-of-mouth and detailed records available to the hiring manager. But fewer outside hires means less new and diverse process knowledge being added to the company, and the Silicon Valley-style cross-fertilization of innovation between companies in a hot new field can't happen.

Hiring managers are aware of this, and the smart ones do their own search and bring in new people by effectively bypassing HR. The larger and more bureaucratized companies make this more difficult, which tends to slowly degrade their competitiveness; think of a regulated utility's staff versus a growing software company's. An older company in a regulated business will always be less dynamic, but can do well staffing an internal center for process and technology innovation by giving its manager complete staffing freedom and ignoring the usual rules.

In the reverse situation, many an innovative, fast-growing company has been gutted after an acquiring company begins to impose its own HR and personnel policies. Not only do innovators sense a loss of freedom to act without a committee's permission to get things done, but the new hires vetted by the acquirer's HR department are more likely to be clock-watching rule-followers who don't want to be responsible for success or failure of their teams. Gradual decline ensues, and after the frustrated innovators leave, the slow to catch on will dutifully work at their jobs until the parent company gives up, then move on to the next slot.

HR can resist this tendency, but only with leadership from the top—both CEO and a carefully-chosen head of HR can choose and groom HR staff to avoid this mistake.

Thought leaders in today's HR specialize in jargon and "aspirational" BS—they want HR heads to be seen as visionaries leading their companies to a Nirvana of fulfilled, productive, and most of all *diverse* staff. Plenty of lip service is paid to productivity and beating the competition with quality and service, but the focus is more often on community and fulfilling interpersonal relationships. That there might be some value in interpersonal *conflict* and *disagreement* over technological and market development doesn't enter their discussions.

But as we will see later, surveys show the most productive and best teams are those whose members feel they have been able to demonstrate their talents. A team that is always harmonious may not last long if their products are the result of groupthink unchallenged by the idiosyncratic few—it's hard to be happy when your company is losing its market share and your team is laid off. Diversity of opinion and good management judgement are key to being right and besting your competitors, who may be forced to spend too much time watching diversity training videos and becoming cynically detached.

Here are some HR thought leaders, excerpted from the book *The Rise of HR: Wisdom From 73 Thought Leaders,*[114] published by the HR Certification Institute and obviously meant to be a sales tool for their services:

> ...We have always provided employees with talent development opportunities in compliance with affirmation action and equal employment opportunities. However, a clear and unabashed focus on diversity and inclusion to advance organizational excellence and success may be unfamiliar to some. HR must help instill a new mindset—one that goes beyond merely complying with non-exclusionary laws, but truly commits to core values and believes that, with guidance, every employee has the capacity to perform at high levels.[115]

This is "No Child Left Behind" view of staffing. Leaving behind the old view where the best candidate should be hired or promoted regardless of race or class, in favor of the social work view of HR: that candidates can be chosen for inclusion and groomed, trained, and managed to be great performers regardless of native talent and background. Businesses that can afford to view staffing as a kind of social uplift effort are few—mostly government agencies where there's guaranteed funding and no competition is allowed.

Anyone who wants to see the trends in HR should skim this book. It's full of uplifting visions and short on accounting and business nuts and bolts. Those visions are lovely aspirations—but demonstrate how easy it is to make pretty speeches or TED Talks disregarding the realities of human nature and competition in teams.

Not everyone is an airhead, however. China Gorman writes:

> The best way to protect your culture's integrity is to be meticulous in only hiring people who fit within it. Yes, it will be tempting to hire people who have amazing skills but may not fit your culture. Don't do it. Don't even think about it! Just as one bad apple can spoil the bunch, so can one bad hire throw a wrench in all the hard work you and your company have invested in creating a unique and wonderful culture. Always remember that skills can be taught, but culture fit is like style—people either have it or they don't. Great culture is about

never settling. It's about doing the right thing, even when it's hard. So wait for the right person. You'll be glad you did, and so will everyone in your great workplace culture.[116]

This is *true*. If your workplace culture is focused on winning and growing in a free market, hiring those whose values are centered on whining about grievances and collecting rent on the value of the work of others through political power is going to poison your workplace culture and reduce morale. Now when HR managers in Silicon Valley talk culture fit, this is code for under 30, no family responsibilities, can work over 60 hours a week, and will put up with the preferred sports, progressive causes, and after-hours socializing of the other low-level staff. And not-so-subtle discrimination against even the most productive who don't fit this mold is common in startup culture. But a culture which encourages employees to have rich family and personal lives away from the workplace doesn't have to be less competitive—just smarter. Your best workers don't work the longest or stay at the office until 10 PM; they're experienced and knowledgeable enough to get their work done in less time, and your company won't sink when your junior employees grow up enough to realize they've been cheated out of a life and leave for more sustainable workplaces.

Fortunately, hiring managers aren't stupid, and (except in highly-regulated industries) they have resisted the HR pressure to hire too much diversity deadwood. And companies are still free to discriminate against people whose *culture* won't be helpful—which is why management needs to be careful not to hire those gender and ethnic studies graduates who seem to want to be social justice activists on someone else's dime.

The Personnel and successor HR department's primary role has been to deal with the discovery, retention, and separation of employees in a way that would keep both managers and companies out of trouble with the law—both Federal and state (especially in the case of progressive-dominated superstates like California and New York) labor laws and regulations, as well as private lawsuits. Much airy HR lip service is paid to the ideal of employees as valuable assets to be nurtured and trained, but as always the bottom line rules and employees can be valued assets one day and discarded the next, should business conditions require a layoff to keep earnings on track.

Concern for corporate survival in the face of government hostility is not paranoid. Corporations are just a legal way to organize a company to limit liability for owners and provide a framework for management, but the charter is controlled and revocable by the state, and corporations are occasionally subject to the death penalty (as in the case of Arthur Anderson, a venerated accounting firm that was destroyed when it was indicted by the Justice Department in the Enron case.) More commonly, tangling with authorities or being found guilty in a lawsuit are major financial hits and make it more likely current executive managements will be fired by the board, a black mark managements will work hard to avoid.

By relying on an HR department to keep its managers out of employment law troubles, companies reduce the risks of penalties and blemishes to their reputation. But as the number of laws and regulations increase, compliance has become more time-consuming and HR staffing has increased. HR departments have gone from a minor cost of doing business to a central factor in success or failure of the enterprise, and managements who let them metastasize without carefully controlling who staffs them and what effect they are having on personnel decisions are making a huge mistake.

CEOs and managers coming up from operations or marketing and sales may be tempted to see HR as a secondary issue, a source of trouble and interference to be put off or ignored whenever possible. That's an error similar to the general citizenry's error in voting for continuity unless times are really terrible, imagining a bird in the hand (stable leadership) to be better than two in the bush (a reform and growth-oriented candidate.) Neglect of HR's role in determining who staffs your teams and how productive they are will slowly degrade morale and performance, and leave you with a shell of a company after your best people move on to more fulfilling workplaces.

The overall role of the government in determining personnel policies has vastly increased since 1900 as progressives created and expanded the administrative state, a less-accountable fourth branch of the federal government which has authority delegated by Congress to legislate regulations, administer and interpret them, and adjudicate cases without the normal protections of courts. As we've seen with the EEOC, these agencies are dominated by true believers, union members, and apparatchiks of the Party of Government. The regulatory agencies' control over policies HR is required to enforce creates a kind of Stockholm Syndrome for HR department staff: HR must work to neutralize and remove company managers who oppose and act out against government regulations, so HR staffers may come to identify with the administrative state and neglect the interests of the company they work for, unless CEOs make sure their HR staff is regularly reminded otherwise. It's no coincidence that HR staffers in the US tend to identify as Democrats regardless of industry, and easily move between private and government employment.

If your HR staffers support a government which micromanages company and individual affairs; if they spend more time writing memos and going to conferences about increasing hiring of minorities and women instead of finding the best fits for each position; if they cooperate more readily with fellow travelers in government and nonprofits than the managers they are supposedly assisting—consider very seriously how you might reform your HR department to truly support your corporate goals.

If you're not in a sector where unions are an important part of workplace life, you might want to skip this chapter. Private sector unions, while helping to create the state and Federal labor laws HR is now in the business of enforcing, are no longer much of a factor in most industries. But if you have to deal with them, this chapter will explain why unions are contributing to the Great Slackening, the stagnant economy, and underemployment.

Private sector unions aren't the force they once were in the US. Manufacturing employment has dwindled, since production of things has moved overseas to a great extent (though the US is still producing a lot of high-end manufactures) but even more importantly, automation and process improvements have eliminated most low-skilled jobs in the sector. And globalization means a union that hobbles its domestic host industry with high wages and inflexible work rules will kill its host, as the UAW nearly killed US auto manufacturers. Stepping back from confrontation and destruction to see themselves more as partners with domestic manufacturers, today's US private sector unions are more often constructive.

Where global competition is not a factor, as in building trades and healthcare, unions are still imposing higher costs and restricting production. In an industry with a unionized workforce, HR's role in setting rules for management treatment of labor is limited, and in some industries like local building trades the union itself determines who is hired and fired. This has led to stresses as union locals tried to resist affirmative action efforts, treating union jobs as favors to be given to relatives and friends.

Efforts to force trade unions to employ more minorities have had scattered success, but the urban political power of such unions and their tribal nature has limited affirmative action plans. This 1995 report in the *New York Times* tells the story of Philadelphia:

The Philadelphia Plan, American labor's longest-running experiment
in affirmative action, is faltering. More than 25 years after the
Government set about trying to break the white monopoly in this
city's construction industry, renewed struggles over a shrinking pie
and constant changes in the rules of the game are eroding the
program's initial gains.

At one time the plan was a model for similar efforts elsewhere in the
country. But the backsliding here has now become another symptom
of the national decline of affirmative action, once viewed by blacks
and other minorities as a Federal commitment to their economic
progress but now seen increasingly as something of a hollow victory.

The Philadelphia Plan, based on an executive order issued by
President Lyndon B. Johnson, was put in place by the Nixon Labor
Department in 1969 to increase jobs for minorities, mainly blacks, in
high-paying skilled trades, which were tightly controlled by the
unions. The goal was to employ them in proportion to their numbers
in the area's work force.

For a while there were gains. The unions opened their ranks and
pitched their apprenticeship programs to train more blacks. The
ironworkers, electricians, carpenters, heavy-equipment operators and
other skilled trades unions now have a black membership of about 15
percent, up from zero in the 1960's.

But... the blacks do not obtain much work these days. A recent tour
of construction sites in Philadelphia turned up very few members of
minorities working at skilled jobs. And Government officials say the
picture is the same in other cities.

Keeping blacks out of union jobs is potentially damaging for
organized labor. Nationwide, black workers join unions more
frequently than any other group, Labor Department data show. One
of every five blacks employed in America belongs to a union. For
them, union jobs are a path to middle-class incomes. But the skilled
trades unions, which control nearly one million jobs that often pay

$18 an hour and up, still resist their presence.[117]

Public employee unions are now larger and far more politically powerful, having entered into coalition with the Democratic Party and playing a key role in campaign finance. Mandatory union dues now support a powerful corrupt feedback loop that works to increase government spending and employment, which results in more campaign contributions, which elects more representatives favoring more government programs. The effort to establish universal public pre-K education shows how this works—unionized government employees will displace private, lower-paid childcare workers, then funnel some of the new public spending to the pols who support expanding the program. The next book in this series will cover civil service and public employee union corruption, but for now we'll just look at private sector unions.

Normally, union strikes and threats of violence would be seen as violations of antitrust and racketeering laws. How did unions become exempt from most scrutiny and elevated to sacred cow status? A little history tells the tale...

The advent of industrialization and large workplaces encouraged formation of worker associations. Facing a powerful employer, workers that joined in a union could send a message about compensation or working conditions with less fear of individual reprisal. In the United States the union movement coalesced in the late 1880s, about the same time Wilson and the Progressives were formulating their program to mold the citizenry through government directives and regulation.

Since unions threatened the interests of powerful industrialists and employers, conflict was inevitable. Violence broke out between management and labor forces, with contract security agents ("company men") from Pinkerton infiltrating and fighting union members during extralegal labor actions. Unions were illegal in some places, and union tactics like picket lines enforced by union violence were met by violence from company goons.

In one incident, the Homestead Steel Strike of 1892, steelworkers

union members fought Andrew Carnegie's Homestead Steel
Company managed by Henry Clay Frick. Frick intended to break the
strike and had hired an army of three hundred Pinkertons to help get
strikebreakers into the Pittsburgh-area riverside plant, bypassing the
strikers' picket lines by boat. With both sides armed with guns and
thousands of workers and local citizens joining the battle, fighting
went on for days, killing nine strikers and seven Pinkertons. Martial
law was declared and public opinion turned against the union,
resulting in deunionization of most US steel plants.[118]

Union activity was seen as a threat to the social order and unions
themselves were feared as introducing "socialist" ideas. Conspiracy to
join together to raise pay had been illegal under English law, and US
law had followed suit. Many typical union tactics—picket lines and
harassment of workers and suppliers trying to get into plants,
secondary boycotts, and sabotage of equipment—were illegal. Yet
unions could perform a valuable function in communicating worker
views to management, and many thoughtful employers were able to
work with unions as an outlet for worker grievances.

The Depression and FDR's New Deal administration brought
much more government recognition and support for union activities.
The new administration believed overproduction and low prices were
the key reason for economic weakness, and so favored controls on
agricultural and industrial production to reduce quantities and raise
prices—so the administration also supported union activity
restricting the entry of low-priced labor and increasing wages for
union members. Much New Deal legislation protected and
encouraged labor unions, and the National Labor Relations Act of
1935 (the "Wagner Act") guaranteed the right of workers to form
unions and bargain collectively in the private sector. Nonunion
industries were organized, strikes increased, and wages rose in those
sectors. For those left out of unions, notably black men, prospects of
employment were diminished, and the economic recovery as a whole
is thought to have been delayed by the New Deal's legalized cartels
and restraints on competition.

Clarified rules and legalization of a constrained right to strike under the law defused most of the violence and disorder associated with union activity. Private-sector unions became another accepted part of the American scene, and the big labor union coalitions like the AFL-CIO joined in disavowing Communism to rid themselves of "un-American" associations.

The simplistic narrative of the noble union is usually set in a one-company town, say a coal mine, where workers have little choice of employer, while management is free to take advantage of their monopoly on local employment to gouge and mistreat workers. In a modern urbanized area, these conditions rarely occur, and workers have a choice of employers vying to hire them, which provides a competitive environment that tends to improve compensation and working conditions as productivity increases.

In reality, unions grew powerful where a choke point existed—where a large and expensive plant, fixed rails, or docks prevented re-routing the business activity elsewhere during a strike. Unions did best where workers were low-skilled and interchangeable, and where the workplace could not be moved and had a lot invested in it, or where a government monopoly existed, as in transit and garbage in many cities. Unions could raise worker compensation and write work rules tailored to union preferences in such situations, making the union job preferable to any competitive nonunionized work, with the union as a barrier to entry of new workers—those already in the union got more money and protection from competition who might be willing to take the job for less.

Unions in private industry with free trade and low barriers to entry tend to harm their hosts and eliminate themselves over time due to high costs and loss of flexibility. As a result, entire US industries were either offshored or automated, and private-sector union employment as a percentage of total private employment has fallen from a peak of around 35% in the mid-1950s to 7% today.[119] Unions are no longer a significant drag on the private sector, and remaining private-sector unions are much more aware of their need to cooperate with company management to produce high-quality, competitive products in a globalized world.

The special rights granted to unions under Federal law make them semi-permanent, unelected, and often unaccountable powers over both workers and companies. Union elections are often rigged, and retribution against challengers is common. The typical union has controlled its workplace for so long that very few current employees voted to authorize it:

> Most commentary claims unions represent workers and discuss (either in sorrow or matter-of-factly) how much union membership has declined. Few analysts will explain an incredible fact: Hardly any unionized workers voted for union representation.

> Analysis of NLRB election record shows 94 percent of unionized (private sector) workers did not vote for their union. 94 percent! Just 6 percent of unionized workers voted for it. Overwhelmingly union members have representatives they never asked for.

> This happens for a few reasons. First, unions do not have to regularly stand for re-election. They remain in office indefinitely unless workers petition for a decertification vote. Consequently most unionized workers inherit a representative that other workers choose decades ago. For example, the UAW organized General Motors in 1937. That decision still binds current employees.

> Second, requesting a decertification vote is very hard. Complicated legal requirements (and union harassment) stymie most attempts before they get off the ground. That is why less than 1 in 1,000 union members voted in a decertification election last year.

> Third, unions are increasingly bypassing secret-ballot elections altogether. They frequently wage negative PR campaigns designed to hurt non-union businesses. They only agree to stop if the firm waives their employees' right to a secret ballot. When firms succumb unions can organize a plant on the basis of publicly signed cards—cards that often do not reflect employees' true preferences.

> The upshot of these policies it that most unionized workers have

representatives someone else chose. So when media personalities claim unions represent millions of workers, remember that's not quite true. Only six percent of those workers asked for union representation.[120]

Nor do the kind of industry-wide unions like the UAW, which gained coercive power from the ability to shut down the entire auto industry instead of one plant or company at a time, contribute to productivity. Unions lobbied government to gain the power to organize entire industries just so they could exercise this power to shut down all production of a good; otherwise a strike would harm only one plant or company, while leaving their competitors free to take up the slack, which would not create the kind of public crisis unions needed to disturb the public and motivate politicians to muscle the companies to settle on union terms. These mega-unions were disastrous for their industries and the economy as a whole.

The history books, they say, were written by the victors. "...The victors of a social struggle use their political dominance to suppress a defeated adversary's version of historical events in favor of their own propaganda, which may go so far as historical revisionism."[121] Progressive journalists and historians have manufactured a rosy narrative of unions as protecting American workers from predatory employers, and continue to claim union shops contribute to productivity. While the New Deal is long gone, the saturation propaganda then and since has left this view as the conventional wisdom, rarely challenged.

Prof. Richard Epstein of the NYU School of Law did a remarkable interview where he took on the conventional wisdom:

> Now what about workers and the efficiency gains? One of the things that many companies do is they actually encourage the formation of worker committees of one kind or another because they have no market power to shut you down but they can give you a flow of information which you could then use to improve your processes and the sensible firms says if we put up a suggestion box and we use your

suggestion, you get a little bump in the paycheck if it's a small thing and a big bump in the paycheck if it's a big thing in terms of what you're doing.

One of the things they did under the labor statute in section 8-2 at the time was they made company unions illegal. Now why did they do that? Because they knew that the efficiency gains that a company union could supply to a firm would make it more difficult for them from the outside to unionize it as part of an international brotherhood.

Indeed one of the sensible compromises that you could have in legislation is you get rid of all of the inter-firm unions which have cartel powers and you allow unions to form on a plant by plant basis because they have very little market power that they could exert. But the progressive story as told by Brandeis and Frankfurt and so forth is done with such an abysmal ignorance of economic circumstances and empirical circumstances that it shows this particular deep contradiction.

Progressives always talked about the need for empirical evidence, right? And detailed study. They didn't do a lick of work in that direction at any time. You read the famous Brandeis Brief and Muller against Oregon. It is a series of string quotations to mindless sociological reports from the United States and Europe about the importance of government protection in labor. There's not a single normative argument they have, a single descriptive argument there, which asks the question, "Hey, are you guys telling the truth?"[122]

Discussing the Progressive era changes to law and court cases that allowed unions to escape the enforcement of normal antitrust and criminal laws:

...one of the two or three centerpieces of the 1912 presidential campaign, in which Wilson was a strong believer in unionization. He was a progressive coming out of New Jersey in Princeton. Credentials like that never lead you in the right direction even in 1908 and he's strongly supported and the Clayton Act was passed in 1914.

What it does is it introduces a separation between these two areas that the 1908 decision had denied. So they tighten the protections against businesses merging and so forth under section seven saying in effect we can enjoin various kinds of mergers [resulting in] substantially less competition.... But section six said labor is not an article of commerce. Agriculture is not an article of commerce and therefore these guys are all exempted... from the antitrust laws when they engage in their activity.

So you could see what they're doing. They basically overturn that. Come 1920, 1921, there's a case called Duplex against Deering and this is another one of these Pitney opinions. You could see what's going on. There are a bunch of companies that are unionized and what they tell their – what the employers tell them is we're not going to sign another union contract with you in an area where there's no sort of national labor relations act unless you take this fourth plant and you unionize it.

So they start running all sorts of boycotts of the—on the secondary nature against these guys and the question is since they were aided by management, are they out from underneath the exemption and is a very tough statutory construction question and Brandeis says no, they are protected and Pitney who wrote the yellow dog contract said no, that they're not probably the correct result both under the statute and certainly as a matter of principle.

The key thing to learn about this, if your unions are efficient, right? Then they should say, "Oh my god, this other plant is non-unionized. We have such a competitive advantage over there. Please don't unionize." But they said exactly the opposite.[123]

So already-unionized companies conspired with their unions to organize other companies in that industry, since otherwise the still-free companies would have a competitive advantage! This explains why once unions have organized part of an industry, the rest will face increasing pressures to go along even though it is not to their advantage.

Epstein goes on to discuss the advantages gained by union workers at the expense of consumers, workers who are shut out of jobs by union control, and society as a whole:

> [Re: benefits to union workers] Well, the answer is if you're a member of a cartel and your wages are increased by virtue of union intervention... That's why majority of people support the unions. We're putting aside here the dissenters like in the Friedrichs' case recently of which there were always some. But the thing to understand is the only way unions could raise prices is essentially to reduce the number of workers available.

> So you want to do this thing systematically. You have to figure out what happens to the welfare prospects of those individuals who don't make it into union memberships and they don't make it into union memberships because these monopoly powers become partly inheritable by saying I'm an electrician in the union. My son will now join the union in preference to anybody else and take my slot when I start to require.

> So you have to do that if you're doing a social welfare thing. Then you got to figure out what about the cost of union goods to other individuals when they want to pay for it and those costs go down. So their fortunes are going to be somewhat reduced and the fact that you are better [off] is true of every monopolist who makes these consumers worse off by raising prices.

> Then of course unions are much more dangerous than monopolies in terms of what they do because monopolies have no reason to interrupt production because it's only going to hurt them. Unions are bargaining with a manufacturer or an employer and they will often pursue high-risk, high-return strategies. We will go out on strike. We will disrupt production. We will get higher wages.

> In the meantime, people have to do without necessities. Children can't go on school buses. They have to stay at home. It's just all sorts of absolutely chaotic third party effects and when I took labor law, I

was told that these things ought to be ignored. I said, "Why would you ever ignore them? You guys start writing about monopolies and there's no disruption to supply. You talk about high prices and so they're wrong. You're right about that. So why somehow does that thing not apply here?"

So, the answer to this is that solipsism is not the same thing as an argument which explains not why unions benefit the people who join them and profit from them, but why they are socially desirable. Nobody in the labor union tries to do this. The irony to understanding this, I'm talking about social welfare functions and how competition leads to optimality across all persons and all resources. These guys are talking about provincialism and then what they do is they turn around and say, "The problem about you professor actually is you're a rugged individualist."

They got it exactly backwards. They are the ones who are essentially working against the public welfare under these circumstances and the bromides that you hear from higher political figures essentially simply obscure that particular fact by using these sorts of nebulous terms, fair shot, fair share and all the rest of that stuff. You could drown on sharing this unfairness if in fact it's just a substitute for what cartelization is.

…You don't want to induce monopolization because what that does is it creates disruptive bargaining, holdout situations. It makes everything look like the inefficient transaction at the back fence. So in this regard, unions are an unmitigated disaster relative to a straight, smooth, competitive economy, which is why it is that the 95 percent of the labor force now, which is non-unionized doesn't have any of the burp and hiccups that the union sector does unless these poor people are working in a union firm where a strike will disrupt their particular employment prospects.[124]

Union work stoppages impose heavy costs on others, not just on the employers. By taking away individual rights to trade and travel and using extortionate threats of violence as a tool, unions worked to keep traditionally white workforces white:

[Re: Unions trying to keep black people from undercutting their wages]: Oh, sure. I mean, look, the key case – this is a case called Steele against the Louisville and the Nashville railroad and it arises under the Railway Labor Act, which I mentioned earlier in this podcast, right? Where I said—in fact in 1926, what they did is they made a single union having sole monopoly power over everybody.

Prior to the existence of this statute, essentially there were competitive unions. One was black and one was white. The reason they segregated on voluntary lines is that the element of trust within the races particularly in those days was vastly greater than the element of trust across the races.

So what the employers would do is play off one union against the other and essentially the black firemen and the black helpers worked [for] about the same amount of money as the white firemen and the white helpers in their particular union.

[A] case called J. I. Case Co. introduced the situation in which the union can abrogate all previous contracts of all bargaining members. Once their majority is chosen, you don't have two separate unions. You have one union 65 percent white, 35 percent black say. What they do is they now run a democracy. So they vote and this is what happened to say that every job in the particular union which was high-paying belong to white workers and every job that was low-paying belonged to black workers. They said to the firms, "You accept this or we will go out on strike."

So they got 21 railroads or something like that to go along with it. Now, this is absolutely outrageous and it kind of shows you how it is a majority can vote to confiscate the wealth and prosperity of a minority, which shows you why it is unvarnished popular democracy in the union context works no better than it does in the political context …[125]

But Epstein sees a place for unions that are voluntary worker associations, able to aggregate and communicate worker concerns and help management improve working conditions and processes:

> [Supporting voluntary employee associations]: ...there is an
> incentive to have company unions in these cases because a lot of
> times, workers may have an instinctive distrust that an organization
> will help them overcome and that means in effect that they can
> basically do better in coordinated activities than they could have
> done without a union. Most firms understand that. I mean yeah, I've
> been an employer.

> Every time I have a particular problem, I'm quite happy to put
> together a worker's committee if I think they're going to be able to
> solve this thing and to give them a charge and the important thing
> that you do as a boss is you actually endorse and support their efforts
> and you can't do that if it's a union because they're always stealing
> information from you in order to figure out how to run the next
> collective bargaining negotiation.

> So what happens is unions kill cooperation down at the molecular
> level. They create the lousy form of labor regulations that a good
> employer will try to avoid.[126]

The entire interview is worth reading if you're interested in the real
power relationships and political forces that allowed unions to escape
normal laws and gain their undue influence.

Court decisions that allowed unions to use extortionate threats
with impunity are now coming into question, and public officials who
cooperate are being criminally charged:

> There was nothing subtle about the labor battle between an electric
> workers union and a Louisiana utility. Workers fired high-powered
> rifles at company transformers. They drained oil from company
> machinery. They blew up a transformer. And the Supreme Court
> ruled that their actions didn't violate federal law because they were
> part of union activity. That early 1970s ruling—known as the
> Enmons decision—helped set parameters for acceptable union
> activity—a question now at the heart of a federal inquiry into union

actions in Philadelphia, Buffalo, and, most recently, Boston.

In the Boston case, three Teamsters members were sentenced last year to federal prison for threatening to "shut down" events run by businesses that hired nonunion workers. In another local pending case, five Teamsters members are accused of disrupting the filming of a television show in an attempt to extort jobs from a production company that hired nonunion workers. A City Hall official has since been indicted in relation to that case, and is also accused of withholding permits to a music festival to force the hiring of union workers.

Kenneth Brissette's indictment appears to stem from the federal investigation into the city's dealings with Boston Calling. In each of the union cases, the union members declared their innocence; their lawyers have cited the Enmons Supreme Court decision as protection for their actions. The recent prosecutions, and the ongoing federal investigation into union tactics that has reached into City Hall, have led legal observers to wonder: What's the line between advocacy on behalf of working people and unlawful coercion.

Legal analysts say that the Supreme Court could be asked to revisit the question, saying the 1973 Enmons decision no longer sets the standard in labor prosecutions. "It was a case decided in a different time, a different era," said Wally Zimolong, a Philadelphia-based construction attorney who has monitored the cases there, in Buffalo, and in Boston.

Another point that remains unclear is whether the Enmons decision protects public officials such as Kenneth Brissette, the city's director of tourism, sports, and entertainment, who was indicted this month for threatening to withhold permits from a music festival that had hired nonunion workers. Brissette would have been acting on behalf of the union, though he wasn't a member.[127]

The overall effect of union activity in the US has been to slow growth, reduce total incomes of most workers so that a unionized minority can make more, and further corrupt government, which gave unions their economic power. Politicians in union pockets continue to promote them at the people's expense. Thomas E. Woods, Jr., writing for the Mises Institute, sums up the staggering costs:

> The ways in which labor unionism impoverishes society are legion, from the distortions in the labor market described above to union work rules that discourage efficiency and innovation. The damage that unions have inflicted on the economy in recent American history is actually far greater than anyone might guess. In a study published jointly in late 2002 by the National Legal and Policy Center and the John M. Olin Institute for Employment Practice and Policy, economists Richard Vedder and Lowell Gallaway of Ohio University calculated that labor unions have cost the American economy a whopping $50 trillion over the past 50 years alone.
>
> That is not a misprint. "The deadweight economic losses are not one-shot impacts on the economy," the study explains. "What our simulations reveal is the powerful effect of the compounding over more than half a century of what appears at first to be small annual effects." Not surprisingly, the study did find that unionized labor earned wages 15 percent higher than those of their nonunion counterparts, but it also found that wages in general suffered dramatically as a result of an economy that is 30 to 40 percent smaller than it would have been in the absence of labor unionism.[128]

Labor lawyers and labor economists have historically been supported by labor unions and their cooperating Democratic legislators, who fund labor-leaning academic institutions. As a result, HR degree programs and faculty begin with a bias toward the labor laws and union-style thinking of academics in the field.

Social scientists generally lean left. Industrial Relations (IR), the field of labor-management studies, also leans sharply left.[129] Social science professors are overwhelmingly Democrats.[130] And the faculty in most HR degree programs are similarly biased, which means the typical new graduate from these programs has been indoctrinated to accept the necessity and essential fairness of the labor laws and regulations they will be expected to help enforce in their postings in private industry or government agencies. While we have seen that these new graduates tend to be tempered by exposure to real workplace life and management influence, they retain their political affiliations and continue to lean toward progressive causes and regulations.

Verdant Labs' survey of political affiliation by occupation based on FEC campaign contribution reports doesn't separate out HR staffers, but does cover HR execs and similar functions:

HR Executives 66% D, 34% R
Compliance Officers 72% D, 28% R
Administrative Manager 70% D, 30% R[131]

It's easy to see why people whose careers involve administering government rules would tend to support the party that maintains even more regulations are useful and necessary, because no one would want to work at something useless or even counterproductive. People who want to work long hours and enjoy the freedom to run risky but successful enterprises aren't likely to be found in HR degree programs. This political tendency is valuable in cooperating with government overseers, but can cause HR staff to overlook the need for the organization they work for to improve productivity and compete with overseas firms not so hampered.

What is the leftist tendency? It is the view that people's economic decisions are to be supervised and regulated by the state for the common good. Communists and Socialists took the simplistic extreme form, taking direct ownership of the means of production—factories, farms, and businesses—to be managed by the workers collectively or the larger state. Every country that tried this failed eventually because it turns out self-interested management by owners is vastly more productive, and no collective can decide as well as an owner with direct access to local and market information.

The leftist fallback position—after millions of deaths and multiple failures of true Communist and Socialist states—has been to leave property and the means of production in private hands, but thoroughly regulate and control what the owners may do with it. This leaves at least some incentive for owners to produce and invest in production facilities, but leaves many important investment and employment decisions in the hands of a political body—a legislature, or agencies given power to oversee employers. And while some socially-harmful decisions (like pollution of the common air and water, discrimination against black people in employment and accommodation, and tolerance of dangerous working conditions in mines and factories) are thereby prevented, many other decisions are made poorly by collective bodies with little or no knowledge of local conditions. The freedom of both worker and employer to balance their interests and negotiate the most favorable contract is often limited by rigid labor regulations, as when workers who would like to work more hours to make extra money are not allowed to do so.

Union labor views were an offshoot of the socialist ideal, where the management of a business—the employer—is viewed as the enemy of the workers, constantly trying to cheat and enslave them. Enlightened managers, of course, have a much broader interest in the health and welfare of employees, and know that respect for their needs and independence makes for a happier, more productive, and loyal workforce ideal for long-term competitive advantage. But the cartoonish 1930s views of oppressive, wealthy capitalists still live on in many minds.

The labor laws dating from the progressive New Deal era embody the *dirigisme* (French for top-down direction of the economy) of that era, and are still with us, though many reforms have taken place. The US is now a patchwork of different labor regimes in different industries, as some unionized manufacturing has become less so, while public employee unions have grown in strength and power. Meanwhile, "right to work" laws in some states limited private sector union power and encouraged more foreign investment like the auto plants now dotting the South.

To see the negative results of heavy regulation of labor, one only has to look at parts of Europe that went all-out to protect and micromanage employment by heavily regulating hiring and firing. As an example, look at France—a highly-developed mature economy with heavy regulation of labor and so much legal job protection that employers are reluctant to hire any long-term employees for fear they can never be let go. Youth unemployment hovers around 25%, and the economy has been stagnant for decades. The BBC reports:

> France has a lot going for it. It has "an enviable standard of living", according to the Organisation for Economic Co-operation and Development (OECD). "Inequality is not excessive and the country has come through the [financial] crisis without suffering too heavily," it says....
>
> But all is not well. Unemployment is high and the government's finances are weak. "France's fundamental economic problem," the OECD says, "is a lack of growth." The latest figures for economic activity (gross domestic product or GDP) for the first quarter of the year show growth of 0.5%. That's better than was expected though it's probably best described as reasonable rather than strong. The longer term picture is more downbeat.

So what is the French economic problem? The most obvious social and economic evidence that something is amiss is unemployment. About three million people are unemployed—10.2% of the workforce. That compares with a figure of 4.3% across the border in Germany. The rate in France is almost the same as the average for the eurozone. That really is nothing to be proud of when you consider that the average reflects some jobless nightmare stories such as Spain and Greece. The French figure is also the second highest among the G7 leading developed economies. Youth unemployment is a particular problem, as it is in a number of other European countries. Almost one in four of those under 25 who want a job don't have one.

The government's finances are also in indifferent shape. France is also in the throes of an EU procedure that tries to impose discipline on governments' finances. The annual budget deficit and the accumulated government debt are both higher than they are supposed to be under the rules.... Behind the problems lies persistently weak economic growth. Gross domestic product per person—a rough and ready indicator of average living standards—grew more slowly between 1995 and 2007 than in any other OECD country (mainly the rich nations) except Italy [which also overregulates labor.]

By the end of last year, economic activity was only 2.8% up from its peak level at the onset of the financial crisis. Why then is France struggling? Many younger people get work on a short-term basis only.... The view of many, including the OECD and the European Commission, is that the labour market is at the heart of the problem, though it's not the only factor. That reflects a persistent complaint from business: that it's too expensive to hire workers and to fire them or lay them off if they need to. France is a prime example of what is known as a "dual labour market": insiders have higher pay, job security and often promotion prospects, [while] others, especially younger people, get only short-term work or none.

The OECD says in its assessment of the French economy: "To reduce the duality of the labour market, the procedures for laying off employees, particularly those on permanent contracts, need to be simplified and shortened.... France ranks among the countries with the strictest legislation of dismissal for open-ended and temporary contracts." The cost of labour to employers in France also includes social security contributions that are higher than in most other countries. There is a catalogue of other issues, including welfare, that is alleged to discourage people taking low-paid work, and extensive regulation of business. The result, it is argued, is a persistent unemployment problem....

President Hollande has accepted the case for labour reform, and his Labour Minister, Myriam El Khomri, has introduced legislation intended to address some of the things that business voices say make it too expensive to take on new workers. The reforms would: lower existing high barriers to laying off staff; allow some employees to work more—far more—than the current working week, which is capped at 35 hours; give firms greater powers to cut working hours and reduce pay. That has met protest and the provisions have been amended in response. One supporter of reform said it was turning into a "veritable catastrophe".[132]

Compared to France, the US has a free and dynamic labor economy,[133] but the signs of the Eurodisease are starting to show—an inflexible labor market with few professional openings for young people. The common joke about children returning to live in their parent's basements is becoming a way of life for many. Increasingly, new college graduates are forced to take low-paying, unskilled jobs in service industries when they find work at all:

Recent college graduates are ending up in more low-wage and part-time positions as it's become harder to find education-level appropriate jobs, according to a January study by the Federal Reserve Bank of New York.

Jeanina Jenkins, a 20-year-old high-school graduate from St. Louis, is stuck in a $7.82-an-hour part-time job at McDonald's Corp. that she calls a "last resort" because nobody would offer her anything better.

Stephen O'Malley, 26, a West Virginia University graduate, wants to put his history degree to use teaching high school. What he's found instead is a bartender's job in his home town of Manasquan, New Jersey.

Jenkins and O'Malley are at opposite ends of a dynamic that is pushing those with college degrees down into competition with high-school graduates for low-wage jobs that don't require college. As this competition has intensified during and after the recession, it's meant relatively higher unemployment, declining labor market participation and lower wages for those with less education....

"The underemployment of college graduates affects lesser educated parts of the labor force," said economist Richard Vedder, director of the Center for College Affordability and Productivity, a not-for-profit research organization in Washington."Those with high-school diplomas that normally would have no problem getting jobs as bartenders or taxi drivers are sometimes kept from getting the jobs by people with college diplomas," said Vedder...

The share of Americans ages 22 to 27 with at least a bachelor's degree in jobs that don't require that level of education was 44 percent in 2012, up from 34 percent in 2001, the study found. The recent rise in underemployment for college graduates represents a return to the levels of the early 1990s, according to the New York Fed study. The rate rose to 46 percent during the 1990-1991 recession, then declined during the economic expansion that followed as employers hired new graduates to keep pace with technological advances....

"College graduates might not be in a job that requires a college degree, but they're more likely to have a job," she said. Less-educated young adults are then more likely to drop out of the labor market. The labor participation rate for those ages 25 to 34 with just a high-school diploma fell four percentage points to 77.7 percent in 2013 from 2007. For those with a college degree and above, the rate dropped less than 1 percentage point, to 87.7 percent.

"At the complete bottom, we see people picking up the worst types of jobs or completely dropping out," Beaudry said. The share of young adults 20 to 24 years old neither in school nor working climbed to 19.4 percent in 2010 from 17.2 percent in 2006. For those ages 25 to 29, it rose to 21.3 percent from 20 percent in that period, according to a Federal Reserve Bank of Boston report in December.

Those with the least education have trouble securing even the lowest-paid jobs. Isabelle Samain looked for work in Washington from April until September of last year. As prospective employers continually passed over her applications, the 40-year-old mother of two from Cameroon realized she was missing out because she lacked a U.S. high-school diploma. "I don't even remember how many places I applied," Samain said of the "frustrating and discouraging" search. Samain passed the General Educational Development test in December and recently started working at Au Bon Pain in Washington for $8.50 an hour for 36 hours a week.

A year-long survey ending in July 2012 of 500,000 Americans ages 19 to 29 showed that 63 percent of those fully employed had a bachelor's degree, and their most common jobs were merchandise displayers, clothing-store and cellular phone sales representatives, according to Seattle-based PayScale Inc., which provides compensation information....

The share of recent college graduates in "good non-college jobs," those with higher wage-growth potential, such as dental hygienists, has declined since 2000, according to the New York Fed study. Meanwhile, the portion has grown for those in low-wage jobs paying an average wage of below $25,000, including food servers and bartenders.[134]

The Party of Government perpetually campaigns on "doing something" about the problems of the little people. Meanwhile, the agencies of the administrative state, like all bureaucracies, keep busy and justify their growth by proposing additional and extended regulations. When regulations address a real problem—some externality requiring private parties to be restrained from damaging a common good or harming each other through force or fraud—there is an optimal point where the additional costs of more regulation are greater than the likely benefit. In labor regulation, the pols and regulators rarely consider the collateral damage they are doing by narrowing the freedom of contract—labor laws are always behind the curve of technology and custom, impeding creative solutions that both employer and employee would benefit from.

This "it's always good to do more" mindset results in laws that are simply propaganda exercises, like the Lily Ledbetter Fair Pay Act of 2009, which extended the statute of limitations for equal pay suits to make it a bit easier to file suit against ongoing patterns of pay discrimination against women.[135] Unequal pay for women was actually outlawed in 1963 by the Equal Pay Act, but Democratic politicians in pursuit of women's votes continue to promote the "pay gap" myth and then offer to "do something" about this imaginary unfairness. Each time they pass a new law or regulation, one might expect improvement in the unfair situation they claim to be addressing, yet the problem remains for the next election, when they will promise to fix it again.

The latest example of harming many by ratcheting up the regulations is the Obama administration's enlargement of the number of employees covered by the Dept. of Labor's overtime regulations under the Fair Labor Standards Act (FLSA), increasing the salary limit for exemption from $23,660 to $47,476 per year, which vastly increases the number of workers covered. At first glance, this sounds good for those employees—time-and-a-half for overtime, baby! But that ignores the likely response of managements to the new rules:

> If an employer could pay Jim, a frontline manager at a retail store, for a 50-hour workweek—40 hours at his regular hourly rate and 10 hours at time-and-a-half—or, instead, pay Jim and Jane 25 hours each at straight rates, what would the employer do?

> Unless the business is a philanthropy, or unless Jim exhibits pure brilliance in directing rank-and-file employees to stock shelves, the

employer is going to choose lower labor costs over higher ones.

This is precisely the question raised by, and the likely effect caused by, new overtime rules under the Fair Labor Standards Act ("FLSA"). Given the basic economics of the workplace, the new rule—which raises the salary threshold under which an employee is entitled to overtime—is just as likely to create less work for individual employees as it is to increase the amount of overtime American employees collectively earn.[136]

The required estimate of costs of the new regulation was lowballed, pulled out of thin air by the DoL under orders from the union-friendly administration to further cripple nonunion businesses by increasing their costs. Independent calculations of the cost were more realistic:

How reliable are projections from the Department of Labor about the cost of the President's ambitious new extension of overtime entitlements to salaried workers ....? The "administration refuses to allow others to check its math. The Florida Department of Economic Opportunity, the state agency that I lead, in August requested the specific data and methodology the Labor Department used to calculate its estimates. Our request was denied." So the department went ahead with its own analysis. "The rule will supposedly cost $2 billion the first year. Our math shows $1.7 billion for Florida alone."[137]

Even House Democrats found the new rules damaging:

It's not clear whether the Obama administration's forthcoming edict on overtime will apply to legislative staffers, but House Democratic leadership decided it would be prudent for their members to at least gesture toward the spirit of the controversial rule by preparing for compliance. Now "the rule is creating administrative headaches" and more:

"We don't have a set-hour kind of situation here; some kids work 12,

14, 16 hours a day, weekends, and I feel terrible that I cannot afford to give raises to the staff," Rep. Alcee Hastings (D-Fla.) told Bloomberg BNA Feb. 11.

With $320,000 slashed from members' representational allowances (MRAs) over the past four years, "I don't see how we could pay overtime" for the "17 or 18 people that each of us is allowed to have —that's problematic for me," added Hastings, a senior member of the House Rules Committee.

Some members fear that an overtime mandate will result in having to send staffers home at 5 p.m., leaving phones unanswered and impairing constituent service. "Most members are of the sentiment that it's impractical to be paying overtime," said former Virginia Democratic Rep. Jim Moran, now a lobbyist, who suggests that members choose to close one of their district offices or reduce constituent correspondence to adjust to a smaller staff number.

If only there were some way for the U.S. Congress to influence federal labor law![138]

For decades, many large corporations have been "stack ranking" their employees—doing performance evaluations and on a relative basis, ranking their employees by performance along a bell curve. The practice of ranking, then laying off or forcing out the bottom performers is known as "rank and yank." GE CEO Jack Welch, who employed it heavily, now says that wasn't what he was doing at all—he wants to use the term "differentiation":

> Differentiation starts with communication—exhaustive communication—of a company's mission (where it's going) and its values (the behaviors that are going to get it there). I'm not talking about putting a plaque on the lobby wall with the usual generic gobbledygook. I'm talking about a company's leaders being so specific, granular, and vivid about mission and values that employees could recite them in their sleep.
>
> Why? Because the "guts" of the differentiation management system are performance appraisals that candidly evaluate employees at least once (and preferably twice) a year on how their results are advancing the company's goals and how well they're demonstrating its values. Two points here:
>
> First, candor is absolutely essential to make differentiation work. Second, differentiation's performance appraisals are not—I repeat, are not—just about "the numbers." Yes, the system does assess quantitative results—say, an employee's sales numbers or inventory turns. But it also looks just as carefully at behaviors, the qualitative factors. Does this person embrace the company value of sharing ideas? Does the employee relish building leaders? What about going the extra mile to delight customers?
>
> Now, one of the most common criticisms of differentiation is that it destroys teamwork. Nonsense. If you want teamwork, you identify it

as a value. Then you evaluate and reward people accordingly. You'll get teamwork, I guarantee it.

Another criticism of differentiation is that it requires managers to let every employee know where he or she stands—how they're doing today, both quantitatively and qualitatively, and what their future with the company looks like. Are they a star in terms of both results and values (say, in the top 20% of the team), about average (say, about 70%), or not up to expectations (the bottom 10%)? Note: The 20-70-10 distribution is not set in stone. Some companies use A, B, and C grades, and there are other approaches as well.[139]

The faddish management belief of the era was that you must measure first to manage effectively, this process was copied by most companies, but not always with the commitment to full communication and honesty Welch suggests. If every time a layoff is needed you fire the worst-ranked, the company soon finds itself hiring people in the next upturn who may or may not be any more effective than those recently laid off. Since these evaluations are both subjective and sensitive to the worker's local environment, employees who might be highly effective in another position or on another team find themselves bounced out, often not for any failing but for failings of their team or manager. Because managers know the rankings will be used to lay off people, there is a temptation for them to game the system to eliminate people they dislike working with, for whatever reason.

Measuring "effectiveness" is similar to the *credit assignment problem*[140] from machine learning algorithms: given a complex, multistep process with many actors, how does a supervising manager decide which actors should be given credit for the success or failure of the production? Any simplification tends to misallocate credit, and adjustments based on incorrect credit scores will be less likely to improve performance in future problems.

After decades in use, it was widely recognized that "rank and yank," at least as practiced at most companies, was actually degrading the workforce and damaging morale, and companies like Microsoft modified or abandoned it.[141] Qualitative performance measures can be useful, but using them to name and shame underperformers and identify layoff candidates may do more harm than good. From *Vanity Fair's* story on Microsoft's morale issues when CEO Steve Ballmer left:

> Eichenwald's conversations reveal that a management system known as "stack ranking"—a program that forces every unit to declare a certain percentage of employees as top performers, good performers, average, and poor—effectively crippled Microsoft's ability to innovate. "Every current and former Microsoft employee I interviewed—every one—cited stack ranking as the most destructive process inside of Microsoft, something that drove out untold numbers of employees," Eichenwald writes. "If you were on a team of 10 people, you walked in the first day knowing that, no matter how good everyone was, 2 people were going to get a great review, 7 were going to get mediocre reviews, and 1 was going to get a terrible review," says a former software developer. "It leads to employees focusing on competing with each other rather than competing with other companies."
>
> When Eichenwald asks Brian Cody, a former Microsoft engineer, whether a review of him was ever based on the quality of his work, Cody says, "It was always much less about how I could become a better engineer and much more about my need to improve my visibility among other managers." Ed McCahill, who worked at Microsoft as a marketing manager for 16 years, says, "You look at the Windows Phone and you can't help but wonder, How did Microsoft squander the lead they had with the Windows CE devices? They had a great lead, they were years ahead. And they completely blew it. And they completely blew it because of the bureaucracy."[142]

Given that few employees can be numerically evaluated by anything as simple as dollar value of sales closed or number of widgets assembled, companies often use a distributed subjective evaluation which relies on not only the employee's manager's rating but adds in the views of peers and subordinates, thought to be more nuanced than stack ranking. This is called *360-degree feedback* or multi-source assessment:

> ...due to the rise of the Internet and the ability to conduct evaluations online with surveys, multi-rater feedback use steadily increased in popularity. Outsourcing of human resources functions also has created a strong market for 360-degree feedback products from consultants. This has led to a proliferation of 360-degree feedback tools on the market.
>
> Today, studies suggest that over one-third of U.S. companies use some type of multi-source feedback. Others claim that this estimate is closer to 90% of all Fortune 500 firms. In recent years, this has become encouraged as Internet-based services have become standard in corporate development, with a growing menu of useful features (e.g., multi languages, comparative reporting, and aggregate reporting). However, issues abound regarding such systems validity and reliability, particularly when used in performance appraisals.
>
> Many 360-degree feedback tools are not customized to the needs of the organizations in which they are used. 360-degree feedback is not equally useful in all types of organizations and with all types of jobs. Additionally, using 360-degree feedback tools for appraisal purposes has increasingly come under fire as performance criteria may not be valid and job based, employees may not be adequately trained to evaluate a co-worker's performance, and feedback providers can manipulate these systems. Employee manipulation of feedback ratings has been reported in some companies who have utilized 360-degree feedback for performance evaluation including GE...[143]

One manager I talked to gave me this bullet-pointed assessment:

- 360 degree reviews in a hierarchical structure have inherent flaws
- No one can give honest feedback
- Encourages incredible political maneuverings and self-sustaining cliques of incompetence
- Team structure can be vicious in excluding those who are "different"

- ...but the #1 question still remains: How to get rid of incompetent bosses...and why HR allows such islands of incompetence to exist (see self-sustaining... above)
- "Forced Ranking" of employees from most valuable to least valuable (in order to prune the least valuable) generally ignores a number of ancillary factors such as time-in-grade, training, salary, trend analysis. Currency bias is rampant (and generally, too).
- Annual goal settings at employee review time are a joke a) 100% in companies operating at "internet speeds"; b) and 99% of the time otherwise
- Such annual reviews are completely CYA and are done to comply with the dictates of the Legal Dept in cases when the company gets sued for discrimination---they really serve no other purpose
- Companies with traditional HR evaluation systems will be forever plagued by an exodus of competence as those folks won't stand for 3% raises while their less competent / hard-working brethren get 2.5%.[144]

So the desire of upper management and HR to "grade" employees and measure performance numerically, while understandable, can be bad for morale and encourage cynical gaming of the system. And one thing people are good at is gaming—looking at the reward system and doing what is necessary to get themselves money and security, which may be far from focusing on the job or the team's mission.

Performance evaluations are also used to decide on promotions, with the idea that metrics are a fair way to make decisions that will promote a more diverse workforce. That really doesn't work:

More than 90% of midsize and large companies use annual performance ratings to ensure that managers make fair pay and promotion decisions. Identifying and rewarding the best workers isn't the only goal—the ratings also provide a litigation shield. Companies sued for discrimination often claim that their performance rating systems prevent biased treatment.

But studies show that raters tend to lowball women and minorities in performance reviews. And some managers give everyone high marks to avoid hassles with employees or to keep their options open when handing out promotions. However managers work around performance systems, the bottom line is that ratings don't boost diversity. When companies introduce them, there's no effect on minority managers over the next five years, and the share of white women in management drops by 4%, on average.[145]

Performance appraisals live on, of course. In many companies, mid-level managers spend almost as much time completing and evaluating 360-degree performance reviews and making salary and promotion decisions supposedly based on them as they do focused on the projects they are assigned.

So why does a management system, so widely acknowledged as fundamentally flawed and so much a product of ancient history, live on in today's modern workplace? There are several reasons. The principal one is that today's crop of unimaginative HR managers and their consultant cronies don't actually appear to have any better ideas. "You can't stop doing performance appraisals," they scoff. "It's like playing a game without keeping score"— a statement which reveals how broken and outdated their thinking is.

Because work in the 21st century isn't a game. Sporting analogies have little relevance to today's workplace. Sportspeople train and practice for 95% of the time, in preparation for the 5% when they have to perform. It's the other way around in the world of work. Success in the world of sport, even in team games, is largely defined by the brilliance of individuals. In today's collaborative workplace, virtuoso performances are far less critical to the overall productivity of the business and its supporting teams (although still important, of course: no-one wants a workplace full of "cultural fit" clones, do they?)

Another reason managers are reluctant to consign performance appraisals to the Welchasaur dustbin of history is that, well, we have to have some way of rewarding the good performers, don't we? And to help (or weed out) the bad ones?... So why persist with the divisive and arbitrary "rating" of employees, the vast majority who are motivated by professional pride as much as a pay-check?

The pernicious apogee of this thinking was, of course, the infamous Welchasaurus refinement of the performance appraisal that came to be known as "rank and yank". "Neutron Jack's" rank and yank system rated workers on a three-step scale, based on a line manager's assessment of his team member's individual goals and performance, and then force-fitted to a "bell-curve". The top 15% were told they were "1s," the middle 75% were designated "2s" and the bottom 10% were assigned "3s." And the bottom 10% got canned. This process was rolled out every year.

(What happened when a team got hacked down to less than ten people? Did managers start firing people's body parts? "Your brain, heart and lungs meet expectations but here's the P45 for your liver...?").... But it ain't going to happen [at Yahoo.] Because someone has advised her that what Yahoo's downtrodden employees really need are rank and yank bucket ratings. As a result, "talented Yahoos are refusing to work with other talented Yahoos for fear of landing in the wrong bucket (or worse, are actively undermining each other), managers are trading rankings like baseball cards to meet bucket quotas, and employees are arbitrarily placed inside bad buckets for hallway remarks or executives who said, 'He just annoys me'"....

Of course, this type of "performance appraisal" is really only about one thing: Headcount reduction. It's a system devised by consultants for weak and lazy managers to hide behind when it comes to the nasty business of firing people. It allows them to stick labels on people they don't like and support it with a paper trail that leads their victims to the exit door. It also ensures that as many productive employees as unproductive ones leave the company: talent will not hang around in the toxic environment that "yank and rank" generates.[146]

Another HR manager, Anitha Rathod, shares her unhappiness with such systems:

> ...HR insists all [too] frequently that employees set goals for themselves, goals that are all too frequently rendered obsolete by events almost before they are set. The result is employees that are dinged for goals that they didn't have any more because their jobs changed and the goals were no longer relevant. All that happens in the end is massive employee dissatisfaction.

> Yet HR insists on keeping score as if a workplace is a game. And maybe, for them it is. Rate everybody and get rid of the people they don't like. Purge and reduce headcount. And they've convinced management in these time that this is a good idea.,,.

> I loathed the time when I as an HR [staffer] had to sit with a manager to force rank his team of 10 employees and identify the bottom performers despite the fact that the team had achieved all its targets and all the employees had given their best to achieve the team results. Every manager is expected to force rank and identity the bottom and top performers in the team and that's how the entire organisation starts to resemble a normal curve....

> Enormous amount of time goes into calibrations and writing reviews by the managers and the opportunity cost seems much bigger to offset the benefit that may or may not be derived from this tiresome process. A study by the Society for Human Resource Management found 90% of performance appraisals are painful and don't work. Most employees seethe [at] the process and it leaves them more agonised than ever, resulting in friction with the managers, the ripple effects of which can be seen on their productivity. Hence the very principle that governs the appraisals to motivate higher performances is a fallacy and organisations are left more devastated with good performers leaving. And the ugly truth still remains that the operational costs are too high.[147]

Annual performance reviews can be a good time for a manager to communicate with the employee, go over the year's successes and failures, and talk about the employee and the team's future goals and plans for improvement. But the formalized version complete with numeric ranking and forms to be filled out to put those plans and goals into a database can feel forced and is often badly timed to meet some corporate calendar. And if the employee hasn't received a lot of feedback and support along the way, it can feel like one of those stressful judgement days that make everyone nervous and give managers ulcers. Then it becomes a rushed chore against an arbitrary (for that team) outside deadline, and can easily be rushed and pro forma. The knowledge that the performance evaluation may also greatly affect upcoming promotion and compensation decisions also makes it less constructive and more stressful. Many companies end up with performance review cultures where everyone is above average—many managers are unwilling to deal with the extra work required when an employee "fails" a performance review. The managers may have learned from experience to avoid rocking the boat by giving blandly positive ratings to everyone.

One simple reform that may help: make the performance review more frequent and cap every major project end with a mini-performance review of that project. Make those promotion and compensation decisions on whatever timetable is required by the corporate calendar, but keep them separate.

Ashley Goodall from Deloitte Services, LP, and Marcus Buckingham wrote an article in the *Harvard Business Review*[148] on Deloitte's performance evaluation experiences and reforms which is densely packed with ideas and data—if you're interested in reforming your companies, it's worth a thorough reading. One thing they discovered: their complex 360-degree feedback process took up 2 million person-hours a year, with much of that spent in meetings discussing how to use the results to manage personnel—in other words, to influence them toward what managers wanted to do anyway. They decided to try to shift those hours from ratings and inter-manager talks toward communicating with employees more directly about their performance and careers.

This is what they discovered when they looked over the research on rating systems:

> The most comprehensive research on what ratings actually measure was conducted by Michael Mount, Steven Scullen, and Maynard Goff and published in the Journal of Applied Psychology in 2000. Their study—in which 4,492 managers were rated on certain performance dimensions by two bosses, two peers, and two subordinates— revealed that 62% of the variance in the ratings could be accounted for by individual raters' peculiarities of perception. Actual performance accounted for only 21% of the variance. This led the researchers to conclude (in How People Evaluate Others in Organizations, edited by Manuel London): "Although it is implicitly assumed that the ratings measure the performance of the ratee, most of what is being measured by the ratings is the unique rating tendencies of the rater. Thus ratings reveal more about the rater than they do about the ratee." This gave us pause. We wanted to understand performance at the individual level, and we knew that the person in the best position to judge it was the immediate team leader. But how could we capture a team leader's view of performance without running afoul of what the researchers termed "idiosyncratic rater effects"?

Deloitte examined a large study done by Gallup (the polling firm) of over 1.4 million employees on 50,000 teams in 192 organizations. They found almost all the variations between high- and low-performing teams were explained by a small number of factors, notably agreement with the statement "At work, I feel I have the opportunity to do what I do best every day."

The implication: *not* doing what you do best every day is a major cause of dissatisfaction, poor morale, and low team performance. This might be because, say, employees have to stop working on projects they feel productive working at to spend hours doing yearly performance evaluations, or budgeting, or expense reports, or going to unnecessary meetings that interrupt their flow state of work!

How did Deloitte Services use these findings to reform

performance evaluations?

> ...to recognize each person's performance, we had to be able to see it
> clearly. That became our second objective. Here we faced two issues
> —the idiosyncratic rater effect and the need to streamline our
> traditional process of evaluation, project rating, consensus meeting,
> and final rating. The solution to the former requires a subtle shift in
> our approach. Rather than asking more people for their opinion of a
> team member (in a 360-degree or an upward-feedback survey, for
> example), we found that we will need to ask only the immediate team
> leader—but, critically, to ask a different kind of question. People may
> rate other people's skills inconsistently, but they are highly consistent
> when rating their own feelings and intentions. To see performance at
> the individual level, then, we will ask team leaders not about the skills
> of each team member but about their own future actions with respect
> to that person.

One way to look at that: since the manager under their old system
would spend hours discussing employees with other managers with
the goal of getting the actions that manager wanted anyway, just ask
the manager what *actions they would want to take* regarding that
employee. This is vastly faster and, it turns out, more accurate at
evaluating that employee! And it gets directly to the result—which is
a return to the era when the team's immediate manager decided,
based on their local knowledge, how to assign, reward and nurture
team members. And both managers and team members are happier
not wasting all that time on efforts imposed on them by HR!

Combined with an effort to give more immediate performance
feedback, and not confining meta-communications (meetings about
the team process and each member's performance in it) to a once-
yearly ordeal, the feedback is fresher and doesn't break into project
timetables or waste everyone's time filling out HR forms to put formal
evaluations in a permanent database.

Deloitte came up with a plan to increase regular check-ins to
provide more frequent feedback:

Research into the practices of the best team leaders reveals that they conduct regular check-ins with each team member about near-term work. These brief conversations allow leaders to set expectations for the upcoming week, review priorities, comment on recent work, and provide course correction, coaching, or important new information. The conversations provide clarity regarding what is expected of each team member and why, what great work looks like, and how each can do his or her best work in the upcoming days—in other words, exactly the trinity of purpose, expectations, and strengths that characterizes our best teams.

Our design calls for every team leader to check in with each team member once a week. For us, these check-ins are not in addition to the work of a team leader; they are the work of a team leader. If a leader checks in less often than once a week, the team member's priorities may become vague and aspirational, and the leader can't be as helpful—and the conversation will shift from coaching for near-term work to giving feedback about past performance. In other words, the content of these conversations will be a direct outcome of their frequency: If you want people to talk about how to do their best work in the near future, they need to talk often. And so far we have found in our testing a direct and measurable correlation between the frequency of these conversations and the engagement of team members. Very frequent check-ins (we might say radically frequent check-ins) are a team leader's killer app.

That said, team leaders have many demands on their time. We've learned that the best way to ensure frequency is to have check-ins be initiated by the team member—who more often than not is eager for the guidance and attention they provide—rather than by the team leader.

"But," say HR staffers, "how will you defend the company against discrimination and other employment lawsuits unless we have detailed performance records in our database to back up a layoff or firing decision?" And the answer is—unclear as yet. The Deloitte reformers at first decided to keep the results of their streamlined evaluation questionnaires secret because managers otherwise were afraid to be frank, but apparently have realized that radical transparency is the likely future course. But they want to increase the *richness* of the employee record so that a fuller, multidimensional view of performance is captured. Instead of a ranking, employees would have a portfolio of projects and results. Dimly we can see how this would create just as defensible a record of performance (or lack thereof) for justifying decisions made by managers to outside authorities.

But the radical notion of *returning to employment at will*—the standard contract of employment a century ago, but surrounded by understandings and traditions not lightly broken by either party for reputational reasons—might end up being the best for all involved, in an age where every company action might be viewed and criticized online. The gradual encroachment of bureaucratic ways picked up from civil service and union contract workplaces ended up being a drag on productivity, employee satisfaction, and ultimately growth—time spent on "paperwork" is time not spent developing new and better ways of doing things, and slowing growth means slowing income growth for employees.

A return to employment at will and freedom of contract won't happen anytime soon. But reform of federal and state employment law to allow simplified systems with less recordkeeping and greater satisfaction would certainly be a start.

Systems designed to screen a group of applicants by objective measures of merit were a focus of civil service reforms. Standardized tests, certification and degree requirements, experience records, and proof of language proficiency and residence are often part of this process, and many private employers also try to make their consideration of new hires and promotions more objective using such evaluation systems.

In trying to remove inappropriate biases (like racism, sexism, nepotism, and cronyism) in hiring by establishing objective screening criteria, organizations lost control of factors which they now find politically necessary to satisfy, like diversity goals. It is now common for objective merit criteria to be discounted or ignored as needed to achieve more minority or female representation. But since it is also technically illegal to use race or sex as a factor in hiring, organizations watched closely by the public and the courts find themselves surreptitiously subverting their previous commitment to merit—instead of openly declaring diversity to be a goal so important that merit becomes a secondary factor, underhanded deck-stacking methods are used to get the desired politically-acceptable hiring mix.

There is nothing improper about diversity goals in certain situations. For example, many big-city police forces were overwhelmingly white and sometimes mostly Irish around 1950, and the lack of representation of minorities in the force increased tensions with poor largely black neighborhoods. City policies to require new hires to be city residents and the removal of exam requirements which favored the more cognitively-adept applicants allowed enough minority hiring to redress this imbalance for good political reasons, though little thought was given to instead modifying the tests to measure policing skillsets and only policing skillsets. Organizations like police and fire departments struggled mightily to comply since they had been run as patronage havens for friends, family, and ethnic groups influential in the cities' political machines.

The wave of affirmative action programs starting in the 1970s weakened civil service exam requirements. Courts found many exams discriminated against minorities, especially when it was clear the exams included cognitive skills not required for lower-level jobs. Some affirmative action programs race-normed the passing grades, which allowed more minorities to qualify with scores that would otherwise have failed. Many positions were entirely removed from examination requirements. Where the qualifying standard had been "top 3" or "best," it became "good enough" or "adequate."

The needs of a bureaucracy may not always favor hiring the most intelligent or skilled candidate. As in private industry, some managers would prefer to hire people who are bright enough and skilled enough, but not too much more than that, lest they be unhappy in the job or liable to be hired away by others—the brilliant scientist who wants to work as a police officer while writing papers on theoretical physics in her spare time is out of luck. In Connecticut, a Federal judge ruled the state was not discriminating unlawfully when it denied an applicant the opportunity to interview for the police force because his intelligence test score was too high.[149] Not rocking the boat is valued over ability in many hierarchies.

But these are just entry-level positions. What happens when promotion from within is favored, while entry-level employees are screened to ensure the very bright or overqualified are kept out in favor of desired race, sex, or residency? Entry-level positions in organizations are often open to all in theory, while in practice networks and connections of family, ethnicity, neighborhood, and religion can assist in placing people at the bottom rungs. If higher-level positions are filled from within this can result in entire organizations dominated by a single affiliate group, for example the Irish-dominated police forces of early nineteenth century cities.

Large companies also had set up screening systems, often using aptitude testing for initial hires. This gave bright but inexperienced young people a chance to prove themselves on the job. But the court rulings against testing and any other screening which might disfavor minorities led to most of these screening systems being modified in favor of degree and certification requirements. Today many entry-level jobs require a college degree, which has delayed entry into the workforce for many and shut others out completely.

In an interesting paper, "Gerrymandering in Personnel Selection: A Review of Practice" by Michael A. McDaniel of Virginia Commonwealth University,[150] the term "gerrymandering" is used to mean any rigging of a system of merit selection designed to subvert it to allow the less-qualified to be hired. Such rigging of the system is accomplished by insiders, either with or without organizational approval, to favor candidates by race (for affirmative action purposes), sex, membership in a political machine, ethnicity, or simply to allow managers to hire the people they want instead of the people who come out on top in a systematic, objective evaluation process. While these insiders keep the appearance of merit selection, they achieve their own goals by subtly adjusting parameters they do control to favor their desired hires. This can be done by tweaking the system itself or by inserting personal judgment components that can be "adjusted" to overcome more objective factors like test scores.

I've adopted "rigging" instead of McDaniel's "gerrymandering," which has a specific meaning in electoral districting. He begins:

> Although [rigging] can be used to benefit a specific individual (e.g., manipulating the system to get one's cousin hired), [it] is often designed to benefit a group of applicants. For example, a group of applicants might be defined with reference to race (e.g., minorities), sex (e.g., females), political affiliation (e.g., Democrats), family associations (e.g., children or spouses of current employees) or type of applicant (e.g., applicants who currently work for the organization versus external applicants).

> [Rigging] is typically in conflict with the goals of a merit-based personnel selection system which seeks to hire the most qualified applicant for a job... efforts focused on groups are typically an attempt to subvert merit-based personnel selection in favor of some

other goal such as racial or gender diversity. The author knows of no example where [rigging] efforts focused on groups were consistent with the goal of a merit-based personnel selection practice.... usually in conflict with merit-based goals, it is consistent with other goals, such as increasing the demographic diversity of organizations or promoting the growth and stability of political organizations.... Because some [rigging] practices in personnel selection are illegal and because most of these practices are seldom transparently applied or openly discussed, it is difficult for the author to estimate how frequently a given practice is used.

Increasing the representation of minorities and women in a workforce based on standardized testing screenings is difficult when those groups on average underperform white males on certain cognitive measures. Males tend to have more extreme results on aptitude and intelligence tests, with more males scoring either very high or very low than females. This implies (if such tests are valid indicators of ability, and they are) that males will tend to be overrepresented in positions requiring extremely high cognitive skills, like STEM professorships and Nobel prizes, quite aside from the cultural factors that encourage more males to concentrate on work and avoid familial care obligations. Physical job requirements, too, can favor some groups over others; upper body strength tests for firefighters and combat soldiers will pass far more males, while black males dominate basketball teams partly for genetically-determined reasons of height and coordination[151] as well as cultural factors.

> Ignoring the cumulative evidence to the contrary, United States employment regulations and some case law are based on the false assumption that minority-white differences in personnel selection tests are uncommon. Specifically, when the use of a personnel selection test results in a lower percentage of minorities hired than whites, the disparity in hiring rates is termed "adverse impact" under the Uniform Guidelines for Employee Selection Procedures (Equal Employment Opportunity Commission, Civil Service Commission, Department of Labor, & Department of Justice, 1978). When adverse

impact is present (and it typically is), it becomes the responsibility of the employer to defend the job-relatedness of the personnel selection system. Defending job-relatedness in an adversarial setting is a time consuming and expensive process. Thus, employers seeking to avoid validation and litigation expenses have substantial motive to [rig] their selection process to hire more minorities.

So the pressure to increase diversity could only be satisfied by quietly rolling back an organization's previous commitment to hiring the best person for the job. Since discrimination against white or male applicants on the basis or race or sex is also technically illegal, if rarely litigated, organizations and HR departments use a variety of techniques to rig their systems to preserve the hollowed-out façade of previously merit-based hiring systems, obscuring the reality of racial spoils systems.[152]

These disguised methods for stacking the deck or putting a thumb on the scale of hiring are hypocritical at best, but now so ingrained in HR and civil service procedures that aside from continuing jokes about "diversity hires" (which can themselves be cause for an EEOC complaint as contributing to a "hostile work environment") there is little awareness of just how much the focus has changed from merit and accountability to politically-based hiring and retention of mediocre and less productive employees.

Reasons for rigging the hiring process:

• For the benefit of one group and the detriment of another. This includes: increasing numbers of minorities or women, for affirmative action/diversity goals; aiming to give preference to members of a political machine or party to continue patronage practices; and preferring members of a tribe, ethnic origin, or extended family group that controls the workplace.

• For the benefit of a single preferred candidate which hiring managers or team members prefer, or the reverse

Methods of rigging the hiring process:

• Tailor personnel selection tools like tests and requirement lists more closely to the position. This can be a positive step toward merit selection when general aptitude tests are replaced by specific job knowledge tests; for example, instead of eliminating use of testing entirely as has happened for many Federal civil service jobs, California's state government adopted dozens of job-specific knowledge tests. This allows those applicants who aren't as good at general aptitude tests and abstract reasoning to demonstrate real job-related knowledge. But it is far more common for tests to be removed entirely from the process so that it can be manipulated to achieve the politically-desired outcome.

• Remove cognitively-loaded (either general aptitude or area knowledge) tests from selection systems. Even tests tailored to the job expertise required will tend to filter out more minority applicants and make reaching diversity goals difficult. McDaniel observed that "a county government stopped using a job knowledge test to screen librarians due to the poor test performance of minority applicants. A measure of training and experience was substituted based on the assumption that minorities would obtain higher scores." Since college degrees and other certifications requiring lengthy programs and cognitive skills challenges also tend to screen out minorities, substitution of on-site training programs advertised only to minority candidates and experience measures also assist in getting minority hires and promotions up.

Companies and agencies under pressure to increase minority numbers faced immediate penalties if they failed, but the longer-term negative effect of forcing hiring of less competent candidates on performance and morale was beyond the effective time horizon of individual executives in upper management. By 2016, of course, the HR departments and government managers who implemented the dumbing-down of their workers have long since retired, replaced by a generation who have been trained in the diversity mantra and have less concern for productivity or performance.

• Add apparently job-related requirements or tests that the desired candidates can do better on, which dilutes the purely subject matter knowledge or cognitive skill component. These might be personality tests, which can be helpful in weeding out candidates who lack emotional intelligence or demonstrate problematic syndromes, or additional screening factors like residence or previous work experience which favor the desired outcome. McDaniel cites one example where a city wanted to keep a workforce stuffed with patronage employees:

> In a large city, Democratic ward committeemen were charged with getting out the Democratic vote on election day. These ward committeemen were often hired as city building inspectors, in part, because the jobs paid well. In addition, building inspectors have been alleged to enhance their income through accepting bribes. A civil service law was passed that required that the incumbent building inspectors pass a civil service examination to be eligible to retain their jobs. The employer was concerned that the external job applicants had substantially better job knowledge than the internal job applicants, which would result in the Democratic ward committeemen losing their jobs (this concern proved justified because most of the external applicants scored higher than the internal applicants). The employer supplemented the job knowledge test with a single biodata item. This item asked whether the applicant had job experience as a building inspector in the city government. To be placed in the highest selection band, the applicants had to have experience as a city building inspector in the jurisdiction where the employment screening was taking place. The passing point of the job knowledge test was set below the lowest scoring incumbent. The addition of the one item biodata test coupled with a low cut-off score, permitted the city to retain all the incumbent building inspectors...[153]

• Add requirements that aren't directly job-related and which appear neutral, yet discriminate against the undesired categories of applicants. Local governments often require residency in their jurisdiction, for example, which seems like a good idea (residents are more likely to understand and want to assist their similar neighbors), but can be used to keep the city's work force racially disparate (either a largely minority city can keep out suburban white and Asian workers, or a lily-white suburb can block minority workers from the city.) Requiring certain language proficiencies: fluent English requirements for garbage disposal workers, for example, would bar many immigrants from the job unnecessarily, and the Canadian federal government's requirements for bilingual proficiency (French and English) even in single-language areas like Alberta and rural Quebec is a politically-motivated effort to glue together disparate regions by creating an elite Federal bureaucracy detached from regional loyalties.

• Add subjective human judgments to the screening. If application evaluations are done by a small group of people who understand they are supposed to favor one person or group over others—as is the case with college admissions decisions—these biased evaluations can be used to make up for the favored group's failings in more objective measures (like grades and test scores.) McDaniel cites one personal experience of this technique:

> The author observed a possible example of [this technique] using an interview that took place in a large city jurisdiction that had been unable to promote anyone into vacant Fire Battalion Chief positions due to a court order stemming from a U.S Department of Justice lawsuit. The employer convened an oral interview panel that rated minority candidates somewhat higher than majority candidates, on average. Because the minority candidates obtained substantially lower scores than whites on the objectively-scored job knowledge test, one might infer that the interview raters evaluated candidates in a race-conscious manner that resulted in higher mean minority scores. When a composite of the interview and the knowledge test

was formed, the interview was given sufficient weight such that the composite score showed near-equal means between minority and White applicants. The court overseeing the hiring permitted the city to hire Fire Battalion Chiefs using the composite test score.[154]

• Changes in relative weights of scoring criteria. Adjusting the weighting of some test scores or requirements relative to others allows manipulation of the resulting composite scores. The scoring calculations can also be fudged directly as needed to obtain the desired composite result, since only a few people are involved and their work is generally not examined to detect cheating.

• Collapse scoring into bands. This is a very common technique to achieve affirmative action goals—most frequently a low cutoff score allows many candidates to be declared qualified for the job, then the desired class can all be offered jobs despite scoring lower in the evaluation than others. This "good enough" style of mediocrity-supporting score-rigging was discussed in "Best vs Good Enough." Applicants above the cutoff point are passed to the hiring manager, often without the actual scores, ensuring that no clue to the relative merits of candidates will be allowed to affect the hiring manager's decision. As McDaniel says:

> Often large companies belong to industry-specific consortiums that offer consortium-developed employment tests conditional upon the company following the rules of the consortium with respect to how test scores are used. The author is aware of one such consortium that requires the setting of a cut-off score, albeit not necessarily a low cut-off score, and then forbids the test scores of the passing applicants to be shared with the hiring manager. This requirement most likely reflects an attempt to promote the hiring of minorities by hiding the score differences between the minority and majority applicants... In banding, applicants are rationally or statistically segmented into groups and all members of a group are asserted to be of equivalent eligibility for hire. Because employment tests are linearly related to job performance, the assumption is clearly false and the low cut off

scores can substantially compromise the merit selection process. The problem is not solely one of hiring less-qualified minority candidates, but also one of not hiring the most qualified non-minorities. When scores are withheld from the hiring manager, it also impairs the ability of the hiring manager to differentiate among the non-minority applicants. In race or gender-conscious banding, the bands are set to ensure that there is at least one minority (or female) in the band. For example, the author observed that a county government would set the cut score for the highest band immediately below the highest scoring minority and then pressured hiring managers with vacancies to consider the minority applicant....

For those looking for clever ways to equalize scoring schemes to make poor-scoring group members look better, the academic article "The diversity–validity dilemma: strategies for reducing racioethnic and sex subgroup differences and adverse impact in selection," by Ployhart, R. E., and Holtz, B. C., in The Journal of Personnel Psychology, 6 Feb. 2008 is a comprehensive survey.[155]

• Give favored applicants the answers to exam questions in advance. These cases often involve public agencies like police and fire departments trying to wire in their preferred "good old boy" candidates:

> ...fifty-five police officers in Nassau County, New York, including many who started their police career in a minority police cadet program, were investigated for giving false statements on autobiographical test items. It was alleged that the answer key for the test was obtained and used to coach applicants[156]. [T]he coaching program [was]conducted by a police sergeant involved in the test validation.[157] The sergeant would offer hypothetical questions and preferred answers. Example questions and answers:

> Q: How many of your relatives work in law enforcement? A: Three.
> Q: Which hobbies do you engage in at least once a year? A: Hunting.

> All of the police cadets passed.

Because releasing an answer key to applicants might be considered fraud, employers who use this strategy need to know the applicants well enough to trust that one or more applicants will not publicize the release of the answer key. Therefore, this strategy is likely to be primarily used in promotional settings.[158]

Coaching a favored candidate allows staff to get their favored candidate on board despite a supposedly neutral process. McDaniel shares anecdotes:

The author is aware of a jeweler whose employees interviewed applicants prior to the applicants taking a standardized integrity test. The employees did not like it when their preferred applicant was not hired due to the applicant's performance on the integrity test. Although the employees did not have the answer key to the test, they had enough information to coach preferred applicants (e.g., never admit to theft or knowing anyone who steals; endorse strong punishment of those who steal) such that all coached respondents passed the test.

Concerning completing a test for an applicant, the author is aware of an insurance office that was required to administer an insurance consortium biodata test to applicants. As with the jeweler example above, the employees did not like it when their preferred applicants failed the test and could not be hired. To [rig] the selection process, the employees kept a copy of the answer sheet from a past applicant who did well on the test. The office employees then used the answers from the successful past applicant to serve as the answers for all future applicants they wanted to hire. Finally, the sharing of the answer key sometimes has a financial motive. The author worked in the same organization as a personnel analyst who allegedly charged $2,000 per applicant to alter the scores on a physical abilities test for firefighters. The analyst was eventually imprisoned....[159]

• A strategy now outlawed: simply add points to the scores of all affirmative action candidates as necessary to equalize their average scores with non-minority candidates. This method was recommended and used for affirmative action by the US Dept. Of Labor using the general Aptitude Test Battery (GATB) for civil service positions until it was outlawed by passage of the Civil Rights Act of 1991.[160]

• Influence hiring managers to choose the desired candidate or choose from preferred candidates. This happens through unofficial channels, by verbal discussion or constant HR and upper management emphasis on getting diversity numbers up and the neglect of emphasis on job performance or fit. Since the hiring manager is often also rewarded or punished based on team performance, this requires the manager to balance short-term problems with bucking clear HR and upper management directives to increase diversity against the longer-term pain of having to add likely less productive people to the manager's team.

So hiring by supposedly objective standards, like performance evaluations, is often rigged and gamed by managers in a tug-of-war with HR responding to external political pressures. As with performance evaluations, why go through the time-consuming and cynicism-producing mummery, when you can simply let the hiring manager decide based on local knowledge?

To a great extent that's why many competitive industries can still function despite the political interference. Hiring managers route around candidate lists provided by HR, and many hires come instead through personal and industry contacts. The remaining quality recruiters still contribute, but there are fewer of them every year.

Failures are growing, and many positions go unfilled for months or years as hiring managers fail to find good candidates and reject those brought to them by HR. Why do candidates screened by HR so often fail?

One problem was termed (by David Hunt, an engineer) "The Quest for the Purple Squirrel."[161] This is the search for a candidate satisfying an impossible checklist of skills criteria, typically in technology though the same phenomenon happens in other fields— the job posting requires candidates who have experience in all five of these technologies, plus the usual social skills and positive attributes needed to work on a team. Hunt wrote:

A month or so ago I had a conversation with a recruiter who had posted a contract position on LinkedIn. It sounded intriguing so we talked. They described the position, and the company's business... they also added that the company was in crisis mode and that they really needed someone who could jump in with minimal ramp-up time. The clear implication was that things were behind, very behind, and they needed a take-charge person with the complete desired skill set. I asked, "Is this <company X>?" They confirmed that it was, and asked if I was already submitted.

First, I said, "Yes"; I had already applied to the company directly. Then I dropped a bombshell. I said that, based on the description, I had interviewed for that very job over 18 months ago. Think about that. No company brings a person into an interview not believing that, based on the resume, they might work out—no company would waste so much of its employees' time. Yet, apparently, in a year and a half of, doubtless, interviewing multiple people, they couldn't find one person who fit the bill. And were now behind the eight-ball.

One jobseeker posted:

> I've seen a lot of postings that say they require several years (2 or more) experience in a relatively small technology or library, something specific to their company. Other times I see 5 or even 7+ years experience required for a language. On their own some of these would be ok, but it gets ridiculous when a small town company says you need 3 years in 2 languages, proficiency in network programming, scripting, databases, and stuff like "experience with large highly redundant business critical systems" all at the same time.
>
> Do they really expect to find someone who has extensive experience working with exactly the same technology set they use? I have a hard time finding a single posting where I don't have at least 1 or 2 holes in my skill set.[162]

This kind of requirements list is put together by people in HR who have converted all the desiderata mentioned by a hiring manager into requirements. The ideal candidate might have all of them, but the ideal candidate is unlikely to exist at all, much less be applying for this position. The hiring manager may be puzzled when months go by and no screened candidates appear in their inbox, while the HR staff don't understand enough about the likely talent pool in the local market to limit the requirements so that they can be satisfied by at least a few reasonable candidates who show the ability to quickly learn any missing skills.

This excessive requirements problem is cited as one of those that tends to slow the career progress of women in STEM—women tend to avoid applying for any position they are not certain they can handle, being on average more risk-averse, while men are more likely to apply even when they know they are weak in some areas. HR staff will sometimes pass along applicants who only partly meet requirements, but they can't pass along applications of women who don't apply. Companies who are trying to increase their female staff especially need to make hiring managers understand too-demanding requirements lists may screen out some of the best candidates. The self-starting dynamo who lacks experience in, say, one required language can easily pick it up in a few weeks and become your most valuable team member, while another who does have such specific experience flounders on the job for other reasons.

Even if the hiring manager is provided with a reasonable list of candidates, no one may be chosen because the hiring manager isn't satisfied—afraid to make the wrong choice, so no choice is made. The project limps along without the supposedly necessary hire. Suzanne Lucas, writing for *Inc.*:

> But Robert N. Charette, writing at *IEEE Spectrum*, makes a pretty convincing argument that there is no STEM shortage. In fact, he writes, there is a STEM oversupply. Wages in computer and math fields, he writes, have stagnated over the past decade. Universities churn out STEM graduates at the rate of 250,000 per year, but there are only 180,000 new jobs per year. That doesn't exactly indicate a need for more H1B visas.

> So what's the problem? Why can't companies connect with these people who are ready, willing and able to work? ...bad recruiting policies and over-reliance on databases.... companies spent over $2 billion last year on databases, such as Monster.com, Taleo, and LinkedIn, only to see a very small percentage of jobs filled through those methods. Only 1.3 percent of jobs are filled through Monster.com.

Another way employers stink is that no matter how good the candidate before them is, they are utterly convinced that there is someone better out there, so they don't make the hiring decision.... a friend was complaining [on Facebook] that her husband had been turned down for a job after interviewing six different times for it. Six times. Six visits to this company. I'd like to say he just dodged a bullet because these people are idiots, but I know he needs a job.[163]

Hunt lays some of the blame on Applicant Tracking Systems[164] (ATS), the software systems widely used to screen applicants and track their progress through an organization's hiring process. He points out that advertisements promise that these systems can find that one applicant in a haystack of applications that perfectly matches a required skill set:

The [software] company then claims they can help locate that Purple Squirrel. The net effect of this, and similar ad pitches, is that hiring managers keep hearing that they can hold out; in the words of one senior person I know, "I want what I want, and will wait until I get what I want." After all, with the labor force participation rate in the 60s, and up to 90+ million people un-or-under-employed, why wouldn't they think that bi-lingual brain surgeon is out there?

There are also no counterbalancing forces on hiring managers to prevent their extending their wait to infinity. Neither do accounting practices formalize the costs of not filling a position to be weighed against the costs of hiring.

Why... aren't hiring managers seeing lots of resumes? ATS portals are infamous for blocking even qualified candidates from being seen by a human. Consider this statistic (emphasis added): "Some sources quote that as many as 75% of applicants are eliminated by ATS systems, as soon as they submit their resume, despite being qualified for the job!"[165]

Peter Cappelli, a Wharton School professor did in an interview in which he made this astonishing statement (emphases added): "One employer told me that 25,000 people had applied for a reasonably standard engineering job in their company and that the hiring systems indicated that none met the requirements."

And a recruiter anonymously told me that a company they knew did a test: they formulated what they—as insiders—considered an ideal, perfect resume. That resume did not get through their ATS filter. Similarly, in an essay of mine on ATS portals where I cited Cappelli's above quote, I noted another datum (emphases in original, slightly edited): "One person [in class] said that his company has a slew of open requisitions, with internal people encouraged to apply – through the ATS portal. Of the people who were already employed at the company, and from my understanding many of whom were already involved to some degree in the project requiring the ramping-up, none were passed through the ATS."

ATS portals are, it seems, one of a company's worst enemies in finding people.[166]

Nick Corcodilos, author of the "Ask the Headhunter" newsletter, outlined why HR departments use ATSs and not more personal recruiting strategies:

I've had HR managers tell me they have no budget or time to actually go out and personally recruit people. There's no money to take anyone to lunch, to go to professional events to find and meet prospective hires or to do anything on a one-on-one level to recruit. It's all done en masse. It's all done with those little keywords. It's all done in databases.

It seems HR will buy anything these "services" sell them, because HR isn't measured by how effectively it hires. It's measured by whether it keeps the ball rolling, so HR pays to outsource the most important job a company has—hiring great workers.[167]

Neil Patrick of 40PlusCareerGuru describes how ATSs work, and often don't work, to screen and present resumes to hiring managers:

> Applicants upload their information, including their relevant experience, educational background and resume into the database. This information is transferred from one part of the system to another as the candidates move through the selection process...

> The problem with applicant tracking systems, is that they are just that. Systems. They lack human intelligence. And that's a big problem for candidates. If your resume isn't formatted how the system expects it to be and doesn't contain the right keywords and phrases, the applicant tracking system may well misread it and rank it as a bad match with the job, regardless of your qualifications. And there're no fail safe checks. That's it. You're out.

> This weakness has been proven by research. In a test last year, Bersin & Associates created a resume for an ideal candidate for a clinical scientist position. The research firm perfectly matched the resume to the job description and submitted the resume to an applicant tracking system from Taleo, the leading maker of these systems. When the researchers then studied how the resume appeared in the applicant tracking system, they found that one of the candidate's job positions was ignored completely simply because the resume had the dates of employment typed in before the name of the employer. The applicant tracking system also failed to pick up several key educational qualifications the candidate held, giving a recruiter the impression that the candidate lacked the educational experience required for the job. This perfect resume only scored a 43% relevance ranking to the job because the applicant tracking system misread it.

> So your only hope for passing through an ATS successfully is to understand exactly how these systems work and to make sure you don't get caught out.

> Many think that applicant tracking systems rely simply on keywords to score the fit between a candidate's resume and a specific job. So they search to identify keywords in the job description and insert these keywords into their resumes. In fact, what matters most to an

ATS isn't the number of word matches found. It's the uniqueness or "rarity" of the keyword or the keyword phrase, i.e. those keywords and phrases specific to that particular job. The ATS then calculates a ranking based on how closely each applicant's resume matches each keyword and phrase and only then how many of the keyword phrases each resume contains.

But scoring shortcomings are not the end of it. An ATS also restricts what recruiters and HR people see when viewing candidates' information on the system. When a recruiter views a candidate whom the applicant tracking system has ranked as a good match for the job, the recruiter doesn't see the resume the candidate submitted. The recruiter sees only the information the applicant tracking system pulled from the candidate's resume into the database. The ATS will try to identify this information on a job seeker's resume, but if a resume isn't formatted in the way the system expects it to be, it won't pull this information into the proper fields. Sometimes, whole sections can be ignored, such as a key skills profile or an executive summary.[168]

Anyone sending out resumes today should read a guide to writing and formatting your resume so that it is not only easily read by hiring managers (who, if you are under serious consideration for a position, will read your original resume) but also can be scanned by an ATS without missing key skills, educational qualifications, and experience. One good online guide is "How to Create a Reader-Based Cover Letter and Résumé," by Marcia LaReau, at http://forwardmotioncareers.com/how-to-create-a-reader-based-cover-letter-and-resume/.

Companies who do critical hiring using an ATS may be saving time by screening out the vast majority of the applications submitted, but they may be missing out on some of the best candidates because the systems fail to capture all of the data in submitted resumes, and can't encode the quality of an applicant's spirit or approach to the work. Putting an automated system between applicants and company hiring managers also risks alienating applicants, who may be snapped up by quicker competitors or tell others about their impersonal experience and the time wasted waiting for a response:

> Putting candidates through a poor background screening process can be particularly costly, said Fishman. "For starters, the most desirable candidates may sour on working for you. Referrals may grow few and far between. Your company's employment brand and marketplace reputation can suffer. And if your background screening process isn't compliant with applicable state and federal laws, you could even be sued."

> Improving the candidate experience means improving communication, educating applicants on the screening process, and providing tools for applicants that increase their visibility into the process, said Trindade. For example, "many companies now provide applicant-facing tools that guide applicants through screening procedures and provide them with opportunities to help manage the process themselves, as well as communicate directly with both the employer and the screening provider. This helps inform and empower candidates and improves their experience with screening, which could have traditionally been a confusing, black-box kind of experience," she said.[169]

There are better versions of ATS systems on the market—some of them are more interactive and allow applicants to track the internal progress of their application themselves, emailing progress reports to remind the applicant to check in. But these are still rare, and you will find many desirable employers still using obtuse systems. Corcodilos reminds us that most good hires come from personal contacts and outreach efforts that route around HR and contact hiring managers directly, and wise jobseekers avoid ATS applications:

> I'm sorry to be so cynical, but the hiring system really is broken. You can use any keywords you like, but there's no telling what the software algorithm is looking for. (I suggest that people just copy and paste the entire job description into their digital resume—maybe that will trigger an interview! Will all the keywords be there then?) If you

use the tools and rules of the job boards and Applicant Tracking Systems, odds are they will reject you. The employers behind these systems never really know whether you can do the job—and that you might be their best candidate.

The solution is pretty obvious. If a system doesn't work, don't use it. Refuse to use it. Go around it. Find your interviews and jobs through personal contacts. Because, while HR and employers have no time or money to go meet people, that's exactly where you should go and what you should do to beat them at this silly keyword game.

Studies show again and again that most jobs are found and filled through personal contacts. I'm sure you already know that. So it's time to use your noggin and trust your good judgment. If it's clear to all of us that this doesn't really work—HR's complaints that employers can't find the talent they need prove it—then just stop.[170]

Hiring managers themselves face an asymmetric risk problem: a bad hire can cost the company more than $50,000[171] and cost the manager time and heartache, while putting off a decision often has no immediate downside for the hiring manager, though it may delay critical projects and cost the company a market edge.

So corporate hiring today is a mess, and about to get worse as progressives try to force companies to give up some of the few tools they have to disqualify criminal or unreliable applicants—with the usual noble motivations, of course. We'll go over these efforts, then look at a new Seattle ordinance designed to limit discrimination in apartment rentals by forcing landlords to accept the first applicant who "qualifies," which will evolve (if not pushed back) to limit allowed requirements until landlords essentially will be forced to take almost anyone. This idea of **forcing acceptance of applicants will most likely soon be applied to hiring,** as the social engineers gradually reduce any freedoms a business manager might have so that their client population can enjoy the benefits of being hardworking, reliable, self-controlled citizens without actually demonstrating any of those qualities. If US labor law ever reaches that late stage equality-of-outcome decadence, productivity will crumble, much as it did in the old USSR where jobs were similarly guaranteed and handed out based on pull. This kind of micromanagement of free-market employment practices is typical of progressives—to achieve the worthy goal (in this case, limiting invidious discrimination), they try to limit the use of management discretion in operating a business by passing unenforceable laws that tend to do more harm than good.

Progressives are working hard to outlaw use of credit scores or criminal records to screen job candidates. This is, of course, because bad records on either tend to identify less trustworthy, less reliable people that employers quite reasonably want to avoid hiring. The campaign to outlaw application questions about criminal records is called "Ban the Box," and this catchy name means applications that include a box to be checked if the applicant has a criminal record are to be banned by law. Most such laws passed at state and local levels only ban the question on applications for government jobs or government contractors, since the legality of going further at the local level is questionable. But moves are afoot to make it part of Federal equal employment regulations.

It's true that not every candidate who fails such screening would be a bad employee. Both ex-prisoners and bad credit risks might well have reformed, with the black marks on their record not indicating their current state of trustworthiness—and a wise employer might consider them by looking deeper into their background and directly questioning them on how they may have learned from their experiences. But employers who are going to rely on the keeping of promises to show up on time, work hard, and not steal from their employer are not wrong to think these are factors to consider.

Further, studies of "Ban the Box" laws show that they can actually harm the minorities they are intended to help. An employer who loses the ability to check for a criminal record may be more likely to act on prejudice—after all, prejudice and adverse stereotyping are strongest where information is limited. Being able to pass a criminal record check enhances a minority candidate's chance of being viewed as a good risk for the employer. The most recent study demonstrated this effect:

> "Ban-the-Box" (BTB) policies restrict employers from asking about applicants' criminal histories on job applications and are often presented as a means of reducing unemployment among black men, who disproportionately have criminal records. However, withholding information about criminal records could risk encouraging statistical discrimination: employers may make assumptions about criminality based on the applicant's race. To investigate this possibility as well as the effects of race and criminal records on employer callback rates, we sent approximately 15,000 fictitious online job applications to employers in New Jersey and New York City, in waves before and after each jurisdiction's adoption of BTB policies. Our causal effect estimates are based on a triple-differences design, which exploits the fact that many businesses' applications did not ask about records even before BTB and were thus unaffected by the law.

Our results confirm that criminal records are a major barrier to employment, but they also support the concern that BTB policies encourage statistical discrimination on the basis of race. Overall, white applicants received 23% more callbacks than similar black applicants (38% more in New Jersey; 6% more in New York City; we also find that the white advantage is much larger in whiter neighborhoods). Employers that ask about criminal records are 62% more likely to call back an applicant if he has no record (45% in New Jersey; 78% in New York City)—an effect that BTB compliance necessarily eliminates. However, we find that the race gap in callbacks grows dramatically at the BTB-affected companies after the policy goes into effect. Before BTB, white applicants to BTB-affected employers received about 7% more callbacks than similar black applicants, but BTB increases this gap to 45%.[172]

Most of these laws are presented as preventing pre-screening—the employer may still look into criminal records after deciding to offer the candidate a job. But the clear trend is to make ex-criminal status a protected class and outlaw discrimination on that basis. Another paper suggests employers are more likely to avoid even taking applications from minority candidates if these laws are in place, exercising a form of passive resistance that is hard to prevent:

...removing information about job applicants' criminal histories [through Ban The Box (BTB) laws) could lead employers who don't want to hire ex-offenders to try to guess who the ex-offenders are, and avoid interviewing them. In particular, employers might avoid interviewing young, low-skilled, black and Hispanic men when criminal records are not observable. This would worsen employment outcomes for these already-disadvantaged groups. In this paper, we use variation in the details and timing of state and local BTB policies to test BTB's effects on employment for various demographic groups. We find that BTB policies decrease the probability of being employed by 3.4 percentage points (5.1%) for young, low-skilled black men, and by 2.3 percentage points (2.9%) for young, low-skilled Hispanic men. These findings support the hypothesis that when an applicant's criminal history is unavailable, employers statistically discriminate against demographic groups that are likely to have a criminal record.[173]

Not screening hires for criminal records also subjects employers to big negligence awards when consumers are victimized by unscreened employees:

> "Consider these allegations from a 2012 Virginia case," Leeson said. "The employer hired a person to work in a hotel, and allegedly did not perform a background check or ask about the person's criminal history. The person had previously been convicted of a felony sex crime. The person thereafter raped an 18-year-old hotel maid on her third day on the job. The maid sued the hotel for negligent hire. The case settled with the hotel agreeing to pay $675,000 to the former maid." Ultimately, Leeson said, "I believe it is reasonable and prudent for employers to ask about prior convictions as one factor in the overall evaluation of the applicant."[174]

But the laws are spreading rapidly and being applied to private employers as well:

> There are a total of 24 states representing nearly every region of the country that have adopted the policies—California (2013, 2010), Colorado (2012), Connecticut (2010), Delaware (2014), Georgia (2015), Hawaii (1998), Illinois (2014, 2013), Louisiana (2016), Maryland (2013), Massachusetts (2010), Minnesota (2013, 2009), Missouri (2016), Nebraska (2014), New Jersey (2014), New Mexico (2010), New York (2015), Ohio (2015), Oklahoma (2016), Oregon (2015), Rhode Island (2013), Tennessee (2016), Vermont (2015, 2016), Virginia (2015), and Wisconsin (2016). Nine states— Connecticut, Hawaii, Illinois, Massachusetts, Minnesota, New Jersey, Oregon, Rhode Island, and Vermont—have removed the conviction history question on job applications for private employers, which advocates embrace as the next step in the evolution of these policies.

> The majority of ban-the-box laws apply only to public employers, but blanket ban-the-box laws impacting all sectors are on the rise. Many

advocates embrace private-sector ban-the-box laws as the "next step in the evolution of these policies," according to the National Employment Law Project (NELP), a worker advocacy organization....

There are also various city and county ban-the-box laws around the country that apply to private employers...

Many ban-the-box policies exempt employers that have 10 employees or less, but some, such as Minnesota's, do not. And while many private employers have balked at ban-the-box policies, at least two large retailers have jumped on board. National retailers Target and Wal-Mart no longer ask about an applicant's conviction record during the initial phase of the hiring process, according to NELP. In order to comply with the 2013 Minnesota law, Minneapolis-based Target announced it was eliminating the box on its applications. Wal-Mart took that action in 2010.[175]

So if your area doesn't already have a BTB law, it soon will. Now to move on to the use of credit reports to screen candidates: credit reports are already regulated by Federal law, and since they aren't cheap, companies rarely use them to pre-screen candidates. But they are widely used in the final stages of hiring decisions:

Employers get a shortened version of your credit report that excludes any information that would violate equal employment opportunity laws, explains Rod Griffin, director of public education for credit bureau Experian. An employer report also does not list "soft" inquiries, which do show up on the report an individual receives....

According to a 2012 survey conducted by the Society for Human Resource Management, 47% of employers check potential employees' credit reports as part of the hiring process. The same study found that the two most common reasons for reviewing job candidates' credit reports are to decrease the likelihood of theft and embezzlement and reduce legal liability for negligent hiring. According to an article in The New York Times, which cited the same survey:

"Most businesses use credit checks only to screen for certain positions, but one in eight, the survey found, does a credit check before every hire."

But it's important to remember that your employer can't check your credit report without your consent; you must give written permission. Also, an employer won't be seeing personal information, like your account numbers, when he or she reviews your report. The modified version that's provided takes steps to protect your privacy.

Also, 11 states have laws prohibiting employer credit checks and/or restricting how this information can be used in the hiring process. If you live in one of these states, an employer credit check may not be something you need to worry about.[176]

If you're a job-seeker worried about how a prospective employer might view your troubled credit history, here's some good advice:

...if you are concerned that your credit history may reflect negatively, have a discussion ahead of time with the hiring manager or Human Resources about your credit reports.... information honestly disclosed by an applicant has much less impact than information the employer discovers for themselves.

...keep in mind that the only reason you are having this discussion is that the firm is seriously considering hiring you, and has gone through a lot of time and effort to make that decision, including reviewing numerous other resumes.

... applicants need to keep in mind that they have rights. Under the Federal Fair Credit Reporting Act (FCRA), a credit report is only obtained after the applicant has given consent and after a legally required disclosure on a standalone document has been given. Before the employer utilizes the credit report in any way not to hire, an applicant is entitled to a copy of their credit report in what is known as a pre-adverse action notice. You are also required to receive a document called a Statement of Rights, which will list your rights and also information on how to correct information on the report.

> The bottom line: If an employer feels a credit report is job related, keep in mind that the employer has made you a finalist, and therefore has an interest in hiring you. You were evaluated without the employer having any idea of what was in the credit report. Protect your credit history. Think of it as one piece of your reputation. Know what is in your credit report and correct errors. If there are negative entries, be prepared to share it before the credit report is run.[177]

That sounds reassuring. But it turns out many employers are failing to follow the existing laws on use of credit reports, and as a result are getting hit with multimillion-dollar class action lawsuits:

> Last year saw an increasing number of FCRA class-action lawsuits filed and settled for millions of dollars. FCRA violations can range from not making legally required disclosures to not following proper adverse action procedures.

> "Not a month has gone by in over a year when there hasn't been a major FCRA class action on background checks, and that trend has already continued into January," said Nick Fishman, executive vice president at EmployeeScreenIQ.

> We may see an "explosion" of FCRA class-action suits against employers and background screening firms as plaintiffs' attorneys become more familiar with the law and the whole area of background checks, said Rosen. The financial recovery can be enormous—up to $1,000 per person in damages.

> "Given the large statutory damages at issue, the promise of attorneys' fees and punitive damages, along with the fact that there is an open question as to whether an individual need be actually harmed to bring an action, these claims will undoubtedly continue," Devata agreed. Many FCRA claims have nothing to do with a person being harmed, but instead are the result of a mere technicality in the law, she added. ...Employers should be aware that taking an adverse action—terminating an existing employee, rescinding a job offer to

an applicant, denying a promotion—based on a consumer report "requires them to engage in a multistep process and requires close consideration of timed requirements," said Do. "Bottom line, if negative information comes back on a background check, an employer simply can't just pick up the phone and say 'You're not getting the job.' " Failing to provide a copy of the consumer report, failing to furnish a copy of the FCRA summary of rights document, and failing to provide the opportunity to dispute a report's inaccuracies or errors, are common allegations, said Do.

These suits are the most troubling because they are the most avoidable, said Fishman. "These laws aren't that hard to follow. Employers need to continually audit their processes and make sure that they comply with the law."

It's important to train incoming HR staff on the FCRA. "In many cases, with high turnover in HR departments, the sufficient training that was provided when an employer first signs on with a screening firm may not be adequately conveyed to new members. The likelihood that an oversight may result when an undertrained staff member fails to follow protocol then increases," said Do.[178]

Notice how a seemingly well-motivated law not only removes hiring discretion, but with the help in this case of class action lawyers (who are part of the political class feeding off private industry with the help of the pols who write the laws), requires hiring more and more HR staff and consultants to administer and train for it. Every regulation imposed on employers increases non-productive staff and budget, and decreases the freedom to seek out the best employees without fear of government punishment. Every gain in "fairness" imposed by law costs everyone twice as much in lost growth and opportunity.

And banning use of credit checks in hiring has the same perverse effect as "Ban The Box"—it hurts minorities:

...one of the hottest ideas among lawmakers right now is to ban employers from running credit checks on job applicants. Since 2007, eleven states, as well as Chicago and New York City, have passed such laws. Supporters of these restrictions often frame the issue as a civil rights problem. In particular, they say, credit checks impede employment among minorities, who disproportionately have low credit scores.

...But a new study from Robert Clifford, an economist at the Boston Fed, and Daniel Shoag, an assistant professor at Harvard's Kennedy School, finds that when employers are prohibited from looking into people's financial history, something perverse happens: African-Americans become more likely to be unemployed relative to others....

Why did black unemployment go up?

To understand how banning credit checks can lead to unforeseen repercussions, consider the problem from the employer's perspective. A single job opening these days can get hundreds of applications. Since hiring managers can't interview every candidate, they need some way to narrow the field. Filtering out people with bad credit helps them bring the number of applicants down to a manageable size. But if employers can't look into a job-seeker's financial history, they try something else.

"Employers have many screening measures to narrow down who they want to hire," Shoag says. "If you take one away, they'll put more weight on the others."

That's exactly what seemed to happen in places that outlawed employer credit checks. Looking at 74 million job listings between 2007 and 2013, Clifford and Shoag found that employers started to become pickier, especially in cities where there were a lot of workers with low credit scores. If a credit-check ban went into effect, job postings were more likely to ask for a bachelor's degree, and to require additional years of experience.

There are other ways that employers could have also become more discerning, Shoag says. They might have started to rely on referrals or recommendations to make sure that applicants were high-quality. In the absence of credit information to establish trustworthiness, they may even have fallen back on racial stereotypes to screen candidates. The researchers couldn't measure these tactics, but they're possibilities.

Any of these reasons might explain one of the study's strangest findings. In states that passed a credit-check ban, unemployment for African-Americans rose by about one percent compared to unemployment in other states and among other demographic groups. This remained true after controlling for factors like education, age, and gender.

… In the absence of that information, employers had to rely more on other clues about the quality of applicants, including their education and experience levels, but also, perhaps, their interview skills or their recommendations. Whatever the new criteria were, they seem to have put black applicants at a disadvantage.

"This reflects a general movement of legislators monkeying around with the hiring process without thinking about the consequences," Shoag says.[179]

The latest in efforts to restrict information available to hiring companies is the so-far-not-cleverly-named movement to ban asking any questions about salary history. The theory here is that current and past salary history can be used to hold back women, since a new employer may well offer an increase based on the supposedly lower salaries women make under the yoke of discrimination. The practical need for both applicant and employer to discover whether they are even close to a negotiating range is, of course, not considered, because the appearance of helping women make better salaries is all that counts. Now employers may spend considerable effort to decide on a candidate only to discover the salary they were prepared to offer is far too low to interest the candidate.

Massachusetts was the first state to pass such a law.[180] But theirs goes further, attempting to enshrine the concept of comparable worth

—even different jobs with similar labor and standards are supposed to pay the same. This was in response to a suit from largely female cafeteria workers paid just over half of what janitors in the same school system made; the obvious difference in working conditions (social and clean vs. nonsocial and dirty) which explain the relative attractiveness of the positions, and thus the pay differential, seem to be beyond the politicians. This subjective standard will occupy court time and allow more lawyers to extract profitable settlements for themselves.

Meanwhile, attempts to outlaw salary questions at the Federal level are ongoing:

> Under the Pay Equity for All Act of 2016 (H.R. 6030), the U.S. Department of Labor would be able to assess fines up to $10,000 against employers who violate the law by asking questions about an applicant's salary history. Additionally, prospective or current employees would be able to bring a private lawsuit against an employer who violated the law and could receive up to $10,000 in damages plus attorney fees....

> Although many employers may not intend to discriminate on the basis of gender, race or ethnicity, asking for prior salary information before offering an applicant a job can have a discriminatory effect in the workplace that begins or reinforces the wage gap, according to a news release announcing the bill.[181]

Women need a Big Brother on their side to have a chance at negotiating a fair salary for themselves, and the Party of Government is happy to provide one. Or at least pretend to.

You have probably seen news items about companies asking prospective employees for passwords to their Facebook accounts, and similarly outrageous invasions of privacy. What you may not realize is that companies are increasingly looking at the public parts of social media accounts as an additional source of information about candidates. Most notably, Twitter is largely open to inspection by anyone, and Facebook's data on users is often more public than users realize. It is not unusual for Facebook users to fail to set their permissions for privacy of some classes of data, like photos, which leaves those drunken party photos you posted in college visible years later.

This is not much different from past reputational investigations. At the very least, applicants who fail to check their public social media record for red flags and questionable items that might reflect badly on them as possible employees are demonstrating negligence and a lack of discretion, which is good to know for sensitive positions where these indiscretions might embarrass the employer. "New Press Secretary Alicia Barnes Denies Stripping at Cabo Bacchanal" is not a headline one wants to see.

So far there are few proposals to regulate use of public social media data for personnel decisions. Executives have faced firestorms of negative publicity after single tweets, and some people have lost their jobs when the mobs turned on them. Quietly not getting a job offer because of social media negatives is becoming common.

But using social media to screen candidates is risky, say HR experts:

> Many companies will add social media investigations to their background screening process to find out more about who they hire, said Cunneen. But beware of potential pitfalls. "There are discrimination, consent, privacy, legal and sometimes moral issues

that can arise from using social media to screen applicants or monitor employees, not to mention the inability to verify the accuracy of the information found," she said.

Employers need to keep in mind that once something is seen, it cannot be unseen, said Kline. "There are many things that may be discovered in a social media check that fall under protected categories, from race, sex, sexual orientation, religion, etc. Even seeing things like organizations the applicant is a member of or a political party they favor can cause bias," she said.[182]

But that is true of even the simplest contacts: resumes, phone calls, and face-to-face interviews reveal a great deal of information that might be used to discriminate based on illegal factors like race, religion, or national origin. And factors like political leanings and group affiliations are still not protected legally, so employers are free to not hire Young Democrats or KKK members.

Again we have HR professionals not questioning the view that government can and should control all aspects of the hiring process, mediated of course by HR professionals and consultants. It's obviously unfair to have careless social media exposures used against you—but then, as Jimmy Carter said, "Life is unfair." The cost of trying to outlaw human nature by micromanaging hiring and team composition is more than we can afford, and blunts the self-regulating reputational systems that keep the social fabric together. Absolute equality of outcome is hard to achieve, but stagnation and decay as a result of misguided interventions are much easier.

The topic is still controversial in HR circles:

Many HR professionals rely on sites like Facebook, LinkedIn and Twitter to find and recruit promising potential hires. According to a survey conducted by the Society for Human Resource Management, 77 percent of companies use social media to identify candidates for positions. In fact, according to some experts, social media may be one of the best ways to engage with the highly coveted passive candidate, who is unlikely to have posted a resume on a job site.

Yet social media engagement statistics drop sharply when it comes to using these networking sites as a form of pre-employment screening. The same SHRM survey found that only 20 percent of HR professionals used social media to research candidates. Those who did tended to pay the most attention to inappropriate or unprofessional public posts that might shed a negative light on the organization in the future.[183]

Only 20 percent *admitted* to using social media for vetting!

Why do 80 percent of those surveyed by SHRM avoid using social media to vet employees? A majority cite legal risk and the possibility of stumbling upon information that is usually protected including age, race and gender. Even when this information is obtained accidentally, if it has an impact on the ultimate hiring decision a candidate could argue discrimination. Many HR professionals would rather cede the potential benefits of using social media rather than opening the organization up to potential discrimination lawsuits.

That's a good reason not to keep any records of such use, or to farm out social media background checks to a contractor who gives HR deniability by not providing any protected-class data.

Despite social media's vast reach and public nature, candidates remain much more likely to be forthright in a tweet than they are in a job application or in-person interview. Social media sites are a good place to scan for potentially inappropriate behavior, such as overt acts of racism, sexism or other discriminatory behaviors. In fact, according to a Career Builder survey, of the red flags raised by social media, 28 percent are of a discriminatory nature. Hate speech can be a red flag for the HR team that a candidate might not fit into the organizational culture....

Experts say that using social media as a screening tool is all about managing risk. The American Bar Association recommends hiring a third-party vendor to conduct the social media searches. An added bonus: "Most helpful, a third party's web-crawler system can typically review more webpages than an individual hiring manager tapping away at individual websites like Facebook and Twitter," the ABA states. If social media screening must be conducted in-house, never ask for a candidate's passwords. That practice is illegal in several states and opens the organization up to the possibility of violating the Stored Communications Act.

There aren't many hiring managers left who discriminate on the basis of race or sex when presented with an outstanding candidate who is otherwise a good culture fit. Using the public data available on a candidate to detect culture fit and attitude problems that might damage the organization is reasonable due diligence—that campus activist who screamed at invited speakers or vandalized school property might have reformed since graduation, but why take the risk of an expensive and damaging problem hire if you can avoid it? Knowing a candidate might be inclined to proselytize others and disrupt business for political diatribes is a perfectly legal reason not to hire her.

It seems likely that careful hiring managers already do a web and social media search on every candidate under serious consideration, while keeping such checks entirely to themselves. This is another form of passive resistance to HR departments and the legal pressures to make hiring decisions blindfolded. As long as discretion is allowed, hiring managers will use every underhanded tool they can to avoid the costs of a bad hire. And quite rightly.

Movements like Ban The Box and prohibitions on credit screening in hiring are social engineering efforts to eliminate the use of applicant histories in hiring. Their proponents believe jobs are rewards that should be handed out to everyone regardless of merit—if they can't politically swing having government employ everyone, they will chip way at discretion in hiring to make private businesses hire based on need of the applicant rather than win-win criteria. This is presented as "fairness,'" but it is actually quite unfair to those who work and sacrifice to become more productive and build a record proving it.

This means their next move will be to eliminate all discretion in hiring. As a hiring manager or businessman, you will be limited in what requirements you can advertise for a new hire, and you will be forced to take the first applicant that meets them, no matter how unpresentable, larcenous, or disruptive the candidate may be. Face-to-face interviews may be prohibited, and all hiring done through a service that disguises protected class characteristics.

You may doubt that such an outrageous, counterproductive policy could ever make it into law or regulation. But you would be wrong—our progressive ruler-wannabes are thinking along those lines, and soon will move further in that direction. Look at Seattle's new ordinance requiring landlords to rent to the first tenant who comes along who meets their posted requirements...

The latest brilliant idea from the socialist progressives (including the new Socialist councilwoman) in Seattle wins the prize for harmful intrusion pretending to do good: landlords must take the first tenant candidate who meets their qualifications, which must be set forth in advance. This is of course intended to prevent invidious housing discrimination in a city with a shortage of rentals and rapidly-increasing prices as Seattle goes the way of California, inhibiting new housing construction (because that only benefits greedy developers) and then blaming the business of providing housing for the shortage and high prices of same.

From the article "A primer on Seattle's new first-come, first-served renters law," by Daniel Beekman in the *Seattle Times* of August 10, 2106:

> Seattle is apparently breaking new ground by requiring landlords in the city to rent their housing units to qualified applicants on a first-come, first-served basis. Officials say they're unaware of any other U.S. city with a policy like the one the Seattle City Council approved Monday, along with other rental-housing changes.[184]

This might be a clue that your new law might be a bad idea. Good luck with those lawsuits!

> The goal is to ensure prospective renters are treated equally, according to Councilmember Lisa Herbold, who championed the policy. When landlords pick one renter among multiple qualified applicants, their own biases—conscious or unconscious—may come into play, she says.

May come into play! To prevent thoughtcrime, one must banish discretion. A similar law in employment will help even more, when jobs aren't handed out on the whim of those who are responsible for production. Every applicant will have a place in tractor factory! The city will tackle discrimination in mating and friendship next.

> Some landlords don't mind the policy, saying they already operate on a first-come, first-served basis. But others are upset, saying they should be able to use their own judgment to choose the renters they believe will be most reliable.

The landlords who say they don't mind may be running low-end buildings with low maintenance and high turnover. And lying, since they've been trained to discriminate covertly by previous regimes. One of the casualties of socialist systems is truth—everyone pretends and works the system. Underground economies spring up—the best apartments go to the connected who can trade favors or outright bribes to get in, as in San Francisco and New York's rent-controlled units.

> Even proponents of the policy acknowledge it could have unintended consequences, and some details still need to be worked out before it takes effect Jan. 1. "There seems to be a strong common-sense argument for this," said Leland Jones, regional spokesman for U.S. Department of Housing and Urban Development. "But we'll have to wait and see."

As with "common-sense" gun regulations, progressives label whatever micromanaging policy they want that week obvious and sensible. Those who point out the unintended consequences are just standing in the way of progress and fairness for all. Unicorns and rainbows happen when we cut up that pie our way! After all, housing is a human right. Those who own it have to give it to those who need it.

> Before accepting a prospective renter's application materials, a landlord will need to provide the renter with information on the landlord's minimum screening criteria, Kranzler said. When the landlord receives a completed application—in person, electronically or through the mail—the landlord will be required to make note of the date and time. The landlord will be required to screen multiple applications in the order in which they were received and make offers to qualified renters in that order. A prospective renter won't necessarily know her position in line, but she can ask SOCR [Seattle Office of Civil Rights] to investigate by checking the landlord's records. Prospective renters will also have the option to sue a landlord when they think they've been skipped—an aspect of the policy that bothers landlord groups.

To aid enforcement, the next update to the law may require all landlords to maintain an open Internet connection which transmits all changes to their records directly to the SOCR.

Ann LoGerfo, a directing attorney with Columbia Legal Services who pushed for the policy, offered an example: A landlord with two qualified applicants picks a name he associates with his own ethnicity, rather than a name that sounds foreign to him. Under Seattle's new policy, if the latter completes her application first and meets the landlord's criteria, the landlord will be required to offer her the unit.

One Seattle landlord who likes the idea is Jason Truesdell, who rents out a duplex in Madison Valley. Truesdell says he practices first-come, first-served now. "Because my goal is to get a unit occupied as quickly as possible by someone reliable," he said.

While that sounds quite reasonable, Jason, your ability to set those criteria for reliability is being taken away. You won't be allowed to use credit scores, criminal histories, or reports from previous landlords to refuse a new tenant—the next generation of this ordinance will set qualifications that your political masters decide. Your pain and suffering in dealing with bad tenants and the apartments they trash and the good tenants they run off matters not at all; giving protected classes do-overs to cover up their irresponsibilities of the past is more important. Because literally nothing in their lives was ever their fault. The Man has kept them down, and you're The Man now, Jason—we're taking control of your property for reparations.

And Shanna Smith, president of the National Fair Housing Alliance, said the policy means Seattle is taking a leadership role. "We've been asking people to address this issue for years," but landlords always push back, said Smith. "We know landlords skip people all the time, and often the people they skip are people of color, people with vouchers and families with children."

Stupid landlords. What do they know? Shanna knows better. Section 8 people are the salt of the earth and belong in quiet buildings. They can be key in the neighborhood Party Committee that will dole out scarce food and housing to those who support the goals of the Council.

> Not everyone is happy about the policy, however. Don Taylor, who rents out a small building off Aurora Avenue North, said he doesn't need policing. "How do I do it? Part of it is just feel," Taylor said, recalling an instance in which he chose one qualified applicant over another because her salary was lower and he guessed she'd be less likely to buy a home and move out. "The longer you can keep a tenant, the better off you are," the landlord said. "I don't care whether you're black, white or purple."

I was once a landlord in an area where good apartments were in great demand, and this is exactly how a smart landlord thinks. There's little or no racism or improper discrimination involved—I chose black men and lesbians quite cheerfully when they were the most likely to pay the rent, be good neighbors to others, and take good care of the apartment. Taking away all the subtle discretionary factors that go into making these decisions amounts to harming small landlords who are doing it right.

> Sean Martin, spokesman for the Rental Housing Association of Washington, says the group already advises landlords to operate on a first-come, first-served basis—to avoid discrimination claims. But he's worried about unintended consequences. He wonders whether the race-to-apply policy will give an advantage to people with cars, smartphones and free time over people who ride the bus and work three jobs....

> Then there's the question of enforcement. Taylor says he'll keep going with his gut. "I plan to find a way to work around the law," he said.

> False times and dates. Different screening criteria. Pre-application interviews. Those are all possibilities, said [Jason] Truesdell, who plans to adhere to the policy. "I can easily imagine how this could be gamed," he said.

> That's why… the national expert says Seattle will need to ramp up its sting operations. According to SOCR, it will need to add two staffers to handle work related to the first-come, first-served policy—to the tune of more than $200,000 next year.

This unenforceable law will lead to sting operations which require hiring a large staff of enforcers which leads to more guerrilla warfare as owners of property respond to unconstitutional interference with undetectable workarounds of their own. What the progressive social engineers never see are the informal checks-and-balances and social controls of a free market that allowed even the poorest people to find stable places to live in big cities of the past—they tended to be the oldest and least-desirable housing available, but they were always there, before rent control and the progressive blockade on new housing. NIMBYs and progressive lawsuits restrained production of housing in the most progressive-run cities until today, when rents are through the roof, job growth is restrained by the high cost of housing, and homelessness is a severe problem. Native black populations have been forced out of many desirable big cities as a result. Applying yet another layer of control to landlords simply makes rental housing even less likely to be built.

As goes housing, so goes employment. Progressives will not rest until they control every aspect of business down to staffing decisions. Because a few employers might discriminate improperly, all must give jobs to anyone who shows up who "qualifies." And those qualifications will be increasingly limited as standards for college degrees decline below those of 1900s high school graduates. Everyone will have subsidized college and worthless degrees entitling them to stay on the no-standards-no-accountability conveyer belt to a job, where they will be protected from firing for life. This progressive vision is of course not sustainable—it resembles the *dirigisme* of India that held the country back for decades. Stagnation, mediocrity, and poverty are the inevitable result.

We've seen how HR is already mismanaging hiring by using primitive automation tools for screening, and how future progressive regulations may make the situation even worse. Meanwhile, social media and online profiles are providing more honest data on candidates than ever before, but HR is warning hiring managers not to look at it.

The good news may be that AI in smarter screening programs may be able to use online searches and carefully-designed online questionnaires to do a much better job of identifying possible great hires and screening out the deadwood. Meanwhile, leading-edge employers like Google have discovered overly-specific degree and experience qualifications can actually screen out some of the most productive people in the applicant pool. If any company can apply data analytics and AI to hiring and performance management, it would be Google. How did Google do when they tried? The *New York Times* interviewed senior VP of people operations (Google's name for HR, apparently) Laszlo Bock in 2013:

> Years ago, we did a study to determine whether anyone at Google is particularly good at hiring. We looked at tens of thousands of interviews, and everyone who had done the interviews and what they scored the candidate, and how that person ultimately performed in their job. We found zero relationship. It's a complete random mess, except for one guy who was highly predictive because he only interviewed people for a very specialized area, where he happened to be the world's leading expert....

> On the hiring side, we found that brainteasers are a complete waste of time. How many golf balls can you fit into an airplane? How many gas stations in Manhattan? A complete waste of time. They don't predict anything. They serve primarily to make the interviewer feel smart.

Instead, what works well are structured behavioral interviews, where you have a consistent rubric for how you assess people, rather than having each interviewer just make stuff up.

Behavioral interviewing also works—where you're not giving someone a hypothetical, but you're starting with a question like, "Give me an example of a time when you solved an analytically difficult problem." The interesting thing about the behavioral interview is that when you ask somebody to speak to their own experience, and you drill into that, you get two kinds of information. One is you get to see how they actually interacted in a real-world situation, and the valuable "meta" information you get about the candidate is a sense of what they consider to be difficult.[185]

Google used to be known for hiring only people under 30, using those brainteasers to identify top programming talent and relying on academic qualifications, favoring degrees from prestigious universities. That's no longer true:

One of the things we've seen from all our data crunching is that G.P.A.'s are worthless as a criteria for hiring, and test scores are worthless—no correlation at all except for brand-new college grads, where there's a slight correlation. Google famously used to ask everyone for a transcript and G.P.A.'s and test scores, but we don't anymore, unless you're just a few years out of school. We found that they don't predict anything.

What's interesting is the proportion of people without any college education at Google has increased over time as well. So we have teams where you have 14 percent of the team made up of people who've never gone to college.... academic environments are artificial environments. People who succeed there are sort of finely trained, they're conditioned to succeed in that environment. One of my own frustrations when I was in college and grad school is that you knew the professor was looking for a specific answer. You could figure that out, but it's much more interesting to solve problems where there isn't an obvious answer. You want people who like figuring out stuff where there is no obvious answer.

So how are they applying their famous data analytics to hiring for Google? Very methodically, as you would expect:

> In the summer of 2006, Todd Carlisle, a Google analyst with a doctorate in organizational psychology, designed a 300-question survey for every Google employee to fill out… Some questions were straightforward: Have you ever set a world record? Other queries had employees plot themselves on a spectrum: Please indicate your working style preference on a scale of 1 (work alone) to 5 (work in a team). Other questions were frivolous: What kind of pets do you own?

> Carlisle crunched the data and compared it to measures of employee performance. He was looking for patterns to understand what attributes made a good Google worker. This was strongly related to another question that interested his boss, Laszlo Bock, senior vice president of People Operations: What attributes could predict the perfect Google hire?

> …Google was essentially trying to Google the human-resources process: It wanted a search algorithm that could sift through tens of thousands of people—Google's acceptance rate is about 0.2 percent, or 1/25th that of Harvard University—and return a list of the top candidates. But after a great deal of question-asking and number-crunching, it turned out that the best performance predictor wasn't grade-point average, or type of pets, or an answer to the question, "How many times a day does a clock's hands overlap?" The single best predictor was: absolutely nothing.[186]

Much research shows referrals to be the most reliable source of better hires, so Google's early emphasis on ties to computer science professors to recruit the best students for their early programming teams was a good if limited strategy. Referrals are more likely to be "good fits" because the skills needed for good teamwork are more likely to get someone referred:

> The study found that referrals produce "substantially higher profits per worker" who are "less likely to quit," "more innovative," and "have fewer accidents"—all this, even after controlling for factors like college, SAT scores, and IQ. Team-based companies require openness, compatibility, and a willingness to cooperate. Referral programs work because great employees pass along workers who similarly match the company culture.

> Although they account for only six percent of total applications, referrals now result in more than a quarter of all hires at large companies, according to a recent paper from the Federal Reserve Bank of New York and MIT....

> Google, which depends on referrals, once administered up to 25 interviews for each job candidate. Todd Carlisle, the organizational psychology doctorate who administered the company's surveys in 2006, thought this might be overkill. He tested exactly how many interviews were necessary to be confident about a new hire. The right number of interviews per candidate, he discovered, was four. This new policy, which Google calls the Rule of Four, "shaved median time to hire to 47 days, compared to 90 to 180 days," Laszlo Bock wrote in his book Work Rules.

> But Carlisle's research revealed something deeper about the hiring process, which has resonance for every industry: No one manager at Google was very good, alone, at predicting who would make a good worker.

> Four meticulously orchestrated Google interviews could identify successful hires with 86 percent confidence, and nobody at the company—no matter how long they had been at the company or how many candidates they had interviewed—could do any better than the aggregated wisdom of four interviewers.

It turns out that a single Google hiring manager, at least, is often not that good at judging candidates—but when four of their judgments are combined, the result is as good as it's going to get. This convinced the company to drop their over-interviewing policies, which took much candidate and staff time and delayed hiring by months.

So what are the prospects for automating hiring? Aptitude test scores have considerable predictive value in many cognitive jobs, but could one automate the emotional intelligence and teamwork skills testing needed to find good team workers? Google has tried and (at least as far as they've disclosed their practices) failed to find anything better than referrals and face-to-face interviews.

But software companies keep trying to improve ATS functions to do a better job:

> Companies such as Facebook, GE, IBM, Hilton Worldwide, SAP and many others have been slowly adding data analytics into their recruitment practices. A few years ago, it was unheard of to scan candidate resumes for data, but now it's commonplace. Machine intelligence is being used to scan through other aspects of candidate information, such as their social media content, their facial expressions, even their work samples to identify top candidates – and weed out the undesirables.

> "Such practices raise questions about accuracy and privacy, but proponents argue that harnessing AI for hiring could lead to more diverse, empathetic, and dynamic workplaces," says Sean Captain, a journalist with Fast Company.

> ..."corporate recruiting is broken" as a system. It's filled with inaccuracies and black holes where candidates disappear.... "85% of job applicants never hear back after submitting an application." This indicates that some recruiters are still not able to stay on top of recruitment processes, and the candidate experience has a long way to go towards being a positive one.

> Perhaps there is room for more automation and AI in recruitment if it can restore better recruitment practices from the human side of things. Kibben mentions that AI will improve the candidate experience and is a winning proposition for recruiters who will be

able to strategically partner with hiring managers instead of simply filling job requests.[187]

Lots of buzzwords and promises, few real advances. One semi-useful tool now becoming popular is the automated interview system— imagine an online interviewing system where the applicant answers preset questions in front of their PC, laptop, or phone camera, with the video uploaded for later replay by HR staff and hiring managers. This certainly cuts down the overhead of doing interviews—no more paying to fly candidates out and take them to dinner, just video dating-style files to pick up those subtle clues about the candidate normally gleaned from a face-to-face interview.

How does that work out in practice? A company called HireVue claims to analyze video interviews using AI tools:

> The deep dive into a candidate's mind isn't a new idea, says Mark Newman, founder and CEO of HireVue. Founded in 2004, it was one of the pioneers in using AI for hiring. Its specialty is analyzing video interviews for personal attributes including engagement, motivation, and empathy. (Although it also uses written evaluations.) The company analyzes data such as word choice, rate of speech, and even microexpressions (fleeting facial expressions).[188]

But most users of their systems are just looking for a cost-effective substitute for face-to-face interviews, with only a few using "AI" to evaluate the candidate videos:

> ...HireVue Inc., which provides video interviewing software for Goldman Sachs and 600 other firms, said it hosted nearly three million video interviews last year, up from 13,000 five years ago....

> Most video-interviewing programs require applicants to click a link or install an app. Interviews begin with a prompt such as "Tell us about a time you had to deal with a conflict" that stays on-screen for about 30 seconds. Then, the camera turns on and the candidate has anywhere from 30 seconds to 5 minutes to respond before the next

question pops up.

Human-resources staff then review the videos and pass along promising applicants to managers for consideration. Applicants who make the cut are typically invited to a one-on-one interview. That doesn't always mean it will be in-person, though. Varsha Paidi, a software engineer hired by IBM last year, had subsequent online interviews and eventually received her job offer via text message.

Speeding up the hiring process allows recruiters to look at more applicants than before, giving companies wider reach, said Obed Louissaint, the human-resources lead for IBM's Watson division.

Applicants, however, say that computer-guided interviews take some getting used to. Amy Hall was never the type to get nervous during job interviews, but when the 29-year-old had to complete a video interview last year for an internal job switch at Cigna-Healthspring, she recalled feeling apprehensive and camera-shy. She waited until after work hours and used a computer in the IT department. With the door closed, she clicked a link to Cigna's video-interviewing site....

Companies say they seek similar traits in video interviews as they do in traditional interviews. Recruiters at IBM and Cigna said they evaluate candidates based on how well the person communicates his/her thought process, whether the person answers all parts of the question—and whether he/she makes eye contact...

Video interviews might also present some problems because managers cannot ask follow-up questions or engage candidates further on a point, said Carol Miaskoff, assistant legal counsel for the Equal Employment Opportunity Commission. In letters to vendors, Ms. Miaskoff has suggested that companies assign more than one person to review individual videos to ensure hiring decisions aren't made hastily.

Taking robo-recruiting one step further, some HireVue customers have an algorithm review the video interviews for them. Using data about the skills and attributes companies are seeking for a given role, a program called HireVue Insights scans videos for verbal and facial cues that match those skills then ranks the top 100 applicants.[189]

Given that in-person interviews by staff tend to wander and often turn into staff evaluations of whether the candidate will be enjoyable company or not, a fixed format with questions set in advance does actually promise to reduce the element of good-old-boyism. Everyone has experienced the job interview that turns quickly to discussion of sports or hobbies in common—the interviewer pays less attention to skills and attitudes than shared cultural enthusiasms, tending to favor cultural clones of themselves whose company they will enjoy. But notice that most companies still rely on human HR staff judgement to screen the resulting videos, which saves time for hiring managers but still introduces an element of HR prejudice. If your HR staff are primarily left-leaning New England-educated feminists, a white male candidate with a Southern accent and stereotypically male mannerisms will likely be screened out. For once the EEOC advice is reasonable—this type of screening will be more effective if more than one person reviews each video, making it more difficult for prejudice to prevail.

Giving HR staff veto power over candidates seems unwise. Practical considerations require obviously unqualified candidates to be weeded out early when a position attracts large numbers of applicants, but hiring managers and team members should invest the relatively minor time it takes to review these types of video responses themselves, as they are likely to be the best judges of culture fit and attitudes revealed by video.

Applicants encounter HireVue and similar video interviewing systems frequently now, and not everyone is happy—they find the idea insulting and intrusive. One question at Ask the Headhunter:

[The questioner's wife] landed two job interviews with hiring managers within three weeks. Suddenly, a personnel jockey injected himself into the ongoing discussions with the hiring manager. The recruiter insisted that my wife submit herself to a one-way, online digital video taping, answer a series of pre-selected "screening questions," and upload it to who knows where for "further review and screening" by who knows whom.

She found the request creepy, impersonal, presumptuous, Orwellian, exploitative, voyeuristic, unprofessional, and perhaps even unethical. She declined, instantly prompting an automated "Do Not Reply" rejection e-mail. She was not worthy because she wouldn't subject herself to a dehumanizing "HireVue Digital Video Interview."

This new wrinkle in HR practices seems like the most unsettling and counterproductive yet. It not only removes access to the hiring manager, but also live, human interaction. It sounds like "HR pornography," where perverted personnel jockeys huddle around a monitor to gawk at videos of "virtual job candidates," picking apart perceived blunders while they screen you out.[190]

The Headhunter, Nick Corcodillos, suggested the candidate respond in this situation by expressing a willingness to do a Skype interview with the hiring manager, cheaper (no payment to HireVue) and more personal. He suggests HR has an agenda in using such impersonal services: "What they mean is, we don't want you to see the personalities of our personnel jockeys because, face it, they're a bunch of data diddlers that we don't want talking to anyone." I'd say that is correct. In this case the applicant already spoke to the hiring manager, but HR is trying to force use of its process using HireVue for bureaucratic control reasons. If it should come to an EEOC complaint, having anyone escape their uniform process would be seen as evidence of favoritism having disparate impact on minorities.

There's nothing wrong with these video interviewing services—ideally they substitute for expensive and time-consuming travel to meet with HR staff and hiring managers. But in practice, some companies now use them along with ATS screening techniques to completely depersonalize all but the last stages of hiring—the candidate does a lot of work, but no one at the company spends any time on their application at all until pre-screened and pre-interviewed. Meanwhile, candidates who contact hiring managers directly or run into them at professional functions or through work at companies in the same industry get the further advantage of being personally known in advance.

It does cost a lot to hire through HR—the arms race of HR automation leads to candidates using automation to contact far more potential employers, leading to avalanches of applications, leading to more ineffective automation. Hopeful noises about AI assisting are so far just that. In principle, AI could do a good job of analyzing resumes and interview videos and deliver the best candidates to hiring managers. In practice, no one is delivering anything more than hype.

Typical of the hype: HiringSolved, a startup promising Siri-like hiring assistance:

> HiringSolved will soon unveil what it considers "Siri for recruiting," an artificial intelligence assistant for recruiters. His name will be RAI, pronounced like the name Ray, and standing for "Recruiting Artificial Intelligence."

> The company has been working on it for five years, and is still perfecting it. The gist of it is you'd ask recruiting questions to a Chatbot-like system. So, instead of checking off a bunch of boxes, you'd type something like, "I need to find 10 female developers with experience using WordPress, within 10 miles of Milwaukee." Or, perhaps, "What was the most common previous title of a systems engineer at Raytheon?"

> Perhaps later, like with Siri, you'd use voice, not typed, commands.

> HiringSolved's RAI tool could also ask you follow-up questions, not unlike a conversation between a recruiter and a manager. If you, say, want a mechanical engineer, it might ask you to narrow your searches. Nuclear? Petroleum? Aerospace?

The idea is that the artificial intelligence will make you a better recruiter/sourcer, guiding you through questions that very experienced sourcers ask themselves in order to chop through a database and hone in on who they want.[191]

Chatbots and Siri, soon to save the day! Smart employers will pay the price to hire good, connected recruiters who have personal contacts in the industry. AI may one day allow applicants to prove themselves worthy without human intervention, but that day is a long way off.

The culture difference between HR staff and the rest of the workforce causes problems in many industries, but it's worst in high tech. While successful companies like Apple, Google, and Facebook started their HR departments with technology-savvy people, even they eventually succumbed to the bureaucratic disease—with newer HR staff more similar to the risk-averse, non-business-oriented sorts seen elsewhere. It takes constant CEO attention to keep HR from drifting toward bureaucratic focus on process and not results.

Bob Cringely has been observing and writing about the PC world since early days, with his "Notes From the Field" column in InfoWorld from 1987 to 1995, and a now dated but still historically interesting book, Accidental Empires: How the Boys of Silicon Valley Make Their Millions, Battle Foreign Competition, and Still Can't Get a Date. His article "The Enemy in HR" gets directly to the heart of the problem of HR in Silicon Valley. He starts off wondering why companies claim there's a shortage of IT workers requiring large numbers of foreign workers to be admitted under H1-B visas to fill the need, while at the same time hundreds of thousands of (mostly male, mostly older, experienced) unemployed IT workers can't get an interview. What could it be? He states the basic thesis of this book in a few paragraphs:

> ...we can start by blaming the Human Resources (HR) departments at big and even medium-sized companies. HR does the hiring and firing or at least handles the paperwork for hiring and firing. HR hires headhunters to find IT talent or advertises and finds that talent itself. If you are an IT professional in a company of almost any size that has an HR department, go down there sometime and ask about their professional qualifications. What made them qualified to hire you?

You'll find the departments are predominantly staffed with women and few, if any, of those women have technical degrees. They are hiring predominantly male candidates for positions whose duties they typically don't understand. Those HR folks, if put on the spot, will point out that the final decision on all technical hires comes from the IT department, itself. All HR does is facilitate.

Not really. What HR does is filter. They see as an important part of their job finding the very best candidates for every technical position. But how do you qualify candidates if you don't know what you are talking about? They use heuristics—sorting techniques designed to get good candidates without really knowing good from bad.

Common heuristic techniques for hiring IT professionals include looking for graduates of top university programs and for people currently working in similar positions at comparable companies including competitors. The flip side of these techniques also applies— not looking for graduates of less prestigious universities or the unemployed.[192]

Software and hardware engineering work is as far from liberal arts-communications-psychology as it is possible to be, revolving around hard math, heavy-duty abstract reasoning, and specialized language often impenetrable to outsiders. So typical HR staff don't understand the work or the distinguishing characteristics of the most productive workers in the field. A software genius may be inattentive to details of personal hygiene—and the HR staffer who interviews him may conclude from his smell that he's sloppy and undisciplined, and will cause interpersonal issues. Many of the best have Asperger's Syndrome, which could be summed up as deep focus on order and details of problem domains while lacking abilities to communicate or sense the feeling of others through the normal signalling.[193] These are the people who get into trouble with modern feminists because they are clumsy and will continue to crudely pursue sexual come-ons when a woman has signalled disinterest; they are no more likely than anyone else to sexually assault a woman, but modern feminists believe unwanted attention from a male is tantamount to sexual assault—if it makes someone uncomfortable, it should be a firing offense. Female HR staff are likely to find such men unattractive and screen them out as not fitting in.

Meanwhile, hiring managers are more likely to understand the type, and that careful management—hiding the socially-inept from customers and outsiders, and feeding them the hardest problems to solve—can make these people a key strength for the organization. It may become necessary for executive management to make it clear to HR that Asperger's (under the current DSM-5 terminology, a form of Autism Spectrum Disorder[194]) is a recognized disability and that the Americans with Disabilities Act (ADA) requires employers to provide these disabled men with "reasonable accommodations"—special treatment recognizing that they need support to be effective workers with their disability. This puts HR staff on notice that they would be violating the law if they continue to discriminate against the apparently insensitive, overly-focused males the company badly needs to do the most difficult programming jobs!

That warning in place, HR staff will come to see both easily-offended women and socially-obtuse men as victims to be protected. Which would be an improvement over current practice, where a few complaints of bad behavior can get a man fired when no actual malice or assault was intended. Everyone in the workplace should feel safe from sexual pressure and physical assault, but not to the point where perceived rudeness or insensitivity gets you fired, or some of the industry's best workers will be exiled.

Silicon Valley is a magnet for technologists from around the world, and the resulting engineering workforce is skewed toward men, Asians, Indians, and a scattering of Europeans all attracted by the prospect of working with the world's best people for some of the world's highest rewards. Early on, PC and microprocessor companies resembled the defense contractors of the Valley, mostly white male engineering staff and more diverse support staff. As engineers from elsewhere moved to take jobs in the Valley, they brought wives and family, and many of the wives began work in support positions like accounting and HR. Today, despite all their efforts to recruit more women and minorities, an exemplary company like Apple reports their engineering staff is still 77% male[195], and that includes a lot of less focused, more routine positions like release management and QA testing support which usually have more women. Meanwhile, overall diversity numbers have been improved by hiring more women and minorities in support, sales, and HR.

Silicon Valley continues to passively resist pressures to hire based on diversity goals rather than competence. Management understands that engineering excellence can't be compromised away without destroying their company's competitive edge, and promotes diversity recruitment efforts to find capable minorities for core engineering work as well as secondary roles like testing and maintenance the best engineers find unexciting. And still the resulting numbers fail to come close to the US population's minority percentages, with Asians, whites, and males over-represented. So the pressure continues:

Two years ago, the Rev. Jesse Jackson set his sights on Silicon Valley. He promised to push tech companies and venture capital firms to prioritize diversity and inclusion, and to add more employees from historically underrepresented groups like women and people of color.

But the progress he'd hoped for hasn't happened yet, and Jackson is growing restless. On Friday, as Jackson's Rainbow Push Coalition held a conference in San Francisco where industry leaders joined local groups and activists to discuss diversity, Silicon Valley and what new initiatives may help close the gap. The Rainbow Push Coalition also introduced several programs of its own. Hire and Invest Oakland, aimed at engaging tech companies based in or moving into the East Bay, would encourage companies like Pandora and Uber to work with local organizations when hiring workers and looking for merchants. Several such Oakland organizations were on hand Friday to make their presence known to tech leaders.

"You would think companies that have been around for a while, since the 1990s, would not be where they are when it comes to diversity because they've had time to catch up," Jackson said. "But the good news is there's time now to catch up, and it will open up a whole new world of opportunity."

...Pressure to boost diversity at tech companies and remain publicly accountable by disclosure of companies' personnel data has grown over the past several years. Several firms—including Airbnb, Dropbox, Pinterest, Twitter and Yelp—even hired individuals to oversee and coordinate diversity efforts. Others have begun offering implicit-bias training to their employees or broadening their corporate definition of diversity to include intersectional identities— how various attributes combine to create unique experiences for certain people. Earlier this year, group-chat company Slack updated its diversity report to include more intersectional data on women of color and LGBT people.

Intel CEO Brian Krzanich, who announced last year that the company would improve its diversity to reflect the percentage of women and underrepresented minorities in the United States by 2020, and pledged $300 million to aid in the effort, acknowledged at the Rainbow Push conference Friday that the company has received criticism for its outspoken commitment to diversity, according to reports.

"There's no reason why there cannot be a change now," Jackson said. "When I think about this culture of exclusion and how unchallenged it has been for so long—we need to end that. There's responsibility at every level, and we all need to apply social pressure to change things because this is the future: America cannot improve without fully realizing its assets. Imagine baseball without Jackie Robinson. That's where we are."[196]

Or imagine fashion design firms required to recruit straight men, or basketball teams required to include more Asians. There are many excellent female and minority engineers, but for a wide variety of cultural and possibly innate reasons, there are not as many as you would expect if talent and interest in the field was uniformly distributed through the population. Decades of special efforts to promote STEM studies and careers for women and minorities has done about as much as is possible to encourage those who want to succeed in it. Forcing equal representation means forcing less qualified, less accomplished employees on some of our key technology leaders, damaging their ability to stay ahead of overseas competition.

Note in the story quoted above the payoffs made to affiliates of Jesse Jackson's PUSH and minority nonprofit organizations. Activists have learned to make their daily bread by threatening boycotts and lawsuits, then accepting instead payoffs to keep their paychecks going while they pretend to work on the never-ending problems they claim they want to fix. The extortionate style relies on threats of public shaming and political difficulties if targeted companies don't meet his demands:

> The responses [to Jesse Jackson's PUSH efforts] by these information technology leaders could have been predicted. Management at eBay had nothing overt to say, which amounts to tacit agreement. More telling was the response by Google. In exchange for Jackson's demand for the company to release employee demographic data on its U.S. work force, David Drummond, chief legal officer (who, like Jackson, is black), promised that his company would release the numbers. He didn't take very long to deliver. Yesterday, the company issued a report on workforce diversity showing about 60 percent of Google employees are white and 30 percent are Asian (apparently not all racial minorities arouse Jackson's sympathies). Laszlo Bock, Google's senior vice president for public relations, also wrote in a blog: "Put simply, Google is not where we want to be when it comes to diversity, and it's hard to address these kinds of challenges if you're not prepared to discuss them openly, and with the facts." Facebook also gave in, adopting a feckless "we're really, really trying" line. COO Sheryl Sandberg explained in writing: "We have built a number of great partnerships, groups like the National Society of Black Engineers, the Hispanic Alumni of Georgia Tech, Grace

Hopper Celebration of Women in Computing, and Management Leadership of Tomorrow. And these partnerships have been great because they are really helping us get great candidates and reach out."

Jackson's IT gambit has been all over the map this year. Earlier this year, he wrote a letter to tech companies, including Apple, Facebook, Google, Hewlett-Packard, and Twitter, replete with his familiar hectoring style. On March 19, he showed up at the Hewlett-Packard shareholders meeting at the Santa Clara Convention Center to skewer CEO Meg Whitman and her company's record on minority hiring. And just two days ago, appearing on CNBC, Jackson denounced information technology firms for their lack of "diversity."[197]

It is far safer and easier to pay off the diversity blackmailers rather than meeting their hiring demands, and such donations to educational and recruitment efforts for minorities are socially positive and build goodwill. It's better to pay this "diversity tax" outright than to compromise your core engineering, sales, and marketing teams with deadwood employees. If the pressure increases, managements may place more diverse hires in less critical areas, judging this to be the least harmful way of making their numbers look better. But employees that aren't the best you can find for the position impose a greater cost than just their salaries—their presence signals to everyone in the company that excellence has been subordinated to political pressure, and that appeasing the diversity activists is more important than customers or markets. And this damages the morale of those who are working hardest and have sacrificed the most to be at the center of the company's production.

One curmudgeon who openly resisted these kinds of demands, T.J. Rodgers of Cypress Semiconductors, famously wrote a letter to crusading nuns who had pressed for women and minority board members:

The semiconductor business is a tough one with significant competition from the Japanese, Taiwanese, and Koreans. There have been more corporate casualties than survivors. For that reason, our Board of Directors is not a ceremonial watchdog, but a critical management function. The essential criteria for Cypress board membership are as follows:

♦ Experience as a CEO of an important technology company.

♦ Direct expertise in the semiconductor business based on education and management experience.

♦ Direct experience in the management of a company that buys from the semiconductor industry.

A search based on these criteria usually yields a male who is 50-plus years old, has a Masters degree in an engineering science, and has moved up the managerial ladder to the top spot in one or more corporations. Unfortunately, there are currently few minorities and almost no women who chose to be engineering graduate students 30 years ago. (That picture will be dramatically different in 10 years, due to the greater diversification of graduate students in the '80s.) Bluntly stated, a "woman's view" on how to run our semiconductor company does not help us, unless that woman has an advanced technical degree and experience as a CEO. I do realize there are other industries in which the last statement does not hold true. We would quickly embrace the opportunity to include any woman or minority person who could help us as a director, because we pursue talent—and we don't care in what package that talent comes.

I believe that placing arbitrary racial or gender quotas on corporate boards is fundamentally wrong. Therefore, not only does Cypress not meet your requirements for boardroom diversification, but we are unlikely to, because it is very difficult to find qualified directors, let alone directors that also meet investors' racial and gender preferences.

I infer that your concept of corporate "morality" contains in it the requirement to appoint a Board of Directors with, in your words, "equality of sexes, races, and ethnic groups." I am unaware of any

Christian requirements for corporate boards; your views seem more accurately described as "politically correct," than "Christian."

My views aside, your requirements are—in effect—immoral. By "immoral," I mean "causing harm to people," a fundamental wrong. Here's why:

I presume you believe your organization does good work and that the people who spend their careers in its service deserve to retire with the necessities of life assured. If your investment in Cypress is intended for that purpose, I can tell you that each of the retired Sisters of St. Francis would suffer if I were forced to run Cypress on anything but a profit-making basis. The retirement plans of thousands of other people also depend on Cypress stock—$1.2 billion worth of stock— owned directly by investors or through mutual funds, pension funds, 401k programs, and insurance companies.... Any choice I would make to jeopardize retirees and other investors from achieving their lifetime goals would be fundamentally wrong.[198]

Rodgers was expressing the belief shared by essentially all advanced technologists that the "package" workers come in—the skin color, sex, and body type containing the most critical component, the brain— doesn't matter. Finding the solutions to problems matters. Building a great product matters. Getting that product sold and dominating the market matters. Making a good profit matters, so you can do it all again in our capitalist system and pay your investors back for their foresight in entrusting their hard-earned resources and future wellbeing to you. And anyone who can contribute to the project is accepted and rewarded, and anyone who does not, is not. There are many roles in society, many industries and types of work, and it would be strange if various types of people—races, sexes, and cultures —were equally motivated to work in all of them. And so it is not racism or sexism that holds back women and minorities in STEM fields, but cultural factors and motivation. And this diversity is to be celebrated, not artificially eliminated.

There is some pushback from the newer software companies as

well. Leslie Miley, (black) head of engineering at the cloud-based team collaboration tool builder Slack,[199] opposed hiring quotas at a recent tech conference:

"I don't think they work, in particular in think it's another way saying we won't lower the bar," Miley said on stage at TechCrunch Disrupt SF. "What I'm saying is we want a level playing field, you need to have a level playing field. How you level it is, you don't [just] go to places like MIT and [University of California—Berkeley] and Stanford and focus on those places. I don't want to have to talk about this again, I don't believe in quotas, I think they're inherently wrong and I think there are realistic solutions that don't have quotas attached to [them]."…

[Slack] has made a lot of effort to branch out into regions outside of Silicon Valley in order to attract talent in regions that are outside the traditional Silicon Valley mold. And it's looking outside the traditional places that Silicon Valley giants, startups and venture capitalists may be pattern-matching into the best candidates.

That includes looking in unexpected areas in the United States, too, including cities like Detroit, Richmond or even Nashville, Miley said. Those cities are plenty diverse and also have a large pool of highly diverse and talented candidates, and Slack is doing what it can to expand into those areas. And larger tech companies should be doing the same thing, he said.

"[Large tech companies] don't need to set up shop at the same scale," Miley said. "Could you put 200 people, definitely, it's a drop in the hat for Google or Facebook, it's actually cost competitive to areas in India and China. I've had teams, managed over 100 people in India, I know what the cost structure looks like… [Then] people who want advancement know they have to come to HQ, you have people coming to Cupertino, Mountain View. What happens when you hire diverse people—they talk to their friends, their network looks like them. They're gonna hire friends, associates, you start to make inroads in this company."

A big part of the issue is that networks within companies tend to self-select within their own networks, keeping diverse candidates from coming into the company. That leads to a reinforcing cycle where diverse candidates from different regions and backgrounds, which might bring in their own friends to the companies, might not feel welcome in those companies....[200]

Outstanding—a networked company can operate in a distributed fashion in many sites around the world, giving HQ a less central role and encouraging geographic diversity that will increase other kinds of cultural diversity. With the goal being cost-effective excellence by going to where the talent is.

But pressure to hire more minorities and women in tech has existed at least since Jesse Jackson's first run at it in 1999.[201] Why is resistance crumbling almost twenty years later?

First, today's high tech is more software than hardware, with a new generation of executives more willing to appease the activists. Most people in the industry want to be sure women and minorities are fairly treated and feel welcomed, and the networked activists can quickly trash your public image if you cross them. So appeasing donations and lip service are the most common responses by today's execs.

Another new factor is the hardcore third-wave feminists and "critical race theory"-trained products of academia that are making activism their life's work. Many college students are adopting the victim culture and identities as protectors of the weak—women, plus transgender and all the other flavors of other. These newer, mostly upper-class-academic activists are besieging the older engineer-dominated companies as well as the new software giants. The culture wars, where activists infiltrate one cultural area after another then try to demonize and expel any conservatives that remain, have reached the gates of high tech.

"Gamergate" was a skirmish in the culture war; computer gaming companies with corrupt relationships to game-reviewing magazines and sites came under fire, and a full-scale battle between activists and gamers who wanted their games built for fun and not political correctness began. There were well-publicized nasty trolling tactics on all sides (though the activists had more friends in the media to promote their story), and at one point the gamergaters persuaded many advertisers to cancel ads in the offending publications. Intel cancelled some of their ad support, then was subjected to activist attacks. To defuse the issue, Intel pledged $300 million to activist groups.[202] Shortly thereafter, Intel cancelled its sponsorship of the (merit-based) Science Talent Search and cut budgets in research and administration by... $300 million.[203]

Online swarming now results in censorship of speech disagreeing with these activists. One article was withdrawn by Forbes online after activist swarming because it denied that diversity in high tech was a problem. This was an instance of *kafkatrapping*, a mechanism for repressing all contrary thought by labelling anyone who speaks it as racist, sexist, or homophobic—your denial of base motives for disagreement with the activist point of view means you are what you deny, and your speech is hate speech to be suppressed.[204] Badthink must be stamped out so that Goodthink will prevail. The article in question was so extreme:

Repeat after me: there is no "diversity crisis" in Silicon Valley. None. In fact, there is no crisis at all in Silicon Valley. Silicon Valley is doing absolutely gangbusters. Apple has $200 billion in cash reserves and equivalents—and a market valuation of about $630 billion. Amazing. Facebook now garners a billion daily users. This is a nearly unfathomable number. Google is worth nearly $450 billion and has $70 billion in cash on hand.

This is not a crisis. Silicon Valley is swimming in money and in success. Uber is valued at around $50 billion. Companies like Airbnb are remaking travel and lodging. Intel is moving forward into the global Internet of Things market. South Korea's Samsung just opened a giant R&D facility in the heart of Silicon Valley. Google and Facebook are working to connect the entire world. Netflix is re-making how we consume entertainment.

Silicon Valley is home to the next phase of the global auto industry. Fintech and biotech are transforming banking and medicine. The success of Silicon Valley is not due to diversity—or to any bias. Rather, to brilliance, hard work, risk taking, big ideas and money.

Want to be part of this? Great! Follow the example of the millions who came before you. Their parents made school a priority. They took math and science classes, and did their homework every night. They practiced ACT tests over and over. They enrolled in good schools... They took computer programming, engineering, chemistry —hard subjects that demand hard work. They then left their home, their family, their community, and moved to Silicon Valley. They worked hard, staying late night after night. They didn't blog, they didn't let their skills go stale, they didn't blame others when not everything worked out exactly as hoped....

From all over the world, from Brazil and Canada, Nigeria, Pakistan, Russia, Norway, Egypt, fellow humans come to Silicon Valley to work, create, succeed. And they do. Silicon Valley is extremely diverse.

Of course, the iPhone wasn't created because of diversity. Nor was Google. Nor Facebook, nor the computer chip, nor the touchscreen. They were created because a small band of super-smart people who worked very hard to create something better than existed before....

Silicon Valley doesn't just create greatness, it's probably the most open, welcoming, meritocratic-based region on the planet. Anecdotal evidence strongly suggests that disproportionately more Chinese, Indians, and LGBQT succeed in Silicon Valley than just about any place in America. Guess what? Everyone earned their job because of their big brains and ability to contribute.

Is that you? Then come here! It's an amazingly inclusive place.

But be sure to bring your computer science degree, your engineering degree, your proven set of accomplishments. Be sure you are prepared to sacrifice "fun" for long hours and hard work. Offer proof of how well you did in school, in math, in physics. These matter dearly as they are fundamental to what makes Silicon Valley succeed.

Silicon Valley is not perfect. It's certainly no utopia. But if you aren't able to make it here, it's almost certainly not because of any bias. Rather, on your refusal to put in the hard work in the hard classes, and to accept all the failures that happen before you achieve any amazing success....[205]

The coiner of the term kafkatrapping, Eric S. Raymond, was a pioneer in *open-source development*, where widely-dispersed programmers working together build a software project which is free to use, change, or incorporate into larger systems. One of the earliest and most famous of such projects was Linux, an open-source version of Unix originated by Linus Torvalds. Open-source projects have been infiltrated by online activists and "codes of conduct" that let them expel less politically-sensitive participants have been added. Linus himself was threatened by the activists.[206]

Another example of the activist entryists' pressure tactics from Raymond's blog (emphasis added):

> The hacker culture, and STEM in general, are under ideological attack. Recently I blogged a safety warning that according to a source I consider reliable, a "women in tech" pressure group has made multiple efforts to set Linus Torvalds up for a sexual assault accusation. I interpreted this as an attempt to beat the hacker culture into political pliability, and advised anyone in a leadership position to beware of similar attempts.
>
> Now comes Roberto Rosario of the Django Software Foundation. Django is a web development framework that is a flourishing and well-respected part of the ecology around the of the Python language. On October 29th 2015 he reported that someone posting as 'djangoconcardiff' opened an issue against pull request #176 on 'awesome-django', addressing it to Rosario. This was the first paragraph.
>
> ```
> Hi, great project!! I have one observation and
> a suggestion. I noticed that you have rejected
> some pull requests to add some good django
> libraries and that the people submitting thsoe
> pull requests are POCs (People of Colour). As
> a suggestion I recommend adopting the
> Contributor Code of Conduct (http://
> ```

```
contributor-covenant.org) to ensure everyone's
contributions are accepted regarless [sic] of
their sex, sexual orientation, skin color,
religion, height, place of origin, etc. etc.
etc. As a white straight male and lead of this
trending repository, your adoption of this
Code of Conduct will send a loud and clear
message that inclusion is a primary objective
of the Django community and of the software
development community in general. D.
```

The slippery, Newspeak-like quality of djangoconcardiff's "suggestion" makes it hard to pin down from the text itself whether he/she is merely stumping for inclusiveness or insinuating that rejection of pull requests by "persons of color" is itself evidence of racism and thoughtcrime.

But, if you think you're reading that 'djangoconcardiff' considers acceptance of pull requests putatively from "persons of color" to be politically mandatory, a look at the Contributor Covenant he/she advocates will do nothing to dissuade you. Paragraph 2 denounces the **"pervasive cult of meritocracy"**. [Update: The explicit language has since been removed. The intention rather obviously remains]

It is clear that djangoconcardiff and the author of the Covenant (self-described transgender feminist Coraline Ada Ehmke) want to replace the "cult of meritocracy" with something else. And equally clear that **what they want to replace it with is racial and sexual identity politics.**

Rosario tagged his Twitter report "Social Justice in action!" He knows who these people are: SJWs, "Social Justice Warriors". And, unless you have been living under a rock, so do you. These are the people – the political and doctrinal tendency, united if in no other way by an elaborate shared jargon and a **seething hatred of [the]"white straight male"**, who recently hounded Nobel laureate Tim Hunt out of his job with a fraudulent accusation of sexist remarks.

I'm not going to analyze SJW ideology here except to point out, again, why the hacker culture must consider anyone who holds it an enemy. This is because we must be a cult of meritocracy. We must constantly demand merit – performance, intelligence, dedication, and technical excellence – of ourselves and each other.

Now that the Internet—the hacker culture's creation!—is everywhere, and civilization is increasingly software-dependent, we have a duty, the duty I wrote about in Holding Up The Sky. The invisible gears have to turn. The shared software infrastructure of civilization has to work, or economies will seize up and people will die. And for large sections of that infrastructure, it's on us—us!—to keep it working. Because nobody else is going to step up.

We dare not give less than our best. If we fall away from meritocracy —if we allow the SJWs to remake us as they wish, into a hell-pit of competitive grievance-mongering and political favoritism for the designated victim group of the week—we will betray not only what is best in our own traditions but the entire civilization that we serve.

This isn't about women in tech, or minorities in tech, or gays in tech. The hacker culture's norm about inclusion is clear: anybody who can pull the freight is welcome, and twitching about things like skin color or shape of genitalia or what thing you like to stick into what thing is beyond wrong into silly. This is about whether we will allow "diversity" issues to be used as wedges to fracture our community, degrade the quality of our work, and draw us away from our duty.

When hackers fail our own standards of meritocracy, as we sometimes do, it's up to us to fix it from within our own tradition: judge by the work alone, you are what you do, shut up and show us the code. **A movement whose favored tools include the rage mob, the dox, and faked incidents of bigotry is not morally competent to judge us or instruct us.**

I have been participating in and running open-source projects for a quarter-century. In all that time I never had to know or care whether my fellow contributors were white, black, male, female, straight, gay, or from the planet Mars, only whether their code was good. The

SJWs want to make me care; they want to make all of us obsess about this, to the point of having quotas and struggle sessions and what amounts to political officers threatening us if we are insufficiently "diverse".

Think I'm exaggerating? Read the whole djangoconcardiff thread. What's there is totalitarianism in miniature: ideology is everything, merit counts for nothing against the suppression of thoughtcrime, and politics is conducted by naked intimidation against any who refuse to conform. Near the end of the conversation djangoconcardiff threatens to denounce Rosario to the board of the Django Software Foundation in the confused, illiterate, vicious idiom of an orc or a stormtrooper.

It has been suggested that djangoconcardiff might be a troll emulating an SJW, and we should thus take him less seriously. The problem with this idea is that no SJW disclaimed him—more generally, that "Social Justice" has reached a sort of Poe's Law singularity at which the behavior of trolls and true believers becomes indistinguishable even to each other, and has the same emergent effects.

In the future, the hacker whose community standing the SJWs threaten could be you. The SJWs talk 'diversity' but like all totalitarians they measure success only by total ideological surrender – repeating their duckspeak, denouncing others for insufficient political correctness, loving Big Brother. Not being a straight white male won't save you either – Roberto Rosario is an Afro-Hispanic Puerto Rican.

We must cast these would-be totalitarians out–refuse to admit them on any level except by evaluating on pure technical merit whatever code patches they submit. We must refuse to let them judge us, and learn to recognize their thought-stopping jargon and kafkatraps as a clue that there is no point in arguing with them and the only sane course is to disengage. We can't fix what's broken about the SJWs; we can, and must, refuse to let them break us.[207]

Raymond's post is the distilled essence of commitment to engineering excellence and equal opportunity. His opponents are the people trying to tear down standards and replace them with identity politics, tribalists who don't understand how to make the pie but want to get pieces for their friends.

Victim culture identity politics is a US-centric movement promoting narrower and narrower minorities as victims. The earlier Jesse Jackson-style affirmative action movement was supposed to get blacks and women into higher-paying, powerful positions in tech— but most tech companies are worldwide in scope and hiring, and it makes little sense for them to represent local population distributions. Silicon Valley is much more top-heavy with Asians than with white males:

> [Most articles on tech diversity say] the biggest tech companies in Silicon Valley are overwhelmingly white and male. While blacks and Latinos comprise 28 percent of the US workforce, they make up just 6 percent of Twitter's total US workforce and six percent of Facebook employees.

> Of course this is just a lie. Very few people would say a workforce that is 50 to 60 percent white, true of both Google and Microsoft, is "overwhelmingly white." In fact, it's less non-Hispanic white than the US labor force as a whole. I've linked to statistics in this very piece. They take about 10 seconds of browsing search queries to understand this.

> But you don't need to know statistics. Eat at a Google cafeteria. Or walk around the streets of Cupertino. There is no way that one can characterize Silicon Valley as overwhelmingly white with a straight face. Silicon Valley is quite diverse. The diversity just happens to represent the half of the human race with origins in the swath of territory between India and then east and north up to Korea.

> The diversity problem isn't about lack of diversity. It is about the right kind of diversity for a particular socio-political narrative. That's fine, but I really wish there wasn't this tendency to lie about the

major obstacle here: people of Asian origin are 5% of the American work force, but north of 30% in much of the Valley. If you want more underrepresented minorities hiring fewer of these people would certainly help. In particular the inflow of numerous international talent coming from India and China could be staunched by changes to immigration law.

But these are international companies. Though they genuflect to diversity in the American sense (blacks and Latinos), ultimately they'll engage in nominal symbolic tokenism while they continue on with business, with an increasingly ethnically Asian workforce and and increasingly Asian economic focus. Meanwhile, the press will continue to present a false caricature of a white workforce because that's a lot more of a palatable bogeyman than Asian Americans and international tech migrants, and the liberal reading public seems to prefer the false narrative to engaging with reality.[208]

Money and power are being created by disciplined, organized hard work in one of the few US-based growth industries left, the connected computers that make up the Internet and allow cellphone apps to do the world's business. Political parasites are trying very hard to gain entry and position themselves to feed from the resources others generated. While it may seem harmless to throw activists a bone—and Silicon Valley really does want more excellent minorities and women!—feeding the activists only lets them gather more allies to return to demand more. And when they gain power, all of us lose.

Bloomberg BNA has been surveying HR departments for nearly four decades and releases an annual report on the results. These reports show how much HR departments have grown and changed over the years.

Their recent reports show 1.1-1.3 HR full-time staff equivalents per hundred full-time employees, with smaller organizations reporting higher ratios. **HR department budgets are increasing as a share of total spend. From 1997 to 2004, HR spent less than 1% of total budgets, but HR spending rose to 1.4% in 2014, the highest spend percentage ever seen.**[209] This is a natural outcome of ever-increasing regulation and the growth of HR bureaucracy in response. Despite increasing use of outsourcing and online tools, more spending than ever is being diverted from production to protection.

This bloating of HR departments is similar to the expansion of hospital and college administration costs, and it's happening for the same reason: political and legal pressure to manage to meet political goals or be punished.

One survey of costs showed HR expenses of around $750 per employee in large companies (0ver 10,000 employees), but $1500 per employee for companies with less than 1,000 employees. This illustrates how increasing regulation differentially harms companies by size—small companies are more heavily burdened, so large companies can gain a competitive advantage by acquiescing in increasing regulatory schemes. It may cost them something as well, but it cripples small competitors who might otherwise compete to keep margins down. The result is a less-competitive marketplace with higher prices for incumbent large firms, and a harder road for small companies who might be more likely to innovate and undercut the incumbents. The outcome for the economy as a whole is slower growth in employment, innovation, and living standards.

Personnel outsourcing companies like ADP (which generates millions of paychecks every month) naturally fund reports demonstrating how outsourcing can reduce HR costs. Their 2011 report suggests in-house HR departments cost 18% more than the same services provided by outsourcing, especially integrated systems which handle all HR functions in one system:

> The current study set out to measure the Total Cost of Ownership (TCO) of four core business functions—payroll (PR), workforce administration (WA), time & attendance (TA) and health & welfare administration (H&W)—and to analyze factors impacting these costs....
>
> 1. In-house administration of payroll, workforce administration, time & attendance, and health & welfare requires a surprisingly large commitment of time and resources—typically over $1,400 per employee per year (PEPY) for large organizations and nearly $2,000 PEPY for mid-size organizations. "Hidden costs," as defined below, continue to account for more than 50% of the TCO of administering these functions in-house.
>
> 2. TCO for payroll is actually increasing—contrary to our expectation, and despite technological advances, administration costs have actually increased rather than decreased since 2003 as organizations focus on technology transformation rather than process transformation.
>
> 3. Outsourcing continues to deliver overall TCO advantages—using in-house payroll, workforce administration, time & attendance, and health & welfare solutions increases TCO by 18% on average.
>
> 4. Utilizing a common vendor or solution to manage multiple functions, rather than leveraging a "best of breed" approach or maintaining disparate legacy systems, can deliver tangible cost efficiencies—organizations administering these functions using software solutions from multiple vendors spend on average 18% more than those organizations administering them in-house using a

common vendor. Organizations outsourcing multiple functions to a single vendor see even stronger cost efficiency—on average 32%—versus organizations using a multiple vendor or "best of breed" in-house approach.[210]

The direct spend on HR staff can be dwarfed by the indirect costs of the unaccounted-for HR reporting and compliance work imposed on the rest of the company, including time spent on performance evaluations and documenting of personnel issues. And hiring and retention of less competent workers to satisfy HR mandates is even more costly to company performance.

As we've seen, HR costs continue to rise because cost savings from outsourcing are swallowed up by increasing regulatory burdens. The hiring of "Chief Diversity Officers" (CDOs), HR executives making a median salary of $162,588 a year[211] to protect the corporate image from attacks by Jesse Jackson-like activist organizations, is just the most visible sign of these increasing costs.

Who are these people, and what kind of organization is hiring them?

> Deborah Elam, Chief Diversity Officer at General Electric, describes her job in expansive terms. "It's about leveraging the new streams of talent around the world, and responding to the changed face of our customers" she says. Anne Erni, Chief Diversity Officer at Lehman Brothers, has an equally large–and strategic–view. "It's about tapping into the widest possible talent pool ... making sure we create a true meritocracy here at Lehman."

> A few years back, these Chief Diversity Officer positions didn't exist. Today they're firmly established in the executive suite across a range of Fortune 500 companies–at Johnson & Johnson, Aon, Citi and American Express as well as at GE and Lehman Brothers.... So what do these new Chief Diversity Officers actually do?

> Well, for starters, they drive an innovative programmatic agenda that is growing by leaps and bounds. JoAnn Heffernan Heisen, J&J's Chief Diversity Officer, has developed an initiative called the Women's Leadership Initiative which leverages the talents of high potential women around the world. Deb Elam has launched a multicultural woman's "boot camp" which gives diverse women the tools, perspectives and insights to be successful. Anne Erni has designed Encore (an on-ramping offering which welcomes back women who used to work in the financial sector) and rolled out it out in New

York, London and Tokyo.

But how much real impact can we expect from these Chief Diversity Officers? Are they merely tinkering at the edges–designing a few interesting programs–or do they have the muscle power to drive transformational change?

One thing we can be sure of: these new leaders have clout. Most have big budgets and high-caliber dedicated staffs. Many report to a member of the Executive Committee or some, JoAnn Heffernan Heisen of J&J amongst them, report to the CEO. In the words of Melinda Wolfe, Chief Diversity Officer at American Express. "My role is seen as a central driver of employee performance and business results–with continued global expansion the heft of this role is likely going to grow."[212]

This title started in government and academic settings, then made its way into very large financial corporations (who are thoroughly under the regulatory thumb). Notice the signature programs of the CDOs tend to be designed to buff the corporate image through favorable publicity rather than directly impacting minority recruiting for the CDO's organization.

A thriving industry in certification completes the picture of a growth industry. The Society for Diversity's certification offering suggests these benefits of their certification:

The benefits of certification include:
• Higher wages for executives, employees and consultants who possess CDE or CDP credentials.
• A more productive and highly trained diversity resource for employers.
• Prestige for the individual and a competitive advantage over non-certified individuals in the field.
• Enhanced employment opportunities.
• Assisting employers in making more informed hiring decisions.
• Assisting consumers in making informed decisions about qualified diversity providers.

• Protection of the general public from incompetent and unfit practitioners.
• Establishment of a professional standard for individuals in the field of diversity.[213]

All this, for only $3,000-6,000 and good for three years, with continuing education requirements costing more in time and money. This is of course a racket, and these competing certification organizations will work hard to get a certification requirement embedded in law or regulations so they can continue to feed off "diversity professionals," much as teacher continuing education requirements fund connected apparatchiks. Cornell has also entered the market with its "Cornell Certified Diversity Professional / Advanced Practitioner (CCDP/AP)" certificate program,[214] which is cheap at $1,000 and conducted by conference call and an email exam (which of course can be taken by a confederate.)

There's even a *Diversity Officer* magazine![215]

Let's see what HR visionaries themselves have to say about their leadership of corporate diversity programs. First we'll hear from Carole Watkins of Cardinal Health:

• Men often see themselves and their skills differently from women. If there are five requirements for a position and a man has two of them, he will ask for the position. But a woman who may have four of the five qualifications will not likely put her hand up because she doesn't have the fifth. Men who participated in the program now recognize this difference and are reaching out to those women to encourage them to apply for positions rather than waiting to apply.

• Assumptions are often made about women's personal and professional desires. In the past, men were making assumptions without consulting the potential women candidates—for example, assuming a woman who is qualified for a promotion wouldn't want it because she has small children and the job requires extensive travel. Assumptions might seem appropriate and even protective but they are actually self-censoring and limiting. Participants are now allowing potential female candidates to make that call.

• Decisions made without applying a gender lens often have unintended consequences. Initiating conversations with women on their team about gender differences awakened male participants to how decisions they make may have unintended consequences. For example, a leader in our nuclear pharmacy business was finding it difficult to hire women, who today are the majority of pharmacy graduates, to move to some of our newer locations. When he probed more, he discovered that since the nature of the nuclear pharmacy business requires pharmacists to work during the dark early morning hours or late night hours, women were not comfortable with the current locations. He needed to consider location (in safe neighborhoods), good parking, and proper outdoor lighting before he could attract top female pharmacists.

• Day-to-day conversations. Today's business meetings are full of sports and military analogies. After talking to many women, male participants realized many of these were lost on the women in the room. The decision was made to begin a "fine" system. If a sports or military analogy is used, the person has to contribute to a fund donated to a local nonprofit focused on women's issues. PLC participants also reported having different, more meaningful conversations with spouses, partners, daughters, and sons about the impact of unconscious bias, asking them questions about its impact on them and sometimes leading to life and relationship-changing conversations. Meanwhile, at Cardinal Health, female promotions as a percent of total promotions jumped from 33 percent to 55 percent in one year. We believe this program played an important role in the improvement....

We began our program by asking every senior vice president in our organization to select two individuals, one of whom needed to be a female and/or ethnically diverse, to sponsor. This way the SVPs were selecting individuals they could advocate for, give direct feedback to, and promote throughout the organization...

In 2010, Cardinal Health had no female presidents. By early 2014, four of nine presidents were women....

1. We hold dedicated "diverse talent reviews" focused solely on discussing diverse employees, their talents and capabilities, and the next steps for their careers. This allows sponsors to advocate for and recognize their protégés so others are aware of their talents.

2. The inclusion index, which is part of our annual "Voice of the Employee" survey, has increased 10 percentage points.

3. In 2014, turnover for females at the manager level and above is 5.2 percent—which is lower than it is for their male counterparts (6.3 percent).[216]

Note that she is almost entirely focused on increasing women's opportunities and comfort level in her workforce. You have to read between the lines to see how arms are being twisted to remove male-oriented culture like sports terminology and to spend more on workplace environments that feel safer for women (which means abandoning urban locations and the diverse employees that might live nearby for suburban locations where white women feel safe.) The not-so-subtle pressure to mentor and promote women and minorities over others is probably increasing workplace resentments as fairness and merit take a back seat.

Brigette McInnis-Day of SAP sounds almost chipper as she recounts how pressure to hire for diversity quotas rather than merit overcame manager doubts:

I have an example I love to share that illustrates setting big goals. We started a sales graduate program in the US and the team was trying to establish goals (not targets—don't get excited) for diversity. Everyone came with a conservative plan using trends and previous statistics, pointing out all of the risks, and suggested a "careful" target. I challenged the team to think big and differently and reach for a target of 70 percent diversity. Everyone laughed, scoffed at the idea, and told me, "No way!" But I held firm on what I knew we could achieve —and we nailed it. We beat our goal by reaching 72 percent. The lead early talent recruiter said to me, "If you did not put that big goal in my head, I would never have strived for it. Once I believed, it was easy!" Even better, it turned the nonbelievers into believers and they changed their hiring approach going forward.[217]

No doubt these converts were waving little red books as they experienced the epiphany she demanded. How the "72% diverse" new hires did over time is not really her concern—she'll be on to a new and higher-paying post at another company before anyone is allowed to doubt the results.

Even tech companies are getting into the CDO game. Salesforce, which sells CRM and personnel management software-as-a-service to business, announced creation of a Chief Equality Officer position:

Salesforce has taken a leading role on LGBT issues and now it is taking that one step further. The company next week will be announcing its first chief equality officer, who will report directly to CEO Marc Benioff... While [Benioff] has built charitable efforts and equality into his own company, and he admits there is a self-serving component to this, he believes that companies need to give back.

"We can just focus on our own results, our own tech, but you won't get the joy that comes from giving, the real pleasure of helping people. You're not only helping other people, you're helping yourself," Benioff says.

Benioff has put his money where is mouth is, giving millions to public schools and working to overturn anti-gay and trans laws in Indiana, Georgia and North Carolina.

It's widely known that when Benioff and co-founder Parker Harris launched the company, they built the 1/1/1 program into the organization to give back to the community. As they like to joke, there wasn't anything to give at that point, but over the years as the company has grown and become tremendously successful, it has given over $128 million in grants and employees have volunteered more than 1.6 million hours in the community....The Chief Equality

Officer will build those values into the fabric of the organization, bringing a voice directly to the C suite.[218]

The "Diversity and Inclusion" consulting firms suggest documenting the great ROI (Return On Investment) of their programs to convince management to fund more of them. Upper-level management, it seems, would like to see these program costs as investments returning higher revenues and profits. This is another credit assignment problem—how can the impact of costly programs which both generate more fees to vendors and take up valuable employee time for nonproductive counselling and "mind-changing" sessions be measured?

The correct answer: it can't. Unless there's a control company which is very similar at the start but does not undergo diversity training and have diversity programs, there's no way to determine what impact such programs have on the business. Since both direct and indirect costs are high, showing positive profit impact is going to take real evidence. What can't be openly admitted is that companies feel they must have such programs or be punished, either by the EEOC or lawsuits. The program itself is partly protective, demonstrating the company made a good faith effort to promote diversity.

But here are some suggested metrics:

Quick List of Possible Metrics
- Percentage of minorities, EEO targets
- Increase in minority representation
- Increased representation of minorities at different levels of firm
- Employee satisfaction surveys
- Better relationships among diverse staff members;
- Fewer discrimination grievances and complaints;
- Fewer findings of discrimination by adjudicators and government agencies;
- Improved labor relations;
- Reduction of noose, graffiti, and hate incidents;
- More diverse hiring.
- Improvements in productivity.

- More innovation and creativity. (There are various metrics for this, such as patents granted per capita.)
- Improved job satisfaction.
- More career development over time for underrepresented group members.
- Use of bridge positions for lower level employees to bridge to professional positions.
- Better retention.
- Decrease in pay disparities.
- More positive responses on exit interviews.
- Higher ranking of the organization in terms of best places to work.
- Becoming an employer of choice.
- Awards from special interest and advocacy groups.
- Inclusion of diversity in corporate social responsibility efforts.
- Independence and professionalism of the diversity officer.[219]

Your company certainly has a problem if it needs to reduce "noose, graffiti, and hate incidents." But as we have seen in academic examples recently, those benefitting from the diversity movement have taken to false reporting or even producing these incidents themselves to get attention. The solution to such incidents is to fire those creating them or falsely reporting them.

Real "improvements in productivity" would be wonderful, but there is no way to prove a whiz-bang diversity program has any effect on productivity numbers. Surveys of employee attitudes and satisfaction are useful, and to some extent diversity programs have a kind of placebo effect—"The company is making an effort, they care!" being the effect on employees and outside observers of media coverage and advertising generated about these programs, which is why there is sometimes more money spent on the PR about diversity programs than on the programs themselves.

An overview of the literature on workplace social or cultural training—that is, training intended to change employee's cultural attitudes and behavior, like sexual harassment and diversity training —shows that most such programs don't work, or even cause employees to be more cynical and less likely to believe allegations of racial or sexual harassment.[220] Most such programs are mandatory, and many are online, requiring the subject to read every word of an hour or more of slides and answer quizzes before continuing. These programs are often chosen for low cost and minimal work disruption, but are resented by employees as obvious wastes of valuable time, and condescending since most of the employees subjected to them already fully understand the material presented. The abusers among them are not affected at all.

Meanwhile, some positive benefits to attitudes are seen with more interpersonal sessions which allow employees to interact, run by facilitators who don't present their political attitudes as correct. This puts the focus on the feelings of fellow employees, not the compulsory re-education camp atmosphere of sessions run by ideologues. But this takes more time, hours at least, and an expensive on-site facilitator.

Hypocrisy is another side-effect. At most companies the programs are required by liability insurance companies and quietly resented by both management and staff, but no one may officially speak against them—diversity is a sacred cow.

Particularly wasteful diversity programs get some publicity:

The Portland Police Department recently came under attack for conducting a 3-day diversity training for its leadership with a well-known and highly respected diversity consulting firm, White Men as Full Diversity Partners. This company focuses on helping white men, in particular, understand their role in creating inclusive environments.

The criticism largely stemmed from the cost of the training—$56,000 for a three day retreat that was apparently held at a posh golf resort at Mt. Hood called The Resort at the Mountain.

The Mayor, Charlie Hales, who was a part of the training defended the expenditure. He said that the Portland community is becoming more diverse and the police force, which is primarily white males, needs to better understand the communities they serve.

One news account questioned how much time was actually spent in training versus on the golf course. Others said that they did not object to the training but as public servants they should have chosen a less expensive venue.[221]

Prices for diversity training depend on type and length. One site offers half-day facilitated sessions for up to 12 employees for $3750, c. $300 each. Lost work time per employee would add $100-200 to the cost. A company with 80,000 workers would therefore end up paying about $32 million for all employees for this one half-day session alone, and HR will want to repeat the training with the latest and greatest methods in a few years. Online training takes less time and money—a few hours of time of the employee's choosing, for c. $100-200 per employee in direct costs, but having little or negative actual effect.

A few contrarian voices speak out against the sacred cow of diversity training. The Harvard Business Review's piece ("Diversity Policies Rarely Make Companies Fairer, and They Feel Threatening to White Men") from the January, 2016 issue slams it hard:

Are all of these [expensive corporate diversity] efforts working? In terms of increasing demographic diversity, the answer appears to be not really. The most commonly used diversity programs do little to increase representation of minorities and women. A longitudinal study of over 700 U.S. companies found that implementing diversity training programs has little positive effect and may even decrease representation of black women....

[Shielding effect:] In a 2011 Supreme Court class action case, Walmart successfully used the mere presence of its anti-discrimination policy to defend itself against allegations of gender discrimination. And Walmart isn't alone: the "diversity defense" often succeeds, making organizations less accountable for discriminatory practices.

There's another way the rhetoric of diversity can result in inaccurate and counterproductive beliefs. In a recent experiment, we found evidence that it not only makes white men believe that women and minorities are being treated fairly—whether that's true or not—it also makes them more likely to believe that they themselves are being treated unfairly.

We put young white men through a hiring simulation for an entry-level job at a fictional technology firm. For half of the "applicants," the firm's recruitment materials briefly mentioned its pro-diversity values. For the other half, the materials did not mention diversity. In all other ways, the firm was described identically. All of the applicants then underwent a standardized job interview while we videotaped their performance and measured their cardiovascular stress responses.

Compared to white men interviewing at the company that did not mention diversity, white men interviewing for the pro-diversity company expected more unfair treatment and discrimination against whites. They also performed more poorly in the job interview, as judged by independent raters. And their cardiovascular responses during the interview revealed that they were more stressed.

Thus, pro-diversity messages signaled to these white men that they might be undervalued and discriminated against. These concerns interfered with their interview performance and caused their bodies to respond as if they were under threat. Importantly, diversity messages led to these effects regardless of these men's political ideology, attitudes toward minority groups, beliefs about the prevalence of discrimination against whites, or beliefs about the fairness of the world. This suggests just how widespread negative responses to diversity may be among white men: the responses exist even among those who endorse the tenets of diversity and inclusion.

In another set of experiments, we found that diversity initiatives also seem to do little to convince minorities that companies will treat them more fairly. Participants from ethnic minorities viewed a pro-diversity company as no more inclusive, no better to work for, and no less likely to discriminate against minorities than a company without a pro-diversity stance. (Other researchers have seen more promising results of pro-diversity rhetoric and images, but it's clear they're no panacea.)...Currently, diversity initiatives' strongest accomplishment may actually be protecting the organization from litigation—not protecting the interests of underrepresented groups.[222]

Identity politics applied to personnel, in other words, don't do much for diversity, but the constant rhetoric makes the company look like it cares more about skin color and sex than performance. This makes the majority of the workers who think of themselves (correctly or not) as colorblind nervous and wary of discrimination. Meanwhile, it does little to truly support minority employees who may find the rhetoric conceals culture-based discrimination.

Many companies would scrap their diversity regimes if they were not required for legal and PR protection. A corporate culture emphasizing Martin Luther King's standard of "content of character" over color of skin and type of sex organs is both less hypocritical and more easily supported by all employees regardless of minority status. A multicolored, multicultural workforce where everyone shares the goal of winning in the marketplace can be more inspiring for high achievers than one that divides employees by race and sex.

But under current state and Federal law, diversity expenditures and PR are required to protect the enterprise. The detailed followup article in the HBR should be studied by upper managements since it not only blows the whistle on the waste and harm caused by current diversity programs but suggests a path to more cost-effective and productive programs:

> Businesses started caring a lot more about diversity after a series of high-profile lawsuits rocked the financial industry. In the late 1990s and early 2000s, Morgan Stanley shelled out $54 million—and Smith Barney and Merrill Lynch more than $100 million each—to settle sex discrimination claims. In 2007, Morgan was back at the table, facing a new class action, which cost the company $46 million. In 2013, Bank of America Merrill Lynch settled a race discrimination suit for $160 million. Cases like these brought Merrill's total 15-year payout to nearly half a billion dollars.

It's no wonder that Wall Street firms now require new hires to sign arbitration contracts agreeing not to join class actions. They have also expanded training and other diversity programs. But on balance, equality isn't improving in financial services or elsewhere. Although the proportion of managers at U.S. commercial banks who were Hispanic rose from 4.7% in 2003 to 5.7% in 2014, white women's representation dropped from 39% to 35%, and black men's from 2.5% to 2.3%. The numbers were even worse in investment banks (though that industry is shrinking, which complicates the analysis). Among all U.S. companies with 100 or more employees, the proportion of black men in management increased just slightly— from 3% to 3.3%—from 1985 to 2014. White women saw bigger gains from 1985 to 2000—rising from 22% to 29% of managers—but their numbers haven't budged since then. Even in Silicon Valley, where many leaders tout the need to increase diversity for both business and social justice reasons, bread-and-butter tech jobs remain dominated by white men.[223]

As we saw elsewhere, all HR-imposed systems will be gamed and routed around by hiring managers keen to improve the performance of their teams and promote their own advancement. When diversity is mostly lip service and an industry is clubbish, not much will actually change—high-performing minority candidates who would have done well anyway are promoted, but the corporate culture won't change much.

> ...companies are basically doubling down on the same approaches they've used since the 1960s—which often make things worse, not better. Firms have long relied on diversity training to reduce bias on the job, hiring tests and performance ratings to limit it in recruitment and promotions, and grievance systems to give employees a way to challenge managers. Those tools are designed to preempt lawsuits by policing managers' thoughts and actions. Yet laboratory studies show that this kind of force-feeding can activate bias rather than stamp it out. As social scientists have found, people often rebel against rules to assert their autonomy. Try to coerce me to do X, Y, or Z, and I'll do the opposite just to prove that I'm my own person.

In analyzing three decades' worth of data from more than 800 U.S. firms and interviewing hundreds of line managers and executives at length, we've seen that companies get better results when they ease up on the control tactics. It's more effective to engage managers in solving the problem, increase their on-the-job contact with female and minority workers, and promote social accountability—the desire to look fair-minded. That's why interventions such as targeted college recruitment, mentoring programs, self-managed teams, and task forces have boosted diversity in businesses. Some of the most effective solutions aren't even designed with diversity in mind.... Decades of social science research point to a simple truth: You won't get managers on board by blaming and shaming them with rules and reeducation....

Another reason is that about three-quarters of firms with training still follow the dated advice of the late diversity guru R. Roosevelt Thomas Jr. "If diversity management is strategic to the organization," he used to say, diversity training must be mandatory, and management has to make it clear that "if you can't deal with that, then we have to ask you to leave." But five years after instituting required training for managers, companies saw no improvement in the proportion of white women, black men, and Hispanics in management, and the share of black women actually decreased by 9%, on average, while the ranks of Asian-American men and women shrank by 4% to 5%. Trainers tell us that people often respond to compulsory courses with anger and resistance—and many participants actually report more animosity toward other groups afterward.

But voluntary training evokes the opposite response ("I chose to show up, so I must be pro-diversity"), leading to better results: increases of 9% to 13% in black men, Hispanic men, and Asian-American men and women in management five years out (with no decline in white or black women). Research from the University of Toronto reinforces our findings: In one study white subjects read a brochure critiquing prejudice toward blacks. When people felt pressure to agree with it, the reading strengthened their bias against blacks. When they felt the choice was theirs, the reading reduced bias.

Companies too often signal that training is remedial. The diversity manager at a national beverage company told us that the top brass uses it to deal with problem groups. "If there are a number of complaints…or, God forbid, some type of harassment case…leaders say, 'Everyone in the business unit will go through it again.'" Most companies with training have special programs for managers. To be sure, they're a high-risk group because they make the hiring, promotion, and pay decisions. But singling them out implies that they're the worst culprits. Managers tend to resent that implication and resist the message.[224]

One lawyer comments on the same issues:

If they are doing it for legal protection, most employers really don't care whether the training works. It is hardly surprising that training could have counterproductive effects when the attitude often is, "Just do it, and just do it as cheaply as possible." This approach leaves employees feeling cynical and distrustful of the company and in the worse case sows the seeds for conflict.[225]

What can companies do to resist the stagnating effect of HR culture and government micromanagement on their competiveness? Say you're a board member or CEO of a major Silicon Valley company wanting to free your enterprise from diversity activists and an HR department increasingly dominated by social worker types wanting to make a socially-engineered conformist playpen of your workplace.

If it's not too late—if your company is a startup with a handful of mostly technical employees—make sure your first HR employee believes in the free market, profit, and growth (of more than just her salary.) Avoid hiring former college social justice activists or Bernie Sanders-style "everything should be free" socialists. Of course your HR head should be aware of PR and the shibboleths[226] of CSR (Corporate Social Responsibility)—but in a world of wolves in sheep's clothing, your HR head needs to be a wolf, too, even if she wears a dress.

Having leftists in HR is damaging in three ways: 1) The leftist doesn't see a need to provide value for money, and their loyalty is to a larger ideology and not your company; 2) The leftist uses the platform you provide to push ideas and policies that will someday destroy your company if they succeed in biasing hiring toward fellow travelers, and 3) They may damage your brand by identifying your company with leftist goals when half or more of your customers don't share them. That last is becoming a problem for ESPN and its parent, Disney, as sports fans discover ESPN programming now has political content, resulting in loss of audience share and revenues.

Corporate culture is key, and keeping out *entryists*—[227] people whose allegiance is to some conflicting ideology that will gradually subvert your culture—is critical. Airbnb received a $150 million early investment from Peter Thiel, who gave the company some valuable advice:

After we closed our Series C with Peter Thiel in 2012, we invited him to our office. This was late last year, and we were in the Berlin room showing him various metrics. Midway through the conversation, I asked him what was the single most important piece of advice he had for us.

He replied, "Don't fuck up the culture."

This wasn't what we were expecting from someone who just gave us $150M. I asked him to elaborate on this. He said one of the reasons he invested in us was our culture. But he had a somewhat cynical view that it was practically inevitable once a company gets to a certain size to "fuck it up." Hmm.. How depressing I thought.

Were we destined to eventually "fuck up our culture?" We talked about it a bit more, and it became clear that it was possible to defend, and actually build the culture. But it had to be one of the things we were most focused on. I thought to myself, how many company CEOs are focused on culture above all else? Is it the metric they measure closest? Is it what they spend most of their hours on each week?

Culture is simply a shared way of doing something with passion…. If you break the culture, you break the machine that creates your products.[228]

If your culture is founded on creating excellent products or services that will win in the marketplace, hiring people who have other goals —righting past wrongs, molding fellow employees' thought processes to conform to their own, shielding everyone from harsh realities to make them (temporarily) feel good and important—will dilute your company's culture, and networks of employees who support each other's willingness to call in outside legal or political forces to win internal battles will form.

Not only do you have to be sure not to take onboard as managers anyone who would engage in racial and sexual discrimination, but you have to be wary of those who would wrongly accuse others of it to gain an advantage. And once you allow a few people to use their protected status to avoid accountability, you damage the rest of your employees' respect for the standard of performance. Why should anyone at your company strive for excellence when the rewards go to cheaters?

So say it's too late to keep them out—they're already inside, and most of your HR management and staff fail to value the survival and growth of the enterprise as the most important goal. It may not be too late—you can outsource the critical functions of HR like payroll and compliance reports, and appoint a new, carefully-selected HR head to downsize the organization, keeping the productive and eliminating the HR staff who spend their time running diversity campaigns and in meetings to write reports about meetings. Throwing back much of the "call in a counsellor" function to managers with outsourced support makes sense. Depending on the industry, hiring can be returned to the hiring managers—who have the incentive to do the best job—or screening for low-level positions can be completely online, with no local HR staff to keep qualified but less-documented candidates away.

Outsourced HR for small companies is being provided by PEOs (Professional Employer Organizations):

> These companies become the legal employer of your staff and handle all the payroll, benefits and HR functions.

> "Most small businesses are under 25 employees, and that means the owner is the most productive, is critical to the success of the business, and has to get out there and generate sales and products," says Milan Yager, president and CEO of the National Association of Professional Employer Organizations. When small businesses outsource non-core activities, "they can focus on the business of their business," says Yager.

> But when does it make sense to hire a PEO? While PEOs aren't for every company, those that do use them can often offer better benefit

packages and thus hire better talent, says Ed Vargas, senior vice president of health and benefits at Aon Consulting. "We help them set up a Fortune 500 package of benefits," he says.[229]

Larger companies may prefer to retain direct legal employment of staff but outsource most of the standard HR functions as they often do payroll. Benefits are one specialized area more efficiently handled through outsourcing—though the provision of health insurance through employment is a costly artifact of history (it began when WW II wage controls kept companies from directly raising salaries to compete for workers) and is likely to be targeted by reform plans, it's still a critical benefit which must be handled by specialists to keep costs down and employees healthy and happy. One good piece of advice:

> As companies turn to business administration outsourcing (BAO) for more and varied functions, the vendors' presence becomes more apparent to the employee end-user. Companies that in the past may have partnered with BAO providers for behind-the-scenes functions —such as open enrollment support or summary plan description creation—are increasingly using the vendors as employees' major point of contact for all things benefits-related.

> ...But no matter how great the time or monetary savings from hiring a BAO provider, the employer should focus on the employee end-user's experience when structuring how the new vendor relationship is going to function...

> While employees are likely to accept an outside company tackling the more administratively burdensome benefits tasks, most companies would be wise to make sure someone internally in HR is sufficiently knowledgeable and readily available to step in when an issue is escalated and unresolved by the vendor. Also, the internal professional should be ready to handle issues that are particularly time-sensitive in nature.

The more hands-off and distant the company's benefits staff is, the more difficult it will be for them to effectively intervene. The space between HR and the outsourced vendor could easily deteriorate into an environment where no one "owns" the issue and no one seems accountable.[230]

When your core HR management is culturally solid and most tasks are outsourced, HR managers can focus on grooming your workforce toward becoming the valuable resource HR visionaries are always talking about. Corporate messaging to larger workforces shouldn't be in the hands of HR, but remain with the executive office. Abdicating culture leadership to HR departments can do great damage unless they are completely on-message with the CEO.

Another useful tactic for the largest companies is to buy off the Democratic politicians who are promoting labor regulations and can be persuaded to go after some other company provided you send them campaign contributions and hire their friends as lobbyists, as Google has. This has the benefit of being relatively cheap and can hobble your competition. Google has used their campaign contributions to enlist US politicians to defend it from EU antitrust enforcement:

> Google has made political donations to 162 members of the US Congress in the latest election cycle, figures show, as concerns grow over the internet giant's lobbying influence in Washington.... Google enlisted American politicians whose election campaigns it had funded to pressure the European Union in a carefully coordinated campaign to drop a €6bn ($6.5bn) antitrust case that threatens its business in Europe.

> The disclosure underlined the close relationship between the company, the US Congress and even the White House, where the chief technology officer is among several ex-Google employees. Critics say that while the firm born in a garage in 1998 tries to present itself as breaking the mould, it has an army of more than a hundred lobbyists and buys influence just as big corporations have done for decades.

Google has reportedly spent more money on federal lobbying than any other company since 2012. And its political action committee has given donations between $1,000 and $10,000 to some 34 senators and 128 members of the House of Representatives in the 2016 cycle, according to data compiled by the Center for Responsive Politics. In the Senate this breaks down as $78,500 to Republicans and $46,500 to Democrats; in the House, as $126,250 to Republicans and $131,500 to Democrats.[231]

Google's earlier violations of age discrimination laws in hiring went unpunished for years. But lawsuits are catching up to them:

> Just over a year ago, two people who had been turned down after applying for jobs at Google filed a lawsuit against the company. They claimed they were rejected because of their age. Both were over 40. A federal court in San Jose is now being asked to decide whether many others who sought jobs at Google and were also rejected can join this case.... Cheryl Fillekes, a programmer and one of two parties in this case, is pressing forward with this collective-action claim... Fillekes, who earned a Ph.D. in geophysics from the University of Chicago and who also undertook postdoctoral work at Harvard, said she was invited for in-person interviews on four different occasions and was rejected each time.

> The lawsuit alleges Google "engaged in a systematic pattern" of discrimination against people over the age of 40. It cited data from Payscale that put the median age of Google's workforce at 29, with a margin of error of 4%. It says the median age for computer programmers in the U.S. is 43.

> The other party to this case, Robert Heath, a software engineer, was rejected after a technical telephone interview....A trial is scheduled for May 2017. A Google spokesman said the company doesn't comment on pending litigation.

> One woman seeking a job at Google said an "interviewer expressed concern about a cultural fit, noting that she might not be up for the

'lifestyle.'"

According to the court document, this unidentified woman assured the interviewer "that she was willing to work long hours," but "the interviewer replied that he was still worried that she was not Googley enough."[232]

Google in its initial growth years was notorious in the Valley for hiring only under-30 academic stars, but they have since been careful to broaden hiring and have taken on more mature employees, especially outside of core programming teams. Their good public relations combined with campaign contributions have so far protected them from the kind of deadening regulation that may await them as jealous competitors lobby foreign governments to restrict their near-monopoly on search and advertising, which was honestly gained by being the best.

Industry lobbying organizations have not been very successful at getting labor laws loosened. In California, old-style labor regulation is constantly added onto by Democratic legislation designed to appeal to voters. Practices that were long accepted like irregular hours, telecommuting, and at-work personal web surfing have been called into question, quite expensively, by class-action attorneys working to win major settlements for minor violations of 1930s-style industrial work regulations. From a labor and employment roundtable sponsored by Fenwick and West, a Silicon Valley law firm:

Mathiason: These cases illustrate that we have employment laws— especially wage-and-hour laws—often manufactured decades ago that are being contorted to fit the current environment. A growing part of the workforce in California may never set foot in California. We have typically applied the law of the physical location of the individual performing the work. Increasingly, technology is making this standard obsolete. With legislative action politically deadlocked, courts are being called upon to balance the new world of work with the original intent of the statutes.

Sulzer: A number of wage-and-hour issues arise in the telecommuting context as well, particularly as we wait for the Brinker decision regarding meal and break periods, and whether they must be "ensured" or "provided." On the flip-side of this, there is a new kind of class action involving employees who are the least mobile—class actions under the labor code related to "suitable seating" for workers... We've seen this in the retail and hospitality industries, but now other industries are concerned about exactly what this trend means. A number of them are looking for an ergonomic defense whereas, in the hospitality or retail industry, there's another defense, which is that if you are customer facing, standing—not sitting—is part of the job.

McCoy: You'll also see these cases in white-collar working environments, such as biotech labs. Sophisticated counsel will take these cases into the high tech sector in the same way that overtime misclassification cases evolved from retail and fast food to high tech.

Johnson: The seating cases are an example of the plaintiffs bar getting more creative with the types of claims they are bringing since the low-hanging fruit has already been plucked. Section 15 of most wage orders require employers to provide a comfortable temperature in the workplace; that could be the next wave of class action litigation. We're getting into the weeds on a lot of the less visible issues in the wage-and-hour area.

Mathiason: Plaintiffs counsel are mining microinequities in the labor code. All of this is driven by the attraction of class action status, the significant costs for litigation, and therefore, the significant settlement value. This will continue until the courts make these kinds of classes hard to certify and they grant more summary judgments....

Sulzer: With plaintiffs looking for different types of class actions to pursue, we frequently see claims based on time rounding. Judges are looking closely at that, and restricting the de minimis argument. Plaintiffs... say, "There's no such thing as de minimis in California anymore." If you underpay somebody by two minutes, you owe them two minutes, plus penalties.

Schachter: In that regard, an enormous area of potential litigation involves employees checking emails on mobile devices. If somebody does that for a minute here and there, to what extent do these di minimis involvements with the workplace trigger an obligation to pay overtime?[233]

Because the plaintiff attorneys are closely connected to the Democratic party legislators and also donate large sums to campaigns, Silicon Valley companies find themselves targets of shakedowns over antiquated work rules those legislators seem never find the time to re-examine. Programmers and other professionals are then subjected to work rules that no one wants—regular hours, prohibition on personal use of computers during the work day, prohibitions on checking work-related email at night or working from home…. It's insane.

Federal rules are not as ridiculous, but still troublesome. The EEOC performs a useful function in investigating and denying most baseless discrimination complaints at low cost, but will occasionally go after a high-profile corporate scapegoat when an administration wants to burnish its image with minority voters.

Pushing back with campaign donations and buying politicians can work only for the largest companies. If small businesses were correctly viewed as disadvantaged by the current system, politicians would create something like a union for them—funded by compulsory dues and charged with representing small business interests in legislation and enforcement.

But in the end the problem at the Federal level is not legislation, but the growing administrative state that has been delegated the power to write and enforce regulations almost independent of Congress. Administrations have grown more corrupt with time, using executive-branch authority to punish and reward certain companies and industries and appointing judges who won't slow the agencies down unless the regulations are exceptional in overstepping legal authority.

It's up to both citizens and corporate management to see that their representatives scale back the administrative state's interference in business operations. Quiet resistance helped companies survive mostly unharmed until recently, but the new level of micromanagement will make it hard to grow and succeed unless it is turned back soon.

And support legislative efforts to return all lawmaking to Congress. Feeble efforts like the CRA (Congressional Review Act), intended to allow Congress to stop abusive rulemaking by executive-branch agencies, have not worked.[234] Streamlining and stripping out-of-control agencies of their improperly delegated legislative and judicial roles is the only way to bring them to heel and reduce their damaging effects on the economy.

The proposed Freedom of Contract Amendment would ultimately dismantle most labor law and regulations, returning employment to a freely-chosen and negotiable contract between employer and employee. Freedom of contract was inherent in the US Constitution, but was eroded in the Progressive era and virtually ended by the post-New Deal changes to the composition of the Supreme Court.[235] Large businesses have been drawn into politics to protect themselves, but find more and more effort is required; clarifying that the powers of the Federal government are not to be used to micromanage business (or personal lives, or education, or...) would keep down the threat and the resulting protection payments. The protective functions of HR would become less necessary.

How can employees resist HR's damaging effects while still appearing compliant? Early drafts of this book elicited a lot of useful responses from people out in the trenches.

One line of defense: the "Irish Democracy" of the Reform and Rebellion chapter. This means individuals refuse to cooperate with HR (and government overseer) efforts to divide and discriminate. Self-identifying as a member of a protected minority class is one way to monkey-wrench the system; if quite a few people adopt this stance, the system cannot function. Letting it be known that you are Native American to reap affirmative action advantages, as Senator Elizabeth Warren (D-MA) did before her tenured position at Harvard Law School was secured, is impossible to dispute. More in-their-face options, like claiming your red-haired, freckled self to be African American, will probably cause unnecessary trouble. But those of mixed and indeterminate breeding should cheerfully claim to be whatever gives them the most benefits. As the number of claimants increase, affirmative action systems begin to break down. "I identify as…" is becoming an all-purpose rebel cry. The social engineers are then forced to begin testing genetics or examining genitalia, making the illiberal Progressive agenda clearer—forcing divisions and classifications on people is an ugly and authoritarian idea, un-American, and contrary to the goal of equal opportunity for all.

Some enterprising TV newscasters are unashamed:

> The anchorman formerly known as David Johnston was stuck in a dead-end job. For six years, Johnston had served as evening anchor at two small TV affiliates in Midland/Odessa and El Paso, Texas. He wanted a shot at a bigger market or a network, but his audition tape never seemed to interest recruiters.

But when Johnston took a job three years ago at KOVR-TV in Sacramento, his career prospects changed dramatically. So did his name. Re-christened on-air as David Ono, the 33-year-old broadcaster has fielded job offers from stations in Los Angeles and Seattle and finally has the networks' attention, thanks largely to his new, ethnic name. "I changed it to my advantage," says Johnston, who still uses his original surname for legal purposes. "I've received a lot of interest. I think the name change could have set that off, in addition to seasoning and just getting better."

Johnston is just one of many broadcasters playing the ethnic name game. Taking advantage of federal affirmative-action rules designed to benefit minorities, a number of reporters and anchors with Anglo-sounding last names have switched to Latino and Asian handles. The trend has led to growing outrage among some news professionals and minority activists, who argue that it cheapens the concept of affirmative action and raises troubling issues of journalistic ethics.

Many reporters who have changed their names claim biracial status and explain that they are just borrowing a relative's last name to accentuate their minority roots—a reversal of the age-old immigrant practice of anglicizing a foreign last name to speed assimilation in the United States. Johnston, for instance, says he is of Asian and white descent, and that Ono is his Japanese mother's maiden name. "It's simple, reflects ethnicity and is very easy to remember," he says.

Reporter Gordon Gary reached back two generations for his new name. On the air at KNBC-TV Channel 4 in Los Angeles, he uses the surname Tokumatsu, which he says was the maiden name of his grandmother, a descendant of Japanese samurai. He switched names shortly after starting his career at KESQ-TV in Palm Springs, he says.[236]

They are providing additional PR-diversity cred to their employers by claiming ethnic and minority identities. And who is going to look into their backgrounds or make them prove their claimed ethnic identification? There are far more blonde women newscasters than can be accounted for by their representation in the population. Is it wrong if women dye their hair blonde to make themselves more attractive to station managers catering to ratings?

One commenter confirms the point that HR directives are resisted when companies require real expertise in a position:

> When there's no way to do the company's work without employees with actual competence, an HR department's preferences and decrees to the contrary will be ignored, whether overtly or covertly. When a clash arises that has nothing to do with law or regulation, the rebellion can be overt, albeit at the cost of open inter-departmental conflict that can have long-term consequences. When law or regulation, or HR's interpretation thereof, manage to intrude, the rebellion must be covert and clever...sometimes to the point of a well concealed act of fraud specifically designed to get around the offending rule.[237]

Another woman chimed in with good advice:

> • HR is the gatekeeper—a clever applicant just has to tune his cover letter to check off all the boxes on the "requirements". The trick is to satisfy them sufficiently to pass you on to the next level, allowing you to talk to an actual person about how your non-standard qualifications are actually BETTER than what HR requests.
> • When you hate an HR mandate, play dumb. Ask for clarification. After enough of those, they may decide to get off your back.
> • Bypass them—walk in to the department that needs you, and talk face-to-face. AFTER that, and with their imprimatur, talk to HR.
> • Don't bother trying to suck up to the women. They HATE all of the non-Liberal Arts types. Only talk to them as a last resort.
> • Realize that they are so annoying, powerful, and yet, underutilized, that they are a prime source of all make-work BS. You will be forced to watch all kinds of videos that are designed to indoctrinate, overpower, and force you into submission. Avoid them, if possible, otherwise, fervently agree with them, and ignore what you can.
> • Arguments don't work with them—they are emotionally-driven, and impervious to logic. Don't waste your breath. If forced to go

along, give them the most smidgenly little you can—i.e., if pressured to give to United Way, don't sign up for monthly pledges, give $5 one time. It will get them off your back, and yet not tick off your boss—who is getting pressured, worse than a loan shark victim, to get to 100% donations.

◆ Keep paperwork—HR has a habit of losing that which you will need—that includes references, administrative correspondence, and credentialing proof. I had to call the state board of licensing, and cry on the phone before I finally got some action on my license. Likewise, I had to drop a dime with the head of HR on a subordinate who was allowing my license to lapse, due to not moving the paperwork through in a timely fashion.

From Silicon Valley, a rebellious male engineer reports:

In my experience, HR departments do more to kill the culture of a tech startup than any other group of people. At some point as a company grows from the "founders + engineers" to "founders + engineers + others," the company has to hire someone to deal with the morass of employment regs. This hire is typically a female, and it typically (in my experience) happens somewhere between 75 and 250 employees.

At that point, you can start to see the culture change. There's never, ever been a situation where there is just one HR female. As soon as you hire one, you've got two or three. Suddenly there are employee handbooks, filled with regulations that employees must abide by, agreements suddenly appear from nowhere, needing to be signed, etc.

What I learned in my experience with these soul-sucking morons is that passive-aggressive noncompliance thwarts them. Women are the masters of passive-aggressive non-compliance—or so they think. Most women know that if they push men hard enough, men rebel and start giving attitude and action back to the women. At this point, the HR drones are in control—they'll have all manner of compliance actions that they can bring down on men who bark back at the hectoring females in HR.

But what happens if one is a good observer of female behavior and you give women the same crap they give men? It drives the typical female HR drone positively NUTS, that's what. Examples:

Female HR drone: "We need you to sign this document that indicates you've received, read and agree to abide by your employee handbook."

Male engineer: "Uh, oh, sorry. I've lost my employee handbook before I read it, so I can't really sign that."

FHRD: "Well, here's another one. Can you please return the agreement, signed and dated?"

Male engineer: "Sure, sure, but I've got a meeting I need to go to right now. I'll get it back to you tomorrow."

FHRD: (next day) "Please return your signed agreement."

Male engineer: "Oh, sorry again. This time, Bob borrowed my employee handbook off my desk, so I still haven't had a chance to read it. The agreement says that I'm signing that I've read and understood the policies, and I haven't had a chance to read them yet."

FHRD: (getting really PO'ed) "We'll get you another handbook."

Next week: FHRD: "Have you read your handbook and signed the agreement?"

Male engineer: "I did, and I found several spelling errors, lots of grammatical errors, several instances of the policies that were in disagreement with the law, case law, etc. So I won't be signing the agreement until those are fixed."

FHDR: *(&(*&*(& "Can you give us your feedback on the handbook so we may issue corrections?"

Male engineer: "Oh, sorry, I passed it off to my lawyer for further review."

FHRD: "!!!! What?!"

Keep this up for three weeks or so, and the female HR drones will a) hate your guts, but b) have nothing with which to hang you, and c) stop wanting to deal with you.

I did this for three weeks, and 10+ years later, had never signed their silly paperwork. HR killjoys avoided me like I was a leper. HR didn't sling code on a schedule for the enrichment of everyone with stock options. I did. Money talks, BS walks. In my case, the BS walked on 3" heels in a tight skirt right out of my boss' office, steamed that he said "He's got more important things to worry about than your paperwork. We've got $50 million in sales hinging on his work, and you want him to fill out some silly form?? Maybe we should call up the CEO and ask his opinion, eh?"

The important thing was to not directly confront them, so as to not provide them with a paper trail of direct refusal, sort of like the girl you ask out on a date, but she's always too busy to make time to go to dinner with you. She never say's 'no', but then again, she never says 'yes' either.

Passive-aggressive. It's the modus operandi of women everywhere. Use it against them. When you're male, heterosexual and otherwise highly masculine, it confuses the hell out of them when you play their game on their terms, but to win.[238]

This kind of extended passive resistance is more effective when you are a key employee. But a less-extended version of this works for everyone—don't comply for what seems like a good reason. You're so disorganized, you lost the paperwork... Wear them down. If HR gets your manager to come after you, explain, and if your manager requests, comply. You will have done your bit to slow down HR's make-work machine.

From Wall Street, a report:

> I work for a large Wall Street firm where 70% of the sales force is male, as is nearly 95% of the top producers. That means you need more women in non-producing roles in order to get to a 50/50 balance. Hence, beyond support positions in sales, women have come to dominate not only HR but also other "soft" staff positions like Diversity, Social Media, Digital Strategies, Strategic Planning, Compliance, Philanthropy, etc.
>
> As a result, all of these department's activities take on a feminists, no, woman's, perspective. How? I have noted that alpha male types that we interview in the sales division sometimes don't make it past the HR interview for no given reason other than "feel" or "fit". Our social media presence heralds all sorts of touchie-feelie events and "appreciation weeks" but does not acknowledge July Fourth nor the day our firm was founded by a few rich white dudes in the early 1900s. We sponsor events for women entrepreneurs at 2X the rate we do for males. Our "green initiatives" are....don't get me started.
>
> I don't expect to make any friends among those whose noses are put out of joint by the above, but the truth is the truth. Ask anyone who works in a bank to give you approximate percentages of males vs females in various departments. It does not take scientific precision to see it...[239]

What should HR look like in the future?

Employees are becoming free agents. The plantation system of near-permanent employment with one company was blown apart by economic change in the late 1990s and the Great Recession of 2008. It had never been a good idea to put all your eggs into one company's basket, but object lessons during that era made it clear—lessons like the tens of thousands of Enron employees who not only lost their jobs but their retirement savings when the company was revealed as an accounting fraud. Corporations no longer hesitate to lay people off to manage their quarterly earnings, and employees have realized that their best career course is often to change companies frequently since they will otherwise be taken for granted and often underpaid. This frequent job change is most easily accomplished in a geographic concentration of similar companies, which is why Silicon Valley became the center of the computer world in the 1980s until today. Easy job-hopping and communication between competitors gave Silicon Valley companies an advantage over other companies not so geographically concentrated.

Loss of loyalty and stability means a rise in contracting out and casual employment. The "sharing economy" of companies like Uber and Airbnb creates an independent labor force, enabled to function as one marketing and accounting entity by an app and its manager. The Ubers of the world will have an interest in curating their partner-workers, but can rely on continuous customer evaluations to weed out bad apples more quickly and effectively than old-line cab companies. The beginnings of analogous fluid staffing of larger organizations can be seen in Silicon Valley's move from centralized new product research to buying hot startups that have pioneered a new product area. Cisco, for example, started buying nearly a company a month at the same time it cut its own research[240]—as the best new technologists preferred the freedom and possible rewards of startups, big corporate research teams lost their edge and couldn't compete.

And companies are no longer the social centers of employees' lives:

> In 1985, about half of Americans said they had a close friend at work; by 2004, this was true for only 30 percent. And in nationally representative surveys of American high school seniors, the proportion who said it was very important to find a job where they could make friends dropped from 54 percent in 1976, to 48 percent in 1991, to 41 percent in 2006.... Focusing our friendship efforts outside work isn't the norm around the world. In surveys across three countries, Americans reported inviting 32 percent of their closest colleagues to their homes, compared with 66 percent in Poland and 71 percent in India. Americans have gone on vacation with 6 percent of their closest co-workers, versus 25 percent in Poland and 45 percent in India. It's not that Americans are less concerned with relationships overall. We're social creatures outside work, yet the office interaction norm tends to be polite but impersonal.[241]

HR as paternalistic referee shepherding employees to better lives is increasingly irrelevant. HR as outward-facing recruiter of new talent has mostly failed, with those old-style outreach efforts cut for budgetary savings and seen as increasingly misguided. The talent net has been extended to lesser schools and the less-credentialed, looking for smart and highly-motivated employees from all social ranks for true diversity:

> Goldman Sachs Group Inc. has always sought to attract the best and the brightest. Now it also wants the most committed from a broader range of backgrounds.
>
> The bank has concluded that helping to widen the pool of candidates beyond those from elite schools like Harvard University and Yale University will enable it to find students loyal to the industry. So it is

making changes in the way it interviews and assesses candidates for summer analyst roles, typically the first-rung jobs for a banking career.

The Wall Street bank is experimenting with video interviews to open up the field to entry-level roles and turn up candidates who aspire to a long-term career in banking, rather than a short stint.

Goldman said Thursday that its recruiters will no longer conduct first-round interviews for summer positions on campus at elite schools like Harvard, Yale and Stanford University. Instead, all candidates for summer analyst positions must complete a video interview, answering prompts from a software program.

While a seemingly minor administrative change, the move alters a rite of passage in finance, in which students don suits and ties for interviews with recruiters or alumni employees. Shifting to video screening allows the firm to cast its net wider and brings it a step toward "leveling the playing field" for recruits from non-elite schools, said Edith Cooper, global head of human capital management at Goldman Sachs.[242]

HR's hiring failures—screening out many of the best candidates and promoting others to satisfy government overseers—hint at how its performance in hiring might be improved:

> Improving hiring requires a radically different approach.... HR should still serve as the conduit between candidates and the company's departments. But they should no longer serve as the gatekeepers, with their arbitrary algorithms ready to dismiss worthy candidates. Instead, the gate should be lifted, the ball should be tossed from the government enforcers to market actors.
>
> Candidates should be evaluated only by the individuals with the requisite knowledge, that is the hiring managers and employees in various company departments. This would result in a higher workload for the departments, but methods for filtering candidates would still be available. An algorithm created at this level, closer to

the knowledge center for the position, would at least be an improvement to HR's central planning algorithm....

But algorithms—no matter at the HR or department level—are not without their faults. Summarizing a candidate into a quantitative score or using a set of logical rules to reject candidates is not perfect and should not replace departmental interviews. A cursory glance at a candidate's application via an algorithm cannot ensure he or she is a cultural fit within the organization....

Hiring cannot and never will be an exact science. But that does not mean that it cannot be improved. Delegating decision-making authority to those closest to the requisite knowledge and emphasizing human interaction over algorithms would better serve departments and candidates.[243]

The evolution of a bureaucracy from small and functional to large and dysfunctional is as old as civilization itself. Governments established law and courts and regulators that intervened in personnel matters, and companies needed more internal employees to keep track of the payroll, taxes, and benefits that legal employment status included. The rules (and the penalties for violating them) grew more onerous, and companies needed more and more HR staff. Taking control from low-level managers and giving HR the authority to approve all personnel decisions protected companies from damaging punishments and lawsuits, but HR staff were more distant from working teams and less concerned about productivity and growth. Like the increasingly bloated and high-paid hospital and college administrations of this era, HR departments developed dual loyalties, with a commitment to ideologies of government and labor law conflicting with employee accountability and productivity.

The widespread decline in growth of high-paying jobs and the economic stagnation now seen in the US is following in Europe's footsteps toward a micromanaged, regulated economy where equality of outcome and protection of big business and existing jobs and social positions suffocates economic dynamism. Incumbent businesses grow larger and less efficient, while the expenses of increased regulation fall heavily on smaller companies. New business starts are down and small business failures up. Most new jobs are low-end service positions—waiters, bartenders, and baristas—not the high-paying professional careers most new college graduates are looking for.

This ossification can only end in widespread collapse as people's hopes and dreams are crushed and the debts can no longer be carried. Marriage declines and new families are less stable because young men can't earn enough to get a good start. Social disorder results as voters turn to politicians who offer authoritarian solutions that won't work.

The solution is an end to the excessive power of administrative state—that complex of Federal and state agencies that has written the rules of employment and micromanages work hours, minimum wages, and affirmative action goals that impede hiring the best employee for the job. "It's none of your business" should be the new watchword for government—it's not a legislature's job to protect every employee from competition, or to right every wrong ever committed by forcing one person to serve another to make up for past wrongs no one alive personally suffered. Freedom to strive and fail and learn and succeed is the key to real self-esteem, and the division of citizens into race, sex, and class-oriented interest groups only hurts everyone in the long run.

And until this reform actually happens, both companies and employees can thrive by downsizing HR departments and remaking them into more functional, less political entities. Workers should seek out companies that reward them for their results and vote with their feet by moving to states and localities where freedom to work is still a priority.

Part Five

Appendixes

When a campaign is underway to regulate a business or a product, it's usually easy to identify two groups promoting increased regulation: "Bootleggers" (people who will benefit because the regulation hobbles a competitor) and "Baptists" (people who sincerely believe the new regulation will help others.) The Baptists naively think goodness will come from outlawing bad things, while the bootleggers are aware of unintended consequences and second- and third-order effects of the proposed regulation that will benefit them personally. Marching together, they agitate for more laws and less freedom of choice.

> Bootleggers and Baptists is a catch-phrase invented by regulatory economist Bruce Yandle for the observation that regulations are supported both by groups that want the ostensible purpose of the regulation, and by groups that profit from undermining that purpose.

> For much of the 20th century, Baptists and other evangelical Christians were prominent in political activism for Sunday closing laws restricting the sale of alcohol. Bootleggers sold alcohol illegally, and got more business if legal sales were restricted. "Such a coalition makes it easier for politicians to favor both groups. ... [T]he Baptists lower the costs of favor-seeking for the bootleggers, because politicians can pose as being motivated purely by the public interest even while they promote the interests of well-funded businesses. ... [Baptists] take the moral high ground, while the bootleggers persuade the politicians quietly, behind closed doors."[244]

Strongly-motivated minorities can move the political process toward satisfying their demands, as Prohibitionists did when they succeeded in getting the Eighteenth Amendment passed outlawing alcoholic beverages in the US, a ban which lasted from 1920 to 1933 before it was repealed by the Twenty-First Amendment. It took a decade of rising organized crime and disrespect for the law to finally rouse the great middle of the electorate to demand repeal. Similar battles still take place on smaller scales. In a recent example,

> Arkansas liquor stores have allied with religious leaders to fight statewide legalization of alcohol sales. The stores in wet counties don't want to lose customers. The churches don't want to lose souls. Larry Page, a Southern Baptist pastor and director of the Arkansas Faith and Ethics Council, which traces its roots to the Anti-Saloon League of Arkansas in 1899, [also recalled]. . .when his group joined with feminists to oppose pornography and cooperated with Mississippi casinos to fight gambling in Arkansas.[245]

The selfish motivations of the "bootleggers" hide behind the naive but high-minded feelings of the "Baptists." How can a politician oppose Goodness in the form of legislated morality?

Here are some other examples of the phenomenon:

Universal pre-K: Who can be against the education of young children, especially those growing up in poor environments for early learning? Surely extending public school to even earlier years will help underprivileged children catch up! And parents can use even more public-funded daycare to ease their burden, right?

While it's common to see articles and editorials accepting the positive benefits of pre-K programs without question, the evidence is thin and suggests that some children can benefit from very high-quality programs, but that such benefits disappear after a few years. The Head Start federal program targeting poor children has been expensive and disappointing, with recent studies demonstrating little permanent improvement in outcomes in the long term.[246]

As often happens, proponents start a few pilot programs, recruit highly-motivated staff and parents, and find significant positive benefits. When expanded and managed via the standard education bureaucracy and with less-motivated, unionized staff, benefits to the children shrink or disappear completely, with some programs actually worse for children than being left in a standard private preschool or home setting.

A well-regarded and funded program in Tennessee was studied by a grant-funded group of social scientists and educators at Vanderbilt who had every reason to bias the study to favor the state's pre-K program. The result? (Emphasis added):

> By the end of kindergarten, the control children had caught up to the TN-VPK children and there were no longer significant differences between them on any achievement measures. The same result was obtained at the end of first grade using both composite achievement measures. In second grade, however, the groups began to diverge, with **the TN-VPK children scoring lower than the control children on most of the measures.** The differences were significant on both achievement composite measures and on the math subtests. ... In terms of behavioral effects, in the spring the first grade teachers reversed the fall kindergarten teacher ratings. **First grade teachers rated the TN-VPK children as less well prepared for school, having poorer work skills in the classrooms, and feeling more negative about school.** It is notable that these ratings preceded the downward achievement trend we found for VPK children in second and third grades. The second and third grade teachers rated the behaviors and feelings of children in the two groups as the same; there was a marginally significant effect for positive peer relations favoring the TN-VPK children by third grade teachers.[247]

The constant drumbeat of publicity promoting Universal pre-K is motivated by the desire of teacher and public employee unions to employ more staff who will provide more revenue and political power for them. They are the bootleggers in the coalition pushing for Universal pre-K at local and federal levels, and the disorganized efforts of those who would be hurt by such programs—operators of private preschools, parents of children who want to choose which daycare they pay for or handle pre-K nurturing themselves—are rarely interviewed, as the propaganda from the government PR offices and unions is well-funded by tax dollars and compulsory union dues.

Free College For All: Bernie Sanders promoted a plan for free tuition at public colleges and universities for everyone. "Education" (in the form of conventional regimented schooling) is a sacred cow, and the belief that everyone is better off being sent to college after high school has been promoted by politicians for years. We've already seen what happens when you make subsidized student loans available to everyone: you get millions of deeply-indebted former students, both those who failed out because they should never have been admitted in the first place and those who learned little of value to the job market. You also get a high rate of inflation in college costs, as these loans allowed colleges to expand and compete for students with less concern for costs or outcomes.

The Baptists in this case are all those well-meaning people who believe everyone should go to college and get a professional white-collar job. The bootleggers are all of those college administrators and employees who benefit from increased funding and enrollment, the prospective students who want to have a free ride, and the politicians who rely on the support of academics. The scribes and government workers who are products of academia themselves write all the narratives in our society, and blue-collar workers and nonacademics who would be taxed to pay for this freebie get no taxpayer funding to tell their own stories.

Let well-known philosopher of labor Mike Rowe explain this:

Consider the number of college graduates today who can't find work in their chosen field. Hundreds of thousands of highly educated twenty-somethings are either unemployed or getting paid a pittance to do something totally unrelated to the education they borrowed a fortune to acquire. Collectively, they hold 1.3 trillion dollars of debt, and no real training for the jobs that actually exist. Now, consider the country's widening skills gap – hundreds of thousands of good jobs gone begging because no one wants to learn a useful trade. It's madness. "College For All" might sound good on the campaign trail, but in real life, it's a dangerous platitude that reinforces the ridiculous notion that college is for people who use their brains, and trade schools are for people who use their hands. As if the two cannot be combined.[248]

Universal Healthcare: The Baptists here are well-meaning people who think everyone should get good healthcare, and because they have been told by propagandists that everyone in Europe and Canada has free, quality healthcare that costs their government far less, they can't imagine why the US shouldn't have it, too. Which ignores the major differences between such programs—only Canada has single-payer without a parallel private-pay healthcare system, and even that is changing, while the Canadian provinces vary in costs and coverages, as well as waiting periods for nonemergency care. Meanwhile, European countries have systems that vary from Britain's NHS, a completely government-owned and run healthcare system with enough problems that its breakdowns are daily news fodder, to Swiss and French programs that are really public-private insurance plans with cheaper basic options. "Medicare-for-All" as proposed by US universal healthcare proponents would expand the Medicare system, which is already headed for financial disaster as the population ages, to cover everyone. It's never acknowledged that rising costs will then require rationing and onerous cost controls that would make the US system start to resemble Britain's NHS—cheaper but lower quality, with worse outcomes for cancer treatments and limited access to more advanced care.

Who are the bootleggers? The ACA co-opted the big health insurance and drug companies to guarantee them a captive market with higher revenues in return for turning the private insurance market into a kind of regulated utility that everyone would be forced to join, which allows regulations to essentially tax younger and healthier people to subsidize the costs of the older and sicker without regard to ability to pay. We now have lower-middle-class working families paying much more than they would in a free insurance market so that wealthy people with pre-existing conditions can get insurance at subsidized rates. While many pre-existing conditions were unfortunate accidents, some were acquired because of poor life choices and self-indulgent health and dietary habits—so now the rich couch potato who drank and ate himself to diabetes and heart problems suffers no penalty, at least financially, since some group of healthy families is paying extra to subsidize his care.

Single-payer, Medicare-for-All is another step toward micromanagement of both citizen lifestyles and medical procedures. The politicians are dreaming of more dependent voters who, as in Britain, vote for a "better" NHS when its problems cannot be solved by a change in administrations because they are due to its structure as a socialized service, with unionized civil service-style employee protections and the accompanying limited accountability for poor service and failure. Once in place, such systems are very difficult to repeal, and their bureaucracies, like today's federal HHS and Medicare bureaucracies, provide a good place for political supporters to collect a paycheck while serving as the party of government's permanent supporting class.

Climate Change: The Baptists here are citizens who believe that not only is global warming a man-made phenomenon resulting from increases in greenhouse gases in the atmosphere (that much is probably true), but that its onset will be rapid and severe enough to justify virtually any costly program proposed to limit the threat (which appears untrue, or at least unproven, as the simplistic early climate models have failed to correctly predict the amount of actual warming.) What price would you pay to save the planet? Even questioning the cost of proposed programs is viewed as heresy by true believers.

The bootleggers are the rent-seeking part of the coalition to "do something," which began when the danger was first popularized and resulted in large increases in research funding for the small number of climate scientists who specialized in climate change research. As momentum built and more governments funded research and activism in the field, whole labs and careers depended on finding the danger to be as large as possible, to justify ever more research funding. Stoking popular fear, politicians could appear to be protecting citizens by promising more and more measures to slow greenhouse gas emissions. It became clear, though, that vested interests would not allow the least-cost, most economically-sound means of reducing emissions: research on solar and nuclear power generation and low, rebated carbon taxes which would allow businesses and citizens to gradually reduce emissions over time without sacrificing current plants and arrangements.

What happened instead: complex emissions credit schemes which allowed politicians to favor some interest groups over others while raking in hidden taxes from consumers; mandates requiring utilities to pay much more to purchase ever-increasing percentages of "green" power, generated at high cost from subsidized windmills and solar power plants which proved to work poorly or have limited service lives; and command-and-control regulations that shut down existing plants and closed down coal mines.

Each of these schemes had bootleggers waiting to profit: politically-connected investors in solar power schemes like Solyndra (bankrupt in 2011, with $535 million in federally-guaranteed loans and $25 million in California tax credits lost) and the Ivanpah steam-solar project ($2.2 billion, obsolete and unable to generate its designed power since the day it opened.)[249] Both Ivanpah and Solyndra were huge bets on the wrong technologies, with standard photovoltaic panels falling in price so much that these huge investments were rendered uncompetitive shortly after they were funded. Ivanpah received $1.6 billion in loan guarantees from federal taxpayer funds, covering investments by its owners, BrightSource Energy, NRG Energy, and Google. The company has delayed payment on its loans and in late 2014 requested an additional $539 million in funding via a federal tax credit program.[250]

Spain's Abengoa, a huge multinational alternative energy company, has filed for Chapter 11 protection in the US, and in March of 2015 filed for bankruptcy. The federal loan guarantees for $1.45 billion for the Solano solar plant[251] in Arizona and the $1.2 billion for the Mojave solar project[252] in California now appear to be US taxpayer losses.[253] Again enormous sums of taxpayer money built scaled-up projects with obsolete technology which could only produce power at many times the cost of natural gas plants.

In parts of Europe and the US, poor and middle-class ratepayers pay much more for electricity because of these state-required green energy programs, while many wealthy consumers avoid paying the inflated rates by installing subsidized solar panels.

Other bootleggers include the large number of government staff now employed to work on climate change issues and propaganda in governments around the world, with the many UN climate meetings in cities like Paris and Copenhagen serving as luxurious junkets for tens of thousands of functionaries.

Even businessmen in the petroleum industry will surreptitiously support green activist organizations they believe will harm competitive fuels more than theirs. Aubrey McClendon, who made and then lost a huge fortune pioneering the fracking production of natural gas in the US, "secretly gave $25 million to the Sierra Club for the Sierra Club's 'Beyond Coal' campaign, for the obvious reason that it would benefit his natural gas company if coal were squeezed by new regulation.":

> But as the Sierra Club and other environmental groups have made clear, once they're done killing coal they're going after natural gas next. Did McClendon think they'd spare him? He was a perfect example of Churchill's description of an appeaser as someone who feeds the crocodile hoping he'll be eaten last. I lost all respect for McClendon when this news leaked out, and it was a great embarrassment to the Sierra Club as well. He was rent-seeking bootlegger. A lot of them died in high-speed crashes back during Prohibition, usually being chased by the law.[254]

Internet Gambling Prohibitions: This is closer to the coalition against alcohol, with many religious and social organizations concerned about gambling addiction joining with casino magnates,

Indian tribes, and state lotteries to try to outlaw a competitor—easy gambling on the Internet. In 2015, Sheldon Adelson, billionaire head of the Las Vegas Sands and numerous high-revenue casinos worldwide, promoted a bill in Congress (The Restoration of America's Wire Act, or RAWA) intended to prohibit Internet gambling at the federal level, superseding state authorizing laws. He hired a lobbying firm, Steptoe and Johnson, which was then also hired by fantasy sports companies—which would be exempt under the proposed Act. By outlawing some forms of online gambling but exempting others, the proposed law would preserve casino monopolies and take control away from states.[255]

Tobacco: Vaping equipment, or e-cigs, provide the appearance of cigarettes and a dose of the nicotine smokers crave in a delivery format (evaporated carrier with nicotine and flavoring) that is much less harmful to smoker's lungs. Many experts recommended smokers switch to e-cigs immediately, since harm to their health would be much reduced. But e-cigs threaten both the makers of the highly-regulated and taxed legacy cigarettes and the makers of smoking cessation products like nicotine gum and patches—often the same companies! So paid "medical authorities" and lobbyists began to work hard to promote the view that the new and untested e-cigs were just as hazardous—if not more hazardous, since their long-term effects were unknown!—than traditional cigarettes. Cato's Regulation put out a good paper on the bootleggers-and-Baptists pattern in this new propaganda war:

> Now consider the situation with electronic cigarettes (e-cigs) and their incumbent competitors: tobacco companies that produce and sell traditional cigarettes and drug companies that produce nicotine replacement therapies (NRTs). The U.S. cigarette market has been regulated, one way or another, since colonial times. Along the way, federal regulation—coupled most recently with the state attorneys general Master Settlement Agreement (MSA, about which we say more later)—effectively cartelized the industry, bringing increased

profits to the industry and higher cigarette prices and reduced cigarette consumption throughout the nation. Falling cigarette consumption gladdened the hearts of health advocates, who fought for the elimination of tobacco products, while higher industry profits brought joy to tobacco company owners.

This happy Bootlegger/Baptist equilibrium is now threatened by the exploding sales of e-cigs, a new technology for delivering nicotine to all who want it without simultaneously bringing the harmful combustion-induced chemicals associated with burned tobacco. Today, there are many e-cig producers and numerous small shops selling e-cigs and customized nicotine-dispensing products. It is a rapidly evolving market that has been relatively open to new entrants and innovation in product design. Given the quick growth in e-cig use (much of which comes at the expense of cigarette sales), previous political deals that stabilized tobacco industry profits are at risk. The major tobacco companies are understandably not sitting idle. They, too, have entered the e-cig marketplace and are responding in other ways to the new competition.

The major pharmaceutical companies have not been idle either. The makers of smoking cessation products, including NRTs such as the nicotine patch and nicotine gum, are major players in the politics of tobacco and nicotine. The producers of traditional nicotine delivery devices and NRTs are at work trying to stop the disruptive e-cig producers. These Bootleggers are joined by health advocates (Baptists) who raise questions about unknown potentially harmful effects that may be associated with e-cig use. Both groups—cigarette and NRT producers on the one hand, and health advocates on the other—would like to stop new e-cig producers or severely crimp their ability to compete.[256]

Lawfare between the tobacco industry and state attorneys general was settled in 1998 with the MSA (Master Settlement Agreement[257]), which set the payments due to the states to compensate them for the additional Medicare and Medicaid costs states would bear because of tobacco products. The agreement was carefully designed to send money to the states while protecting the incumbent manufacturers from competition, allowing them to raise prices more than required to pay the fines.

The heart of the MSA was the promised payment of $206 billion by the four participating cigarette companies to the participating states. Those payments would be tax deductible and the costs would be paid by consumers in the form of higher cigarette prices. (Because cigarette consumption is highly price inelastic, the cost of the price increase was largely borne by consumers rather than producers.) The MSA presented state legislatures with a simple choice: either accept the MSA, in which case they would be able to spend their state's share of the billions of dollars raised from smokers, or reject the proposed statute and their states' smokers would still pay the higher prices necessary to fund the deal but they would lose their claim on the money. Not surprisingly, every state legislature took the money.

Responsibility for the payments was allocated among the cigarette companies in proportion to their current market share, thereby reducing the incentive for the participating cigarette companies to engage in price competition to increase their respective market shares. The structure of the MSA thus provided a powerful incentive for each company to be satisfied with the status quo.

The MSA also attempted to protect the major cigarette companies from new competition. At the time of the agreement, the four participating cigarette companies accounted for about 99 percent of domestic cigarette sales. Increasing cigarette prices to pay for the settlement risked a loss of market share to marginal competitors or new entrants. Therefore the MSA provided that for every percent of market share over 2 percent lost by a participating cigarette manufacturer, the manufacturer would be allowed to reduce its payments to the states by 3 percent, unless each participating state enacted a statute to prevent price competition from non-participating manufacturers (which each state did). The statutes require nonparticipating cigarette producers to make payments equal to or greater than what they would owe had they been participants in the agreement, to eliminate any cost advantage.

The MSA also included restrictions on cigarette marketing practices agreed to by the participating producers. The advertising limits were portrayed as a public health measure because they reduced advertising that could influence young adults and teens. The limits also reinforced the anticompetitive nature of the MSA by making it more costly for new brands or entrants to secure market share through promotional efforts.

The MSA's cartel-reinforcing provisions sufficiently suppressed competition to enable cigarette companies to take advantage of the price inelasticity of cigarette demand and obtain record profits. This made it possible for the major cigarette manufacturers to increase prices by more than was necessary to make the mandated MSA payments.

Having made a deal to get big money for states and attorneys while protecting the companies from competition and raising prices more than enough to make the addicted smokers themselves pay the full cost of the settlement, many of the states decided to grab their money immediately by selling municipal (federal tax-free) bonds backed by the MSA payments expected. California alone issued at least $16.8 billion in such bonds, proceeds being used for both immediate expenses and long-term capital improvements.[258] Legislators appear to have forgotten that the supposed purpose of the payments was to cover smoking-related expenses of future medical care for the state's population, and instead chose to spend the money immediately on unrelated matters while leaving the burden of those health expenses with future taxpayers.

In some cases, however, the bonds are backed by secondary pledges of state or local revenues, which creates what some see as a perverse incentive to support the tobacco industry, on whom they are now dependent for future payments against this debt.

Tobacco revenue has fallen more quickly than projected when the securities were created, leading to technical defaults in some states.

Some analysts predict that many of the bonds will default entirely. Many of the longer-term bonds have been downgraded to junk ratings. More recently, financial analysts began raising concerns that the rapid growth of the electronic cigarette market is accelerating the decline of $97 billion outstanding in tobacco bonds…. Lawmakers in several states proposed measures to tax e-cigarettes like traditional tobacco products to offset the decline in TMSA revenue. They anticipate that taxing or banning e-cigarettes would be beneficial to the sale of combustible cigarettes.[259]

Vested interests including tobacco companies and states now actively seek to suppress e-cigs or at least tax them enough to make up for any lost revenue as they are adopted.[260] This means they are actively working to keep smokers addicted to the most hazardous form of nicotine consumption, with its resultant cancers and other diseases. The original Baptist goal of helping smokers quit the habit to avoid cancer and early death has long since been forgotten.

Minimum Wage: Baptists: voters who want low-paid workers to have better lives and higher incomes, imagining poor families will benefit while businesses will pay the costs. Bootleggers: Politicians needing an issue to show they want to help "working families," and unions who both represent some minimum-wage workers but more importantly the workers who make more than that, who will get even higher wages as a result of escalating wage rates based on the minimum wage in existing contracts and the outlawing of lower-paid laborers who might compete with them.

Economically, it's very clear: minimum wage laws harm inexperienced and unskilled workers by making it illegal for them to be employed at wage rates that reflect the value they can add with their labor. Those workers won't be hired, and many will be replaced by automation as they are priced out of the labor market. Politicians and union bosses won't lose their jobs, even as unemployment among the unskilled increases as a result of the new minimum wage law. Most unionized workers make much more than minimum wage now, so they will keep their jobs while outlawing lower-priced nonunion competition. Economists who study the issue tend to agree there is at least a slight negative effect on employment when minimum wages are increased slightly, but the large increases now proposed may do much greater harm by reducing hours and eliminating jobs for unskilled workers. The economists who find no negative effects tend to be labor economists, who tend to be supported by government and labor union funding and so have some conflict of interest in their researches.

Meanwhile, small business owners are ignored when they explain their response to much higher minimum wages has to be reduced hours, higher prices, and possibly going out of business since many have committed to expensive leases and can't withstand a huge increase in costs:

> [Seattle restaurant owner Grant Chen wrote of] his struggles to stay in business as he faces a 61% increase in his labor costs from Seattle's $15 minimum wage initiative. ... the $15 an hour minimum wage law isn't really ultimately "a political problem as much as it's a simple math problem," as Anthony Anton of the Washington Restaurant Association explained the situation. And Grant Chen and other Seattle restaurateurs like Brendan McGill (owner of Hitchcock Restaurant and Hitchcock Deli) are finding out that the new restaurant math of Seattle's $15 minimum wage is breaking the system.... a 61% increase in wages from $9.32 to $15 an hour is like imposing an annual tax on restaurants of $11,360 per full-time employee. If you understand that a $11,360 tax per employee (and $113,600 in higher labor costs for every 10 employees) would drive many restaurants out of business, you'll understand why the "new restaurant math of a $15 minimum wage" is making Grant Chen's restaurant unprofitable, and why it is driving him out of business."[261]

The Baptists are told hard-working poor families will enjoy richer lives, but it's rarely mentioned that young people looking for summer work or just starting out will find it much harder to reach that first rung on the career ladder.

As Glenn Reynolds of Instapundit says:

> The Los Angeles Times report somehow fails to list union workers among the winners. They earn quite a bit more than the minimum, but many of them have their pay scales indexed to the minimum wage. Unions also give heavily to Democratic politicians who support union-friendly issues like hiking the minimum wage.
>
> And the losers? Anyone whose labor is worth less than $15 an hour, and who is about to learn the hard way that the real minimum wage is always zero.[262]

They Wrote a Book On It: Economist Bruce Yandle (who coined the term "bootleggers and Baptists" in 1983) has a book out with co-author Adam Smith, Bootleggers and Baptists: How Economic Forces and Moral Persuasion Interact to Shape Regulatory Politics.[263] Recommended for further study and examples, notably TARP, a $700 billion emergency response to the economic crisis of 2008 which ended up as a field day for bootleggers and rent-seekers.

There's a natural human tendency to stereotype: to combine cultural and real-life knowledge about correlations between superficial, easily-observed characteristics and traits we cannot immediately observe, like trustworthiness, tendency to violence, and intelligence.

Famously, Jesse Jackson once commented on his own use of stereotypes about young black men: "There is nothing more painful to me at this stage in my life than to walk down the street and hear footsteps and start thinking about robbery. Then look around and see somebody white and feel relieved.... After all we have been through. Just to think we can't walk down our own streets, how humiliating."[264]

This is a good example of use of *heuristics*—simple rules for deciding which may not always be correct but help shortcut the time to decide. Mr. Jackson, like everyone else, discovers he is a little bit racist—he is using a stereotype about his own race to decide whether to be afraid about the man coming up behind him. He may decide to take evasive action if the young man is black, and not if it turns out to be a middle-aged, well-dressed white man.

And who can blame him? While there is some chance the white man is a mugger, the chance is far less than if it is a young black man in urban thug-style clothing. Note that it is not only race that people use to jump to conclusions on limited evidence—clothing, mannerisms, age, and walk also come into play.

Prejudice and stereotyping can harm those whose superficial characteristics are associated with negative judgments. The young black man who is hurt when others cross the street to avoid him is the least of the problems—the black man or woman who applied for a retail clerk's job in the South in the 1950s would often be discouraged; even employers who were not themselves prejudiced would assume some of their customers would be, and hire the less qualified white person instead.

The civil rights movement, and other movements of the 1960s and on, tried to eliminate the harmful effects of prejudice and stereotyping by teaching everyone to internally reject stereotypes as a basis for making decisions. This has worked so well that now when we say the word "stereotype" it is assumed that what we are talking about is false and damaging. This makes us Better People because we do not treat others badly because of some irrelevant superficial characteristic, but may have gone too far.

The problem with today's politically correct rejection of the entire idea of stereotypes is that cultural stereotypes and generalizations are actually remarkably accurate in many areas. Social scientists who study them have reams of data showing this, but rejection of stereotypes is now an article of faith impervious to any contrary data. So we all still make judgments based on stereotypes internally but pretend that we don't! Jesse Jackson's moment of shame was in realizing the inconsistency. And well-meaning white people in the same circumstance will try to avoid taking any action which might be seen as implying they fear the young black man—hoping to avoid hurting an innocent person's feelings. Which can lead to being mugged.

Lee Jussim, Ph.D, writing for Psychology Today, discusses this problem:

> I suspect that, when many of you saw the title, you assumed I would be discussing how inaccurate stereotypes are impervious to change in the face of data. That is how social scientists have been discussing stereotypes for nearly 100 years. Nope!
>
> But we agree that being impervious to data is a bad thing, right? Liberals routinely rail against conservatives' supposedly anti-scientific stands, right? Liberals, in sharp contrast, don't ever oppose data and science, do they?
>
> Great! In that case, you will be interested to discover that:
>
> 1. Stereotype accuracy is one of the largest and most replicable effects

in all of social psychology

2. The fact that this is true has had almost no effect on the frequency with which social scientists claim, assume, or imply that stereotypes are inaccurate.

You probably find this hard to believe. After all, you have been told, over and over and over and over, that stereotypes are inaccurate. This has been part and parcel of the liberal project of fighting oppression and prejudice....

Stereotype accuracy is an empirical question. You can claim anything you want. Your interpretation of your experience is whatever you believe. But combating the well-established flaws and limitations of subjective interpretation of experience is exactly why science was developed. Which gets us to, not your personal experience, but the science. What has scientific research found about the accuracy of stereotypes?

Stereotypes are (Usually) More Valid Than Most Social Psychological Hypotheses

Over the last 40 years, there has been a ton of research assessing the accuracy of stereotypes. The findings are astonishing, at least if you have bought the longstanding line that "stereotypes are inaccurate."

The following data are from my recent review of this area of research (Jussim et al, 2014). It gives the proportion of results for various types of research that are greater than correlations of .30 and .50, respectively, because Richard et al (2003) provided these figures for all of social psychology, which then constitutes an excellent standard of comparison.

Which is more accurate, social psychology or social stereotypes?

Percent of Correlations that are	>.30	>.50
All of Social Psychology	24%	5%
Race, consensual stereotype accuracy	95%	95%
Race, personal stereotype accuracy	47%	18%
Gender, consensual stereotype accuracy	100%	94%
Gender, personal stereotype accuracy	79%	58%

These results are based on over 20 studies of stereotype accuracy conducted by multiple independent researchers and laboratories... Results for other stereotypes (e.g., age, occupation, politics, etc.), are similar. As such, stereotype accuracy is far more replicable than many far more famous "effects" in social psychology (large effects are inherently more replicable, but understanding why that must be involves an arcane statistical discussion that is beyond the scope of this blog entry).

To be sure, there is some evidence of inaccuracy in stereotypes, especially national stereotypes of personality. There is also good evidence that political ideologues exaggerate each others' views. Nonetheless, the BIG picture remains intact: Stereotype accuracy is one of the largest and most replicable findings in all of social psychology.

Why, then, have social scientists been declaring and decrying the inaccuracy of stereotypes for nearly a century? The data don't now, and never have, supported such a claim.

Social scientists don't go around making stuff up to advance their leftish narratives of oppression. Do they?

Disclaimer II: I AM a social scientist. There are LOTS of other social scientists out there who go to great lengths and do a good job of not allowing their politics to distort their science. I admit that making claims that are unhinged from data does no credit to our field and, if taken out of context, can lead people to dismiss the field's value and importance. However, the solution to bad science is not to kill science. It is to pressure and advocate for, and push, enhance, and support good science. Such efforts, which include exposing bad science, should count as a CREDIT to the social sciences.

> So, my liberal friends who embrace science, you are now outraged at
> the anti-scientific stand of all those who deny the scientific evidence
> demonstrating stereotype accuracy, right?[265]

His data show that groups have averaged stereotypical beliefs that are
remarkably accurate, while individuals are less accurate but still doing
much better than chance.

The takeaway lesson: the first-order reaction against stereotypes,
while very useful in correcting poor treatment of individuals, is far
too simple. A second-order or even more nuanced understanding of
the mechanism of stereotyping can salvage their utility while still
removing most of the harm to individuals.

The Enlightenment values of individualism and justice are best
served by recognizing the real world utility of heuristics based on
superficial factors, while always doing more to determine true
characteristics of individuals in truly important matters. All of us are
judged constantly and may do more or less well in interacting with
others based on superficial characteristics and snap judgments; this
cannot be completely removed. Those who wish to gain the trust of
others will always need to signal their reliability. It may not be fair,
but it is human.

A thought experiment demonstrating that cultural cues will
outweigh racist stereotypes:

> Picture this: A young White man, standing in front of a beat-up
> looking house trailer with one broken window patched with a sheet
> of cardboard. On the ground around him, there are bits and pieces of
> trash, including an old crushed water bottle a couple of dented beer
> cans. Now imagine a young Black man, standing on the porch of a
> nicely appointed middle class home in the suburbs, complete with
> healthy trees, flowers, and a green lawn. On the stylish lawn table
> near him is a bottle of New Zealand Sauvignon Blanc and two crystal
> wine glasses. In your judgment, which of these young men is more
> likely to: 1) father children earlier, 2) invest in those children's

education, 3) impulsively get into a fight or steal a car?

According to a recent series of studies, published in the Proceedings of the National Academy of Sciences, stereotypes normally associated with Blacks and Whites are more about ecology than about race. Given no other information, survey respondents tend to assume that a young Black person is more likely than a White person to embody a "fast" life-style—acting impulsively, having children early, and engaging in opportunistic criminal acts. But when the researchers -- Keelah Williams, Oliver Sng, and Steven Neuberg—probed more deeply, they discovered that this assumption was linked to another assumption, that the Black person is more likely to live in a "desperate ecology" (an environment in which dangers are relatively plentiful, but opportunities are relatively scarce, and likely to disappear if you don't take them right away). Indeed, survey respondents assume the exact same "fast" and impulsive characteristics apply to White people living in desperate ecologies.

When the researchers compared stereotypes about Black people living in hopeful ecologies with White people living in more desperate ecologies (as in the example in the opening paragraph above), they found that everything flipped around: Blacks living in hopeful ecologies were assumed to have the characteristics normally associated with "Whites" whereas Whites living in desperate ecologies were stereotyped with traits normally attributed to "Blacks."[266]

The widely-noticed blog post by Jonathan Haidt, "Where microaggressions really come from: A sociological account," starts out this way:

> I just read the most extraordinary paper by two sociologists—Bradley Campbell and Jason Manning—explaining why concerns about microaggressions have erupted on many American college campuses in just the past few years. In brief: We're beginning a second transition of moral cultures. The first major transition happened in the 18th and 19th centuries when most Western societies moved away from cultures of honor (where people must earn honor and must therefore avenge insults on their own) to cultures of dignity in which people are assumed to have dignity and don't need to earn it. They foreswear violence, turn to courts or administrative bodies to respond to major transgressions, and for minor transgressions they either ignore them or attempt to resolve them by social means. There's no more dueling.

> Campbell and Manning describe how this culture of dignity is now giving way to a new culture of victimhood in which people are encouraged to respond to even the slightest unintentional offense, as in an honor culture. But they must not obtain redress on their own; they must appeal for help to powerful others or administrative bodies, to whom they must make the case that they have been victimized. It is the very presence of such administrative bodies, within a culture that is highly egalitarian and diverse (i.e., many college campuses) that gives rise to intense efforts to identify oneself as a fragile and aggrieved victim. This is why we have seen the recent explosion of concerns about microaggressions, combined with demands for trigger warnings and safe spaces, that Greg Lukianoff and I wrote about in The Coddling of the American Mind…. The key idea is that the new moral culture of victimhood fosters "moral dependence" and an atrophying of the ability to handle small

interpersonal matters on one's own. At the same time that it weakens individuals, it creates a society of constant and intense moral conflict as people compete for status as victims or as defenders of victims.[267]

This is very obvious to anyone paying attention to college campuses these days. And as he and the authors of the paper he discusses point out, this new culture of victimhood thrives only where there is very little actual victimization or inequality—under the umbrella of a micromanaging government or university administration who can be called on to recognize your victim status.

> As we dissect this phenomenon, then, we first address how it fits into a larger class of conflict tactics in which the aggrieved seek to attract and mobilize the support of third parties. We note that these tactics sometimes involve building a case for action by documenting, exaggerating, or even falsifying offenses.

And an epidemic of falsification has occurred, with many of the most publicized cases of rape or hate crimes on campus having been revealed to be hoaxes or fabrications. In a world where young people are encouraged to think of themselves as members of oppressed minorities, some of the most privileged—affluent students on university campuses—demand more subsidies and more recognition for their special snowflake natures, and agitate for more grants and more programs to allow them to avoid repaying student loans and to work after they graduate at activist nonprofits.

> In the settings such as those that generate microaggression catalogs [ed. note: I call these settings grievance bubbles in my writings], though, where offenders are oppressors and victims are the oppressed, it also raises the moral status of the victims. This only increases the incentive to publicize grievances, and it means aggrieved parties are especially likely to highlight their identity as victims, emphasizing their own suffering and innocence. Their adversaries are privileged and blameworthy, but they themselves are pitiable and blameless. [p.707-708] [This is the great tragedy: the

culture of victimization rewards people for taking on a personal identity as one who is damaged, weak, and aggrieved. This is a recipe for failure—and constant litigation—after students graduate from college and attempt to enter the workforce]

One issue which is going to be more and more obvious with time: these students are leaving permanent records of their entitled and litigious attitudes in social media and online; I would not blame employers for looking these up and not employing those who have lied or exaggerated their grievances to demand special action.

But let's return to the cultures of individual morality identified in the paper. Honor culture makes every person responsible for maintaining their boundaries with others and acting as necessary to punish aggression against them or their reputation; it is the prevailing system when interpersonal aggression is the dominant form of social control. In societies with hierarchical organizations as in feudal Europe or Japan, persons much above you in status were deferred to while persons much below you were deferential toward you, or else.

A) A Culture of Honor

Honor is a kind of status attached to physical bravery and the unwillingness to be dominated by anyone. Honor in this sense is a status that depends on the evaluations of others, and members of honor societies are expected to display their bravery by engaging in violent retaliation against those who offend them (Cooney 1998:108–109; Leung and Cohen 2011). Accordingly, those who engage in such violence often say that the opinions of others left them no choice at all.... In honor cultures, it is one's reputation that makes one honorable or not, and one must respond aggressively to insults, aggressions, and challenges or lose honor. Not to fight back is itself a kind of moral failing, such that "in honor cultures, people are shunned or criticized not for exacting vengeance but for failing to do so" (Cooney 1998:110). Honorable people must guard their reputations, so they are highly sensitive to insult, often responding aggressively to what might seem to outsiders as minor slights (Cohen et al. 1996; Cooney 1998:115–119; Leung and Cohen 2011)...

Cultures of honor tend to arise in places where legal authority is weak or nonexistent and where a reputation for toughness is perhaps the only effective deterrent against predation or attack (Cooney 1998:122; Leung and Cohen 2011:510). Because of their belief in the value of personal bravery and capability, people socialized into a culture of honor will often shun reliance on law or any other authority even when it is available, refusing to lower their standing by depending on another to handle their affairs (Cooney 1998:122–129). But historically, as state authority has expanded and reliance on the law has increased, honor culture has given way to something else: a culture of dignity. [p. 712-713]

The Enlightenment and the end of feudalism brought in a new kind of moral order, based on law and individual rights, which the authors call a "culture of dignity." Most developed countries have adopted this model, where each person is deemed to be equal under the law and enjoys individual rights that law and state forces will enforce against others. The honor culture continues as an element of many subcultures, notably in the military, law enforcement, and areas where order has broken down, but the boundaries of allowable violence and retaliation are constrained; duelling and violence for retribution is now illegal. Offenses are now to be brought to authorities for resolution and punishment, and grievances below a minimal standard are to be dealt with socially.

B) A Culture of Dignity

The prevailing culture in the modern West is one whose moral code is nearly the exact opposite of that of an honor culture. Rather than honor, a status based primarily on public opinion, people are said to have dignity, a kind of inherent worth that cannot be alienated by others (Berger 1970; see also Leung and Cohen 2011). Dignity exists independently of what others think, so a culture of dignity is one in which public reputation is less important. Insults might provoke offense, but they no longer have the same importance as a way of establishing or destroying a reputation for bravery. It is even commendable to have "thick skin" that allows one to shrug off slights and even serious insults, and in a dignity-based society parents might teach children some version of "sticks and stones may break my bones, but words will never hurt me" – an idea that would be alien in a culture of honor (Leung and Cohen 2011:509). People are to avoid insulting others, too, whether intentionally or not, and in general an ethic of self-restraint prevails.

When intolerable conflicts do arise, dignity cultures prescribe direct but non-violent actions, such as negotiated compromise geared toward solving the problem (Aslani et al. 2012). Failing this, or if the offense is sufficiently severe, people are to go to the police or appeal to the courts. Unlike the honorable, the dignified approve of appeals to third parties and condemn those who "take the law into their own hands." For offenses like theft, assault, or breach of contract, people in a dignity culture will use law without shame. But in keeping with their ethic of restraint and toleration, it is not necessarily their first resort, and they might condemn many uses of the authorities as frivolous. People might even be expected to tolerate serious but accidental personal injuries.... The ideal in dignity cultures is thus to use the courts as quickly, quietly, and rarely as possible. The growth of law, order, and commerce in the modern world facilitated the rise of the culture of dignity, which largely supplanted the culture of honor among the middle and upper classes of the West.... But the rise of microaggression complaints suggests a new direction in the evolution of moral culture.

Highly "evolved" settings are encouraging the culture of victimhood, where one maintains one's status and reputation by competing to be recognized as a victim—the victim Olympics, it is sometimes rudely called.

C) A Culture of Victimhood

Microaggression complaints have characteristics that put them at odds with both honor and dignity cultures. Honorable people are sensitive to insult, and so they would understand that microaggressions, even if unintentional, are severe offenses that demand a serious response. But honor cultures value unilateral aggression and disparage appeals for help. Public complaints that advertise or even exaggerate one's own victimization and need for sympathy would be anathema to a person of honor – tantamount to showing that one had no honor at all. Members of a dignity culture, on the other hand, would see no shame in appealing to third parties, but they would not approve of such appeals for minor and merely verbal offenses. Instead they would likely counsel either confronting the offender directly to discuss the issue, or better yet, ignoring the remarks altogether.[p.714-715]

A culture of victimhood is one characterized by concern with status and sensitivity to slight combined with a heavy reliance on third parties. People are intolerant of insults, even if unintentional, and react by bringing them to the attention of authorities or to the public at large. Domination is the main form of deviance, and victimization a way of attracting sympathy, so rather than emphasize either their strength or inner worth, the aggrieved emphasize their oppression and social marginalization. ... Under such conditions complaint to third parties has supplanted both toleration and negotiation. People increasingly demand help from others, and advertise their oppression as evidence that they deserve respect and assistance. Thus we might call this moral culture a culture of victimhood because the moral status of the victim, at its nadir in honor cultures, has risen to new heights.[p.715]

The culture of victimhood is currently most entrenched on college campuses, where microaggression complaints are most prevalent. Other ways of campaigning for support from third parties and emphasizing one's own oppression – from protest demonstrations to the invented victimization of hate-crime hoaxes – are prevalent in this setting as well. That victimhood culture is so evident among campus activists might lead the reader to believe this is entirely a phenomenon of the political left, and indeed, the narrative of oppression and victimization is especially congenial to the leftist worldview (Haidt 2012:296; Kling 2013; Smith 2003:82). But insofar as they share a social environment, the same conditions that lead the aggrieved to use a tactic against their adversaries encourage their adversaries to use that tactic as well. For instance, hate crime hoaxes

do not all come from the left. [gives examples] ... Naturally,
whenever victimhood (or honor, or anything else) confers status, all
sorts of people will want to claim it. As clinical psychologist David J.
Ley notes, the response of those labeled as oppressors is frequently to
"assert that they are a victim as well." Thus, "men criticized as sexist
for challenging radical feminism defend themselves as victims of
reverse sexism, [and] people criticized as being unsympathetic
proclaim their own history of victimization."[p.715] [In this way,
victimhood culture causes a downward spiral of competitive
victimhood. Young people on the left and the right get sucked into its
vortex of grievance. We can expect political polarization to get
steadily worse in the coming decades as this moral culture of
victimhood spreads]

I'll point out that these environments tend to be artificially
maintained—they are not natural outgrowths of business and
commerce, where every participant has to cooperate with others to
thrive and make a living. They are more like cloistered institutions of
the past, supported by exterior economies, like convents and
monasteries, or royal courts. When we say something is "academic,"
we often mean it's not important in the real world. And the money
supporting it all is partly from parents, but mostly from government,
which pays for research and subsidizes the loans that have allowed
the schools to charge more than ever and hire all the administrators
that make work for themselves by policing student activity.

So I suspect we're seeing peak influence of the culture of
victimhood, and natural corrections—like the refusal of businesses to
degrade their competitive edge by further kowtowing to identity
politicians—will push back. Part of this may be a repudiation of the
Democratic party, which has co-opted much of the third-wave
feminist and identity politics sentiment. Having used it through
several election cycles, they are now so identified with it that any
backlash will damage them. Trump's current support is a result of
decades of suppression of populist speech, and his un-PC style is
actually being rewarded in polls.

Lastly, I'll point out some similar classifications in Jane Jacobs'

Systems of Survival[268]. She identified two syndromes—we might call them meme-complexes, systems of ideas that are internally consistent and self-supporting:

MORAL PRECEPTS

GUARDIAN SYNDROME	COMMERCE SYNDROME
▪ Shun trading	▪ Shun force
▪ Exert prowess	▪ Compete
▪ Be obedient and disciplined	▪ Be efficient
▪ Adhere to tradition	▪ Be open to inventiveness and novelty
▪ Respect hierarchy	▪ Use initiative and enterprise
▪ Be loyal	▪ Come to voluntary agreements
▪ Take vengeance	▪ Respect contracts
▪ Deceive for the sake of the task	▪ Dissent for the sake of the task
▪ Make rich use of leisure	▪ Be industrious
▪ Be ostentatious	▪ Be thrifty
▪ Dispense largesse	▪ Invest for productive purposes
▪ Be exclusive	▪ Collaborate easily with strangers and aliens
▪ Show fortitude	▪ Promote comfort and convenience
▪ Be fatalistic	▪ Be optimistic
▪ Treasure honor	▪ Be honest

The Guardian Syndrome roughly corresponds to the culture of honor, and it naturally evolved in a state where roaming bands of warriors—warlords—compete to control territory which (through agricultural populations or hunter-gatherer bands) generates food and wealth. As agriculture advanced, the warlords became a separate military and governing class, and cities began to develop. Trading and commerce flowered, and the ethos of the Commerce Syndrome developed as technology and trade overtook the produce of the land as a source of wealth. Cities grew, and classes of scribes, accountants, and religious orders became important. Law as a codification of wise rule, and then as recognition of individual rights, became a reliable way of settling grievances without taking up arms. And in the US, the idea of regulating the state itself via a Constitution allowed a free people to coexist with others who believed quite differently by enforcing a neutral code of law.

Interactions between victimhood activists and others are especially vicious because of the mutual misunderstandings of the importance of honor, dignity, and truth to the older cultures. Any disagreement with the claim of victim status is recast as another microagression, and only complete submission to their claims is accepted. When action is taken to address their concerns, it is only satisfying for a brief period before new outrages are identified—there must always be something to complain about, or they would be required to justify their existence and self-esteem via some real accomplishment. Meanwhile, lies and personal character assassination of those deemed incorrect or of the class of oppressors make people who are steeped in the honor or dignity cultures violently angry, and their angry outbursts are used as more evidence of the need to suppress them.

The culture of complaint and victimhood thrives only in those insulated bubbles where government supports institutions detached from customer demand. This includes government itself, especially those bureaucracies which have gained the power to maintain themselves regardless of party in power, but also includes public schools and all the universities which derive most of their funds from government grants and student loans—which is nearly all of them. One way of reducing this detachment from reality and accountability is to cut funding for these institutions and encourage individual and entrepreneurial solutions to the problems they were assigned to address. What we have now is sometimes called the clerisy—a quasi-religious governing structure of scribes and functionaries who act to increase their own power from some protected perch of authority, directing the lives of others with what they think is superior intellect and morality. And there are now so many of them living well on the borrowed and taxed dollars taken from the real economy that their rules and demands are strangling the economy that supports all of us.

A Vox piece by Oliver Lee, who's quitting his job as a professor to find more meaningful work:

> All of these issues lead to one, difficult-to-escape conclusion. Despite all the finger-pointing directed at students ("They're lazy! They're oversensitive! They're entitled!"), and the blame heaped on professors ("Out of touch and irrelevant to a man"), the real culprit is systemic. Our federally backed approach to subsidizing higher education

through low-interest loans has created perverse incentives with disastrous consequences. This system must be reformed[269].

He suggests a smaller, more accountable higher education system, stripped of the excess federal loan funding.

Progressives are asserting a need to control Futurism to bring correct feminist and progressive thought into it.

My opinion: a study recently showed women go into scientific fields in roughly the proportion you'd expect, if you first take out everyone who didn't study much qualifying mathematics. I expect there is a natural aggregate difference in how interested each sex is in planning for the future, preparing for hazards, etc., with men vigilant while women tend to be more focused on immediate needs and alleviating suffering—the Mommy vs Daddy differences. And so you would expect futurists to skew male simply because they are interested (sometimes obsessed) by the topic.

None of this means there aren't women who are interested and good at futurism (e.g., Virginia Postrel.) But an effort to force more women into futurism means less good futurism and more emotionalism as guides to policy and planning. Which means a less dynamic future for everyone.

Rose Eveleth (of "Shirtstorm" fame) has an article in the Atlantic: "Why Aren't There More Women Futurists?"

> There are all sorts of firms and companies working to build robotic servants. Chrome butlers, chefs, and housekeepers. But the fantasy of having an indentured servant is a peculiar one to some. "That whole idea of creating robots that are in service to us has always bothered me," says Nnedi Okorafor, a science fiction author. "I've always sided with the robots. That whole idea of creating these creatures that are human-like and then have them be in servitude to us, that is not my fantasy and I find it highly problematic that it would be anyone's."

> Or take longevity, for example. The idea that people could, or even should, push to lengthen lifespans as far as possible is popular. The life-extension movement, with Aubrey de Gray as one (very bearded) spokesman, has raised millions of dollars to investigate how to

extend the lifespan of humans. But this is arguably only an ideal future if you're in as a comfortable position as his. "Living forever only works if you're a rich vampire from an Anne Rice novel, which is to say that you have compound interest," jokes Ashby. "It really only works if you have significant real-estate investments and fast money and slow money." (Time travel, as the comedian Louis C.K. has pointed out, is another thing that is a distinctly white male preoccupation—going back in time, for marginalized groups, means giving up more of their rights.)[270]

So, let's see—she thinks we need to keep human beings indentured to jobs taking care of the helpless old, for example, rather than have robotic assistants. Of course in her mind it's the obligation of some government to pay all those human assistants, as much as necessary to eliminate all suffering and pain. Robotic assistants are simply Not Needed in the social welfare world of the future, where we can all help each other 24×7 and someone else provides all our needs.

It's also, apparently, desirable that we all die sooner than necessary. We should return to the golden past, where life was short and disease and hunger stalked almost everyone. 25 is old enough!

Of course it's harder to predict what social attitudes will be in the future—and many futurists fail to imagine what's to come in that area, while more easily projecting trends in technology. But that doesn't mean an infusion of women will make such predictions any better.

Science fiction has become more pessimistic about the future, and people like this are a big reason:

> In order to understand what those who have never really felt welcome in the field of futurism think, I called someone who writes and talks about the future, but who doesn't call themselves a futurist: Monica Byrne. Byrne is a science-fiction author and opinion writer who often tackles questions of how we see the future, and what kinds of futures we deem preferable. But when she thinks about "futurism" as a field, she doesn't see herself. "I think the term futurist is itself is something I see white men claiming for themselves, and isn't

something that would occur to me to call myself even though I functionally am one," she says.

Okorafor says that she too has never really called herself a futurist, even though much of what she does is use her writing to explore what's possible. "When you sent me your email and you mentioned futurism I think that's really the first time I started thinking about that label for myself. And it fits. It feels comfortable."

When Byrne thinks about the term futurists, she thinks about a power struggle. "What I see is a bid for control over what the future will look like. And it is a future that is, that to me doesn't look much different from Asimov science fiction covers. Which is not a future I'm interested in."

The futurism that involves glass houses and 400-year-old men doesn't interest her. "When I think about the kind of future I want to build, it's very soft and human, it's very erotic, and I feel like so much of what I identify as futurism is very glossy, chrome painted science fiction covers, they're sterile." She laughs. "Who cares about your jetpack? How does technology enable us to keep loving each other?"[271]

And how does not having technology help us love each other? Fights to the death for food and resources are what love is all about! Kill off a few billion people, return to warm and loving matriarchal villages, and enjoy true humanity... there's no reason we can't have both higher tech, longer lifespans, and love, Ma'am. It's only the current ease of life due to technology and specialization that allows you to believe such ridiculous things.

About the Author

Jeb Kinnison studied computer and cognitive science at MIT, and wrote programs modeling the behavior of simulated stock traders and the population dynamics of economic agents. Later he worked at BBN, doing AI and supercomputer work, then went to grad school and into business. His last career before retiring to write was managing money for Silicon Valley tycoons.

He's written two books on applied attachment theory, *Avoidant: How to Love (or Leave) a Dismissive Partner* and *Bad Boyfriends: Using Attachment Theory to Avoid Mr. (or Ms.) Wrong and Make You a Better Partner,* and a series of three science fiction thrillers, *The Substrate Wars.*

Visit his web site at JebKinnison.com for more: rail guns, Nazi scientists, the wreck of the Edmund Fitzgerald, the 1980s AI bubble, and current research in relationships, attachment types, diet, and health.

If you liked this book and think others would enjoy it, please leave a review at Amazon, or on Goodreads, or wherever you comment on books. As a small publisher, we can't afford advertising or bookstore placement fees, and we rely on word-of-mouth to bring our readers great new work. Every review and recommendation to friends helps! And because we're covering politically-incorrect topics, we expect a lot of one-star reviews from progressives—so it's especially important that you review the book if you want us to be heard.

Acknowledgements

Thanks to my early readers, especially Paul Perrotta, whose assistance was invaluable. Also, special thanks to John Carlton of The Arts Mechanical and Nick Corcodillos ("The Headhunter") for their job search posts and links to sources. Walter Olson (of Cato and Overlawyered) and Glenn Reynolds and Sarah Hoyt (of Instapundit) helped by getting early readers for some chapters. Janet Bloomfield, David Ochroch, and Eric S Raymond contributed useful bits as well. Multiple anonymous contributors gave me some of the more colorful anecdotes—we all know why they remain anonymous.

Online Resources

Please email the author at jebkinnison@gmail.com if you find any errors or have any comments. And sign up for email updates at JebKinnison.com, where you can read about attachment, science, and health topics. There will also be interesting material about science fiction and politics at SubstrateWars.com.

Bibliography

Please visit the Death by HR Bibliography page (http://jebkinnison.com/death-by-hr-bibliography/) at my web site for links that allow you to view the recommended books for further reading.

Endnotes

1. "Why We Hate HR: In a knowledge economy, companies with the best talent win. And finding, nurturing, and developing that talent should be one of the most important tasks in a corporation. So why does human resources do such a bad job—and how can we fix it?" Fast Company, August 1, 2005. http://www.fastcompany.com/53319/why-we-hate-hr

2. Clogs to Clogs in Three Generations - https://en.wiktionary.org/wiki/clogs_to_clogs_in_three_generations

3. *Bourgeois Equality: How Ideas, Not Capital or Institutions, Enriched the World,* by Deirdre McCloskey, Univ. of Chicago Press, 2016. http://amzn.to/2ajzYRK

4. "The Great Enrichment: A Humanistic and Social Scientific Account," by Deirdre Nansen McCloskey, 2016. http://deirdremccloskey.org/docs/pdf/McCloskey_ASSA2016.pdf

5. *Capital in the Twenty-First Century* by Thomas Piketty, 2013. See https://en.wikipedia.org/wiki/Capital_in_the_Twenty-First_Century

6. "Deciphering the fall and rise in the net capital share," by Matthew Rognlie. March 19, 2015 Brookings Papers on Economic Activities. https://www.brookings.edu/bpea-articles/deciphering-the-fall-and-rise-in-the-net-capital-share/

7. "Falling Investment and Rising Trade Deficit Lead to Weak First Quarter" - Dean Baker, Center for Economic and Policy Research, April 28, 2016. http://cepr.net/data-bytes/gdp-bytes/gdp-2016-04

8. *The Great Stagnation: How America Ate All The Low-Hanging Fruit of Modern History, Got Sick, and Will (Eventually) Feel Better,* by Tyler Cowen. Dutton (January 25, 2011) http://amzn.to/1pTybdh

9. "The Struggles of New York City's Taxi King"—by Simon Van Zuylen-Wood, Bloomberg, Augist 27, 2015 http://www.bloomberg.com/features/

2015-taxi-medallion-king/

10. https://www.khanacademy.org/

11. The Future and Its Enemies: The Growing Conflict Over Creativity, Enterprise, and Progress, Virginia Postrel, Simon and Schuster, 1998 http://amzn.to/1SFodo7

12. From Virginia Postrel's web site. https://vpostrel.com/future-and-its-enemies

13. https://substratewars.com/2015/10/30/tomorrowland-tragic-misfire/

14. "The Rate of New Business Formation Has Fallen By Almost Half Since 1978: America's declining 'business dynamism' has affected all 50 states and nearly every single metro area." Richard Florida, Citylab, May 5, 2014 http://www.citylab.com/work/2014/05/rate-new-business-formation-has-fallen-almost-half-1978/9026/

15. From C.S. Lewis's essay anthology "God in the Dock" (1948), viewed 4-28-2015 at http://www.wsj.com/articles/SB10001424052702304527504579170134126854254

16. "Once Skeptical Of Executive Power, Obama Has Come To Embrace It," by Binyamin Applebaum and Michael D. Shear, NY Times, 08-14-2016. http://www.nytimes.com/2016/08/14/us/politics/obama-era-legacy-regulation.html

17. Commenter JAORE, 8-13-2016. http://althouse.blogspot.com/2016/08/an-army-of-lawyers-working-under-mr.html?showComment=1471097558303#c8108980759878368373

18. https://en.wikipedia.org/wiki/Vertical_integration

19. "The Changing Role of Chaebol," Charlotte Marguerite Powers, Stanford Journal of East Asian Affairs, Summer 2010 https://web.stanford.edu/group/sjeaa/journal102/10-2_09%20Korea-Powers.pdf

20. "I, Pencil: My Family Tree as Told to Leonard E. Reed," courtesy of the Ralph Smeed Private Foundation, 1958. https://fee.org/media/14940/read-i-pencil.pdf

21. "U.S. Department of Transportation expands and accelerates Takata air bag inflator recall to protect American drivers and passengers," US NHTSA 13-16, May 4, 2016. http://www.nhtsa.gov/About+NHTSA/Press+Releases/nhtsa-expands-accelerates-takata-inflator-recall-05042016

22. https://en.wikipedia.org/wiki/Smoot%E2%80%93Hawley_Tariff_Act

23. "France labour dispute: Wave of strike action nationwide," BBC, 26 May 2016 http://www.bbc.com/news/world-europe-36385778

24. "How the West (and the Rest) Got Rich —

The Great Enrichment of the past two centuries has one primary source: the liberation of ordinary people to pursue their dreams of economic betterment," Deirdre N. McCloskey, Wall Street Journal, May 20, 2016 http://www.wsj.com/articles/why-the-west-and-the-rest-got-rich-1463754427

25. "The Unrealized Horrors of Population Explosion," Clyde Habermann, New York Times, May 31, 2015 http://www.nytimes.com/2015/06/01/us/the-unrealized-horrors-of-population-explosion.html

26. "'The switch in time that saved nine' is the name given to what was perceived as the sudden jurisprudential shift by Associate Justice Owen Roberts of the U.S. Supreme Court in the 1937 case West Coast Hotel Co. v. Parrish. Conventional historical accounts portrayed the Court's majority opinion as a strategic political move to protect the Court's integrity and independence from President Franklin Roosevelt's court-reform bill (also known as the "court-packing plan"), which would have expanded the size of the bench up to 15 justices, though it has been argued that these accounts have misconstrued the historical record." https://en.wikipedia.org/wiki/The_switch_in_time_that_saved_nine

27. "One top-notch engineer is worth '300 times or more than the average,' explains Alan Eustace, a Google vice president of engineering. He says he would rather lose an entire incoming class of engineering graduates than one exceptional technologist. Many Google services, such as Gmail and Google News, were started by a single person, he says." See http://cacm.acm.org/blogs/blog-cacm/180512-is-there-a-10x-gap-between-best-and-average-programmers-and-how-did-it-get-there/fulltext

28. See https://en.wikipedia.org/wiki/The_Mythical_Man-Month. An excerpt is available online: https://books.google.com/books?id=mt9tF7XMFX4C&lpg=PA287&pg=PA210. The study of software project management has advanced a great deal since the book was first published, but its key points are still ignored in government software contracting.

29. https://en.wikipedia.org/wiki/Levellers

30. https://www.washingtonpost.com/politics/how-the-clintons-haiti-development-plans-succeed--and-disappoint/2015/03/20/0ebae25e-cbe9-11e4-a2a7-9517a3a70506_story.html

31. "In the late 1990s some Haitians working at Teleco told me that 'the Kennedy company Fusion' was getting a special rate discount and that it had an office inside Teleco. I called Fusion to inquire but it would not even confirm whether it did business in Haiti. Then the FCC told me that its file containing the Haiti contracts, which are public documents, was missing.

When the FCC asked carriers for duplicate copies, Fusion coughed up one, from 1999. Then it went to court to block my request to see it.

Fusion lost, and when the contract was released it showed that the company had a rate of 12 cents per minute when the official rate was 50 cents. As one Haitian told me, on one of the busiest routes in the Western Hemisphere, 'it was a gold mine.'

Among Mr. Kennedy's more hilarious claims is that Fusion's sweetheart deal with Teleco was 'an innovative agreement' and an example of 'deregulation of state-owned monopolies.' The FCC has suggested otherwise in another similar situation. In 2008 it fined New Jersey-based IDT $400,000 for failing to file its 2003 Teleco agreement for 8.75 cents per minute, a 66% discount from the official rate.

An American entrepreneur who does business in the Caribbean recently explained the Haitian landscape to me this way: 'We did not bother with Haiti as the Foreign Corrupt Practices Act precludes legitimate U.S. entities from entering the Haitian market. Haiti is pure pay to play. The benefit of competitive submarine cables would be transformative for the Haitians. Instead, they were stuck with Clinton cronies taxing the poor.'"
http://www.wsj.com/articles/
SB10001424052748703625304575116030721437698
32. Calabresi, Steven G. and Price, Larissa, "Monopolies and the Constitution: A History of Crony Capitalism" (2012). Faculty Working Papers. Paper 214. http://scholarlycommons.law.northwestern.edu/facultyworkingpapers/214
33. EEOC letter dated June 11, 2012. "ADA & Title VII: High School Diploma Requirement and Disparate Impact." https://www.eeoc.gov/eeoc/foia/letters/2012/ada_title_vii_diploma_disparate_impact.html
34. "Ban the Box: US Cities, Counties, and States Adopt Fair Hiring Policies," by Michelle Natividad Rodriguez and Beth Avery, National Employment Law Project. http://www.nelp.org/publication/ban-the-box-fair-chance-hiring-state-and-local-guide/
35. "The Rubber Room: The battle over New York City's worst teachers," by Steven Brill. The New Yorker, August 31, 2009 http://www.newyorker.com/magazine/2009/08/31/the-rubber-room
36. http://slatestarcodex.com/2015/06/06/against-tulip-subsidies/

37. https://en.wikipedia.org/wiki/Tulip_mania

38. "Trapped in the Community College Remedial Maze," by Mikhail Zinshteyn, Atlantic, February 26, 2016 http://www.theatlantic.com/education/archive/2016/02/community-colleges-remedial-classes/471192/

39. "Obama Moves to Expand Rules Aimed at Closing Gender Pay Gap," By Julie Hirshfeld Davis, Jan. 29, 2016 New York Times. http://www.nytimes.com/2016/01/29/us/politics/obama-moves-to-expand-rules-aimed-at-closing-gender-pay-gap.html

40. "Harvard prof. takes down gender wage gap myth," by Ashe Schow, 1/13/16 Washington Examiner. http://www.washingtonexaminer.com/harvard-prof.-takes-down-gender-wage-gap-myth/article/2580405

41. "EEOC pay reporting: the better to sue you with, my dear," by Walter Olson, 2/1/2016 Overlawyered. http://overlawyered.com/2016/02/eeoc-employers-must-report-pay-numbers-to-us/

42. "Young women in STEM fields earn up to one-third less than men: Marriage, kids and scientific fields chosen explain gap, study finds,"
by Jeff Grabmeier, May 10, 2016, Ohio State University News.
https://news.osu.edu/news/2016/05/10/stem-gap/

43. "Human Task Switches Considered Harmful," by Joel Spolsky. Feb. 12, 2001 Joel on Software http://www.joelonsoftware.com/articles/fog0000000022.html

44. "What Real Feminists Meant by "Equal Pay for Equal Work," by Jeffrey A. Tucker, August 05, 2016, Foundation for Economic Education (FEE). https://fee.org/articles/what-real-feminists-meant-by-equal-pay-for-equal-work/

45. https://en.wikipedia.org/wiki/Obergefell_v._Hodges

46. "Companies Say No to Having an HR Department," by Lauren Weber and Rachel Feintzeig, Wall Street Journal, April 9, 2014. http://www.wsj.com/articles/SB10001424052702304819004579489603299910562

47. Private communication.

48. "Why We Hate HR: In a knowledge economy, companies with the best talent win. And finding, nurturing, and developing that talent should be one of the most important tasks in a corporation. So why does human resources do such a bad job—and how can we fix it?" by Staff, Fast Company, August 1, 2005. https://www.fastcompany.com/53319/why-we-hate-hr

49. "It's Time For Companies To Fire Their Human Resource Departments," by Kyle Smith, Forbes, April 4, 2013. http://www.forbes.com/sites/kylesmith/2013/04/04/its-time-for-companies-to-fire-their-human-resource-departments/#4f95b0444f7e

50. "Companies Say No to Having an HR Department: Employers Come Up With New Ways to Manage Hiring, Firing and Benefits," by Lauren Weber and Rachel Feintzeig, Wall Street Journal, April 9, 2014. http://www.wsj.com/articles/SB10001424052702304819004579489603299910562

51. "It's Time to Split HR," by Ram Charan. Harvard Business Review, July-August 2014. https://hbr.org/2014/07/its-time-to-split-hr

52. "Household Data Annual Averages," 2015. US Bureau of Labor Statistics. "HOUSEHOLD DATA ANNUAL AVERAGES. Employed persons by detailed occupation, sex, race, and Hispanic or Latino ethnicity [Numbers in thousands]" http://www.bls.gov/cps/cpsaat11.pdf

53. "The New 'Women's Work': On Being A Male Human Resources Professional," by James A. Landrith. The Good Men Project, October 30, 2012. https://goodmenproject.com/featured-content/the-new-womens-work-on-being-a-male-human-resources-professional/

54. Janet Bloomfield blogged in response to a draft of this section:

"Those stereotypes are more or less true. 'Women are more emotional than men' is a polite way of saying women are less able than men to master their emotions. In any given situation, men are just as likely as women to feel a particular feeling – anger, sadness, embarrassment, etc. – there really is not any difference between men and women's capacity for emotion, but men are able to control those feelings and not allow feelings to dictate actions to a much greater degree. This is why you will often find women crying at work, but not men.

"Men consistently display greater affinity than women for logic, rationality and objectivity. Feminists long ago stopped trying to disprove this unfortunate gender difference, and instead switched to insisting that either A) logic isn't valuable, or B) logic isn't real, it's just a tool of the patriarchy. The hilarious irony is that feminists deploy their shaky grasp of logic trying to logically prove that logic isn't real or doesn't matter. They could claim decisive victory if only their arguments were logical....

"Women are absolutely more risk averse than men, for some pretty important evolutionary reasons. Men take greater risks to raise their attractiveness to mates, and thereby increase the likelihood of reproductive success. Women keep their risks to a minimum, because babies are hard to keep alive without a mother. It's a straight forward cost/benefit analysis....

"Sadly, the stereotypes about women being petty and mean and more likely to focus on the trivial and not the larger organizational goals are also true. Not for each and every woman, obviously, but for women as a group, and those tendencies are exacerbated by women's tendency towards collectivism and their intolerance for women who break from the pack. The tendency is so strong, psychologist Meredith Fuller has written an entire book on the subject, breaking the Mean Girls down into categories and offering strategies for how to manage these women. *Working With Bitches: Identify the Eight Types of Office Mean Girls and Rise Above Workplace Nastiness* is a book I recommend men in particular to read. Women reading this book will simply recognize women we've been dealing with our whole lives. Men will learn exactly how women operate to punish, control and oppress other women.... Women are the main sources of misogyny in our culture. Nowhere is that more true than in the workplace, where actual things are at stake." http://judgybitch.com/2016/08/11/give-women-power-and-women-will-create-morally-righteous-ways-to-abuse-it/

55. "Men in HR: A National Geographic Exclusive," by Ben Eubanks, UpstartHR, September 23, 2010. http://upstarthr.com/men-in-hr-a-national-geographic-exclusive/

56. "HR is Female," by John Sumser. HR Examiner, March 30, 2011. http://www.hrexaminer.com/hr-is-female/

57. Comment by "poolboy" found on blog entry "Why are there so many women in HR?" dated 07-15-2013 at All About Human Capital. https://mortenkamp.com/2013/07/15/why-are-there-so-many-women-in-hr/

58. "It's Time For Companies To Fire Their Human Resource Departments," by Kyle Smith, Forbes, April 4, 2013. http://www.forbes.com/sites/kylesmith/2013/04/04/its-time-for-companies-to-fire-their-human-resource-departments/#4f95b0444f7e

59. "60% of compliance officers are women—and that may be a bad thing," by Shanto Atkins, Quartz, March 28, 2014. http://qz.com/191569/60-of-compliance-officers-are-women-and-thats-a-bad-thing/

60. "Human Resources: The Complexity of the Gender Imbalance," by Benjamin Banks of St. John Fisher College, May 2010. http://fisherpub.sjfc.edu/cgi/viewcontent.cgi?article=1002&context=business_etd_masters

61. "The Feminization of Teaching in America," By Elizabeth Boyle, MIT Program in Women's and Gender Studies - Kampf Prize, 2004.

https://stuff.mit.edu/afs/athena.mit.edu/org/w/wgs/prize/eb04.html

62. Boyle

63. Boyle

64. *Job Queues, Gender Queues: Explaining Women's Inroads Into Male Occupations* by Barbara F. Reskin and Patricia A. Roos, Temple University Press, March 3, 2009. http://amzn.to/2b4vuCq

65. "Publishing: A 'Pink-Collar Ghetto'?" by Molly Fischer. The Observer, May 5, 2010. http://observer.com/2010/05/publishing-a-pinkcollar-ghetto/

66. "What are the Core Courses in a Bachelor's in Human Resources Program?" Humanresourcesmba.net, 2016. http://www.humanresourcesmba.net/faq/what-are-the-core-courses-in-a-bachelors-in-human-resources-program/

67. "Economists Aren't As Nonpartisan As We Think," FiveThirtyEight, Dec. 8, 2014. "...macroeconomists and financial economists are more right-leaning on average while labor economists tend to be left-leaning."
http://fivethirtyeight.com/features/economists-arent-as-nonpartisan-as-we-think/

68. UC Berkeley Labor Center. http://laborcenter.berkeley.edu/

69. "Funding Ideology, Not Research, at University of California 'Labor Institutes'," by Steven Greenhut, Reason.com, May 6, 2016. http://reason.com/archives/2016/05/06/funding-ideology-not-research-at-univers

70. "What Your HR Department Could Learn from Hayek," by Harrison Burge. Foundation for Economic Education, August 22, 2016. https://fee.org/articles/what-your-hr-department-could-learn-from-hayek/

71. Personal communication, August 25, 2016

72. https://en.wikipedia.org/wiki/Affirmative_action

73. https://en.wikipedia.org/wiki/Ketuanan_Melayu

74. https://en.wikipedia.org/wiki/Equal_Employment_Opportunity_Commission

75. http://www.eeoc.gov/employees/charge.cfm

76. http://www.eeoc.gov/eeoc/statistics/census/race_ethnic_data.html

77. https://en.wikipedia.org/wiki/Equal_Employment_Opportunity_Commission

78. https://www.eeoc.gov/federal/directives/md-110_chapter_5.cfm

79. https://www.eeoc.gov/federal/directives/md-110_chapter_5.cfm

80. LinkedIn Pulse 2-24-2106, "Employers Deserve ANSWERS about EEOC's Position Statement Policy" https://www.linkedin.com/pulse/employers-deserve-answers-eeocs-position-statement-policy-archer

81. "EEOC: Let Us Imagineer ENDA For You," Walter Olson, Cato At Liberty, July 17, 2015 http://www.cato.org/blog/eeoc-let-us-imagineer-enda-you

82. "EEOC May Face $4 Million in Attorney Fees," by Allen Smith, SHRM Legal issues, 5/25/2016. https://www.shrm.org/legalissues/federalresources/pages/eeoc-attorney-fees.aspx

83. "CRST Van Expedited: Back To the Dunking Booth for the EEOC," Walter Olson, Cato at Liberty, May 24, 2016 http://www.cato.org/blog/crst-van-expedited-back-dunking-booth-eeoc

84. Numbers of disabled are hard to determine because of the definitional issues, and the lack of labor force participation of many. But the BLS tries, showing 29.2 million disabled potential workers out of a population of 247.9 million able workers. See: "Economic news release," BLS, 2014 Annual. http://www.bls.gov/news.release/disabl.t01.htm

85. New York Times, 8-30-2015, David Barstow and Suhasini Raj. http://www.nytimes.com/2015/08/31/world/asia/caste-quotas-in-india-come-under-attack.html

86. The Economist 2-27-2016 http://www.economist.com/news/asia/21693613-higher-castes-demanding-lower-status-make-mockery-positive-discrimination-backward-ho

87. "With Affirmative Action, India's Rich Gain School Slots Meant for Poor" - New York Times 10/7/2012, by Gardner Harris. http://www.nytimes.com/2012/10/08/world/asia/indias-rich-benefit-from-schools-affirmative-action.html

88. "The Licence Raj or Permit Raj (rāj, meaning 'rule' in Hindi) was the elaborate system of licences, regulations and accompanying red tape that were required to set up and run businesses in India between 1947 and 1990. [It] was a result of India's decision to have a planned economy where all aspects of the economy are controlled by the state and licences are given to a select few. Up to 80 government agencies had to be satisfied before private companies could produce something and, if granted, the government would regulate production." https://en.wikipedia.org/wiki/Licence_Raj

89. "Capitalism's Assault on the Indian Caste System: How Economic Liberalization Spawned Low-Caste Dalit Millionaires," by Swaminathan S. Anklesaria Aiyar, Cato Institute Policy Analysis No. 776, July 21, 2015. http://www.cato.org/publications/policy-analysis/capitalisms-assault-on-the-indian-caste-system

90. "How Capitalism Is Undermining the Indian Caste System," by

Swaminathan S. Anklesaria Aiyar, Cato Institute, July 22, 2015. http://
www.cato.org/blog/how-capitalism-undermining-indian-caste-system
91. "Chinese in Malaysia," originally an article from U. Maryland's College of
Behavioral and Social Sciences, copied to: http://www.eng.fju.edu.tw/
worldlit/link/malaysia_chinese.htm
92. Affirmative Action Around the World, Thomas Sowell, Yale University
Press (February 9, 2004), review comments: http://amzn.to/1ZEGTZP
93. "A Never-Ending Policy," The Economist, 4-27-2013 (author unnamed)
http://www.economist.com/news/briefing/21576654-elections-may-could-
mark-turning-point-never-ending-policy
94. The Diplomat, Han Bochen, 11-10-2015. "Malaysia's Chinese Diaspora:
The Other Side of the Story: Conventional narratives overlook the
marginalization of ethnic Chinese in Malaysia—especially the Chinese
poor."
95. "Indian Discontent Fuels Malaysia's Rising Tensions," by Thomas Fuller,
The New York Times, 2-10-2008. http://www.nytimes.com/2008/02/10/
world/asia/10malaysia.html?_r=0
96. "Policy Brief: Affirmative Action: Nigeria," Inter-Regional Inequality
Facility, February 2006. https://www.odi.org/sites/odi.org.uk/files/odi-assets/
publications-opinion-files/4082.pdf
97. "Nigeria and 'Federal Character'; 'Quota System' setbacks," editorial staff,
National Mirror (Nigeria), 9-17-2015.http://nationalmirroronline.net/new/
nigeria-and-federal-character-quota-system-setbacks/
98. "Federal Character And Its Discontents" Jan 31 2016, Reuben Abati
@Abati1990 http://nigeriavillagesquare.com/forum/threads/federal-
character-and-its-discontents.92347/
99. Amazon review of Sowell's book by Sodalug, August 17, 2004. https://
www.amazon.com/review/RBPBZGX2W4O7E
100. Affirmative Action Around the World: An Empirical Study, by Thomas
Sowell, Yale University Press, February 9, 2004. https://www.amazon.com/
Affirmative-Action-Around-World-Empirical-ebook/dp/B00155ZZPE/
101. Mismatch: How Affirmative Action Hurts Students It's Intended to Help,
and Why Universities Won't Admit It by Richard Sander, Basic Books, 2012.
http://amzn.to/2bUt0UP
102. There's little evidence that Obama would not have been admitted on his
own merit to these Ivy League schools without affirmative action
preferences, but there's no doubt he received preference and was virtually
guaranteed to be accepted when others with similar records might not have

been. Discussion here: "Barack Obama: Affirmative Action's Best Poster Child?" by Conor Friedersdorf, The Atlantic, April 28, 2011. http://www.theatlantic.com/politics/archive/2011/04/barack-obama-affirmative-actions-best-poster-child/237990/

103. https://www.law.cornell.edu/supct/html/05-908.ZO.html

104. "Study: Workplace diversity can help the bottom line. MIT economist scrutinizes firm data suggesting diverse offices function more effectively," by Peter Dizikes, MIT News Office, October 7, 2014. http://news.mit.edu/2014/workplace-diversity-can-help-bottom-line-1007

105. "When Passionate Advocates Meet Research on Diversity, Does the Honest Broker Stand a Chance?" by Alice H. Eagly, Journal of Social Issues - Wiley Online Library, 9 March 2016. http://onlinelibrary.wiley.com/doi/10.1111/josi.12163/full

106. "Asian Americans and the Future of Affirmative Action: The way members of the 'model minority' are treated in elite-college admissions could affect race-based standards moving forward," by Alia Wong, The Atlantic, June 28, 2016. http://www.theatlantic.com/education/archive/2016/06/asian-americans-and-the-future-of-affirmative-action/489023/

107. "The Trouble With Harvard: The Ivy League is broken and only standardized tests can fix it," by Steven Pinker. The New Republic, September 4, 2014. https://newrepublic.com/article/119321/harvard-ivy-league-should-judge-students-standardized-tests

108. *Two Cheers for Anarchism: Six Easy Pieces on Autonomy, Dignity, and Meaningful Work and Play,* by James C. Scott. Princeton University Press, 2012. http://amzn.to/2cnRPtj

109. "The term 'Hispanic' was adopted by the United States government in the early 1970s during the administration of Richard Nixon after the Hispanic members of an interdepartmental Ad Hoc Committee to develop racial and ethnic definitions recommended that a universal term encompassing all Hispanic subgroups—including Central and South Americans—be adopted. As the 1970 census did not include a question on Hispanic origin on all census forms—instead relying on a sample of the population via an extended form ('Is this person's origin or descent: Mexican; Puerto Rican; Cuban; Central or South American; Other Spanish; or None of these'), the members of the committee wanted a common designation to better track the social and economic progress of the group vis-à-vis the general population. The designation has since been used in local and federal employment, mass media, academia, and business market

research. It has been used in the U.S. Census since 1980. Because of the popularity of 'Latino' in the western portion of the United States, the government adopted this term as well in 1997, and used it in the 2000 census." https://en.wikipedia.org/wiki/Hispanic %E2%80%93Latino_naming_dispute

110. "Arab- and Persian-American campaign: 'Check it right' on census," by John Blake, CNN, May 14, 2010. http://www.cnn.com/2010/US/04/01/census.check.it.right.campaign/

111. "The Rise of the American 'Others': An increasing number of respondents are checking 'Some Other Race' on U.S. Census forms, forcing officials to rethink current racial categories," by Sowmiya Ashok, The Atlantic, August 27, 2016. http://www.theatlantic.com/politics/archive/2016/08/the-rise-of-the-others/497690/

112. https://en.wikipedia.org/wiki/Demographics_of_France.

113. "The 1994 Election: Did Racial Redistricting Undermine Democrats?" by Steven A. Holmes, The New York Times, November 13, 1994. http://www.nytimes.com/1994/11/13/us/the-1994-election-voters-did-racial-redistricting-undermine-democrats.html

114. *The Rise of HR: Wisdom From 73 Thought Leaders*, edited by Dave Ulrich, William A. Schiemann, GPHR and Libby Sartain, SPHR, published by the HR Certification Institute, 2015. http://www.octanner.com/content/dam/oc-tanner/documents/ebooks/HRCI_TheRiseofHR-dual.pdf

115. "HR as Organizational Leader and Champion of Diversity and Inclusion," by Andy Brantley, from *The Rise of HR*, p. 217-225

116. "CEOs Want Better Performance. Great Culture Can Make It Happen," by China Gorman of Great Place to Work, from *The Rise of HR*, p. 179-188

117. "Union Goal of Equality Fails the Test of Time," by Louis Unchitelle, The New York Times, July 9, 1995. http://www.nytimes.com/1995/07/09/us/union-goal-of-equality-fails-the-test-of-time.html

118. https://en.wikipedia.org/wiki/Homestead_Strike

119. "Union Membership in U.S. Fell to a 70-Year Low Last Year," by Steven Greenhouse, New York Times, Jan 21, 2011. http://www.nytimes.com/2011/01/22/business/22union.html

120. "Labor Unions: Workers' Unelected Representatives," by James Sherk, National Review, September 6, 2016. http://www.nationalreview.com/corner/439701/labor-unions-workers-only-6-percent-support-them

121. Paraphrase from "Society must be Defended" by Michel Foucalt. See discussion: https://en.wikipedia.org/wiki/

Philosophy_of_history#History_as_propaganda:_Is_history_always_written _by_the_victors.3F

122. "What's Wrong With Labor Unions?" Free Thoughts Podcast, March 2016 – Episode 124 of 151. Trevor Burris and Aaron Powell interviewing Prof. Richard Epstein. Transcript: http://www.libertarianism.org/media/free-thoughts/whats-wrong-labor-unions

123. Epstein

124. Epstein

125. Epstein

126. Epstein

127. "Labor law comes under scrutiny in US courts," by Milton J. Valencia, Boston Globe, May 25, 2016. http://www.bostonglobe.com/metro/ 2016/05/24/labor-law-comes-under-recent-scrutiny-courts/ gjclW3OsGnHZwM2Z9mXeLJ/story.html. Also, see "Boston's Labor Day: Investigators probe how far Mayor Marty Walsh's administration may have gone in forcing private firms to use union shops," by Steven Malaga, City Journal, September 4, 2016. http://www.city-journal.org/html/bostons-labor-day-14714.html

128. "Forgotten Facts of American Labor History," by Thomas E. Woods, Jr., in Mises Daily Articles,11/22/2004. https://mises.org/library/forgotten-facts-american-labor-history

129. "The data suggests that the ratio of Democratic-to-Republican voter registration among participants in IR is roughly 10 to one. I find a similar ratio when looking at those who have made contributions to Democratic and Republican candidates for office. I also show that Democratic lopsidedness at the three mainstream IR journals becomes more extreme at the higher stations (officers and editors, as opposed to ordinary members and authors). Also, I analyze the content of the 539 articles for union support and regulation support; the mainstream IR journals are overwhelmingly pro-union and pro-regulation." From article "The Left Orientation of Industrial Relations," by Mitchell Langbert, Econ Journal Watch, Vol 13, No. 1, Jan. 2016. https://econjwatch.org/articles/the-left-orientation-of-industrial-relations

130. "Daniel Klein, one of the authors [of the study] and a professor of economics at George Mason University, said that it demonstrated 'solidly' that most social science professors are 'leftist and statist, and that they have a narrow tent.'" From "Social Scientists Lean to the Left, Study Says," by Scott Jaschik, Inside Higher Ed, Dec. 21, 2005. https://www.insidehighered.com/

news/2005/12/21/politics. Also see: "Economists' policy views and voting,"
Daniel B. Klein and Charlotta Stern, Public Choice 126:331-342, 6 Dec 2004.
http://econfaculty.gmu.edu/klein/PdfPapers/KS_PublCh06.pdf

131. "Democratic vs. Republican occupations," Verdant Labs chart, 2016.
Data source: FEC campaign contribution data. http://verdantlabs.com/
politics_of_professions/

132. "What is the French economic problem?" by Andrew Walker, BBC
World Service, 29 April 2016. http://www.bbc.com/news/business-36152571

133. French leftists sniff at the US and its Anglospheric cousins because the
US economic model (the "Anglo-Saxon model") is more liberal—less
protectionist and *dirigiste*. The cultural backdrop is the French intellectual
distaste for crude money-making and *égoïste* neglect of collective opinion.
See https://en.wikipedia.org/wiki/Anglo-Saxon_model

134. "Low-Wage Jobs Displace Less Educated," by Katherine Peralta,
Bloomberg, March 12, 2014. http://www.bloomberg.com/news/articles/
2014-03-06/college-grads-taking-low-wage-jobs-displace-less-educated

135. https://en.wikipedia.org/wiki/Lilly_Ledbetter_Fair_Pay_Act_of_2009

136. "Deep Impact: New Overtime Rules Will Change Work, Not Overtime
Pay," by Mark A. Konkel and Barbara Hoey, Inside Counsel, August 31, 2016.
http://www.insidecounsel.com/2016/08/31/deep-impact-new-overtime-
rules-will-change-work-no

137. "Lowballing the cost of junior-manager overtime," by Walter Olson,
Overlawyered, November 19, 2015. http://www.overlawyered.com/2015/11/
lowballing-the-cost-of-junior-manager-overtime/

138. "Overtime Brings House Democrats Woe," by Walter Olson, Cato at
Liberty, April 13, 2016. http://www.cato.org/blog/overtime-brings-house-
democrats-woe

139. "Jack Welch: 'Rank-and-Yank'? That's Not How It's Done," by Jack
Welch, WSJ, Nov 14, 2013. http://www.wsj.com/articles/
SB10001424052702303789604579198281053673534

140. "The credit assignment problem concerns determining how the success
of a system's overall performance is due to the various contributions of the
system's components. 'In playing a complex game such as chess or checkers,
or in writing a computer program, one has a definite success criterion – the
game is won or lost. But in the course of play, each ultimate success (or
failure) is associated with a vast number of internal decisions. If the run is
successful, how can we assign credit for the success among the multitude of
decisions?'" From "Dictionary of Cognitive Science" by Dr. Michael R.W.

Dawson and Dr. David a Medler, U of Alberta, Nov 2010. http://
www.bcp.psych.ualberta.ca/~mike/Pearl_Street/Dictionary/contents/C/
creditassign.html

141. "Why Stack Ranking Is A Terrible Way To Motivate Employees," by
Max Nisen, Business Insider, Nov. 15, 2013. http://
www.businessinsider.com/stack-ranking-employees-is-a-bad-idea-2013-11

142. "Microsoft's Downfall: Inside the Executive E-mails and Cannibalistic
Culture that Felled a tech Giant," July 3, 2012. http://www.vanityfair.com/
news/2012/07/microsoft-downfall-emails-steve-ballmer

143. https://en.wikipedia.org/wiki/360-degree_feedback

144. Personal communication by anonymous manager, August 2016.

145. "Why Diversity Programs Fail," by Frank Dobbin and Alexandra Kalev,
Harvard Business Review, July 2016. https://hbr.org/2016/07/why-diversity-
programs-fail

146. From Linkedin Pulse posting by Slucock, quoted by The Arts
Mechanical February 2, 2016. https://theartsmechanical.wordpress.com/
2016/02/02/the-hr-secret-police/

147. "Why Companies ought to move away from bell curve model," by
Anitha Rathod, HR Manager at Blueberry Digital, Linkedin Pulse, January
30, 2016. https://www.linkedin.com/pulse/why-companies-ought-move-
away-from-bell-curve-model-anitha-rathod

148. "Reinventing Performance Management," by
Marcus Buckingham and Ashley Goodall, Harvard Business Review (HBR),
April 2015. https://hbr.org/2015/04/reinventing-performance-management

149. "METRO NEWS BRIEFS: CONNECTICUT; Judge Rules That Police
Can Bar High I.Q. Scores," New York Times, Sept. 9, 1999
http://www.nytimes.com/1999/09/09/nyregion/metro-news-briefs-
connecticut-judge-rules-that-police-can-bar-high-iq-scores.html

150. "Gerrymandering in personnel selection: A review of practice," by
Michael A. McDaniel, Human Resource Management Review 19(3):263-270
· September 2009. https://www.researchgate.net/publication/
222705476_Gerrymandering_in_personnel_selection_A_review_of_practic
e

151. *Taboo: Why Black Athletes Dominate Sports and Why We Are Afraid to
Talk About It,* by Jon Entine. PublicAffairs - Hachette Book Group, 2008. "In
virtually every sport in which they are given opportunity to compete, people
of African descent dominate. East Africans own every distance running
record. Professional sports in the Americas are dominated by men and

women of West African descent. Why have blacks come to dominate sports? Are they somehow physically better? And why are we so uncomfortable when we discuss this? Drawing on the latest scientific research, journalist Jon Entine makes an irrefutable case for black athletic superiority." http://amzn.to/2cCDxVS

152. "Racial spoils systems must involve incessant mischief because they require a rhetorical fog of euphemisms and blurry categories (e.g., 'race-conscious' measures that somehow do not constitute racial discrimination) to obscure stark facts, such as: If Ricci and half a dozen others who earned high scores were not white, the city would have proceeded with the promotions." From the op-ed piece "The Wreck of the Racial Spoils System" by George Will, Washington Post, Sunday, April 26, 2009. http://www.washingtonpost.com/wp-dyn/content/article/2009/04/24/AR2009042402305.html

153. McDaniel

154. McDaniel

155. "The diversity–validity dilemma: strategies for reducing racioethnic and sex subgroup differences and adverse impact inselection." By Ployhart, R. E., and Holtz, B. C. J. Personnel Psychology, 61, Feb 2008. http://onlinelibrary.wiley.com/doi/10.1111/j.1744-6570.2008.00109.x/abstract

156. "55 Suffolk County Officers Accused of Lying About Qualifications on Exams," by Duayne Draffen, New York Times, February 27, 1998.
http://www.nytimes.com/1998/02/27/nyregion/55-suffolk-county-officers-accused-of-lying-about-qualifications-on-exams.html

157. "The Coachability and Fakability of Personality-Based Selection Tests Used for Police Selection," by Miller, C.E. and Barret, G.V., in J. Public Personnel Management, Fall 2008, Vol 37 No. 3 pp 339-351.
http://ppm.sagepub.com/content/37/3/339.abstract

158. McDaniel. https://www.researchgate.net/publication/222705476_Gerrymandering_in_personnel_selection_A_review_of_practice

159. McDaniel.

160. https://en.wikipedia.org/wiki/Civil_Rights_Act_of_1991

161. "The Quest for the Purple Squirrel," by David Hunt, PE. LinkedIn Pulse, July 2, 2015. https://www.linkedin.com/pulse/quest-purple-squirrel-david-hunt-pe

162. http://programmers.stackexchange.com/questions/64822/do-job-postings-exaggerate-their-requirements

163. "There's Not a Talent Shortage. You Just Stink at Hiring," by Suzanne Lucas, Inc. Magazine, November 4, 2013. http://www.inc.com/suzanne-lucas/theres-not-a-talent-shortage-you-just-stink-at-hiring.html

164. https://en.wikipedia.org/wiki/Applicant_tracking_system

165. "Applicant tracking systems – the hidden peril for job applicants," by Neil Patrick, 40PlusCareerGuru, July 10, 2014. http://40pluscareerguru.blogspot.com/2014/07/applicant-tracking-systems-hidden-peril.html

166. "The Quest for the Purple Squirrel," by David Hunt, PE. LinkedIn Pulse, July 2, 2015. https://www.linkedin.com/pulse/quest-purple-squirrel-david-hunt-pe

167. "Ask the Headhunter: Why you can't win the keyword resume game," by Nick Corcodilos, PBS Newshour Making Sense, March 8, 2016. http://www.pbs.org/newshour/making-sense/ask-the-headhunter-why-you-cant-win-the-keyword-resume-game

168. "Applicant tracking systems: the hidden peril for job applicants," by Neil Patrick at 40PlusCareerGuru, July 10, 2014. http://40pluscareerguru.blogspot.com/2014/07/applicant-tracking-systems-hidden-peril.html

169. "Know Before You Hire: 2015 Employment Screening Trends," by Roy Maurer, SHRM, January 27, 2015. https://www.shrm.org/resourcesandtools/hr-topics/talent-acquisition/pages/2015-employment-screening-trends.aspx

170. "Ask the Headhunter: Why you can't win the keyword resume game," by Nick Corcodilos, PBS Newshour Making Sense, March 8, 2016. http://www.pbs.org/newshour/making-sense/ask-the-headhunter-why-you-cant-win-the-keyword-resume-game

171. "How Much A Bad Hire Will Actually Cost You," by Rachel Gillett, Fast Company, April 4, 2014. https://www.fastcompany.com/3028628/work-smart/infographic-how-much-a-bad-hire-will-actually-cost-you

172. "Ban the Box, Criminal Records, and Statistical Discrimination: A Field Experiment," by Amanda Y. Agan (Princeton University - Department of Economics) and Sonja B. Starr (University of Michigan Law School), U of Michigan Law & Econ Research Paper No. 16-012, June 14, 2016. http://papers.ssrn.com/sol3/papers.cfm?abstract_id=2795795

173. "Does 'Ban the Box' Help or Hurt Low-Skilled Workers? Statistical Discrimination and Employment Outcomes When Criminal Histories are Hidden," by Jennifer L. Doleac and Benjamin Hansen, NBER Working Paper No. 22469, July 2016. http://nber.org/papers/w22469?sy=469

174. "Ban-the-Box Movement Goes Viral," by Roy Maurer, SHRM, 2016. https://www.shrm.org/ResourcesAndTools/hr-topics/risk-management/Pages/Ban-the-Box-Movement-Viral.aspx

175. Maurer

176. "Your Employer Won't Be Looking at Your Credit Score—Here's Why," by Lindsay Konsko, Nerdwallet, August 1, 2016. Starts by saying employers don't look at credit *scores*, then segues to how they actually look at credit *reports*. https://www.nerdwallet.com/blog/finance/credit-score-employer-checking/

177. "The Use of Credit Reports in Employment Background Screening," by Lester Rosen, CEO, Employment Screening Resources, and Kerstin Bagus, Director Global Compliance, LexisNexis Screening Solutions Inc., 2010. http://www.esrcheck.com/file/ESR-LN_The-Use-of-Credit-Reports-for-Employment-Background-Screening.pdf

178. "Know Before You Hire: 2015 Employment Screening Trends," by Roy Maurer, SHRM, January 27, 2015. https://www.shrm.org/resourcesandtools/hr-topics/talent-acquisition/pages/2015-employment-screening-trends.aspx

179. "The law was supposed to reduce discrimination. But it made hiring more racially biased," by Jeff Guo, Washington Post, March 23, 2016. https://www.washingtonpost.com/news/wonk/wp/2016/03/23/the-law-was-supposed-to-reduce-discrimination-but-it-made-hiring-more-racially-biased/

180. "Does new law mean real pay equity for women? Not quite," by Shirley Leung, Boston Globe, August 4, 2016. https://www.bostonglobe.com/business/2016/08/04/things-know-about-massachusetts-equal-pay-law/uuiduzYp7EyiIBhxt14pSJ/story.html

181. "Bill Banning Salary History Questions Goes Before House." by Kathy Gurchiek, SHRM HR Today, Sep 16, 2016. https://www.shrm.org/hr-today/news/hr-news/pages/bill-banning-salary-history-questions-goes-before-house.aspx

182. "Know Before You Hire: 2015 Employment Screening Trends," by Roy Maurer, SHRM, January 27, 2015. https://www.shrm.org/resourcesandtools/hr-topics/talent-acquisition/pages/2015-employment-screening-trends.aspx

183. "The Pros and Cons of Social Media Screening," by Staff, Global HR Research, November 13, 2015. http://www.ghrr.com/blog/2015/11/13/the-pros-and-cons-of-social-media-screening/

184. "A primer on Seattle's new first-come, first-served renters law," by Daniel Beekman, Seattle Times, August 10, 2016. http://

www.seattletimes.com/seattle-news/politics/a-primer-on-seattles-new-first-come-first-served-renters-law/

185. "In Head-Hunting, Big Data May Not Be Such a Big Deal," by Adam Bryant, New York Times, June 19, 2013. http://www.nytimes.com/2013/06/20/business/in-head-hunting-big-data-may-not-be-such-a-big-deal.html

186. "The Science of Smart Hiring," by Derek Thompson, The Atlantic, April 10, 2016: http://www.theatlantic.com/business/archive/2016/04/the-science-of-smart-hiring/477561/

187. "How AI and recruiters will work together in the near future," by Tess Taylor, HRDive, September 15, 2016. http://www.hrdive.com/news/how-ai-and-recruiters-will-work-together-in-the-near-future/426291/

188. "Can Using Artificial Intelligence Make Hiring Less Biased?" by Sean Captain, Fast Company, May 18, 2016. https://www.fastcompany.com/3059773/the-future-of-work/we-tested-artificial-intelligence-platforms-to-see-if-theyre-really-less-

189. "Video Job Interviews: Hiring for the Selfie Age," by Dahlia Bazzaz, Wall Street Journal, August 16,2016. http://www.wsj.com/articles/video-job-interviews-hiring-for-the-selfie-age-1471366013

190. "HR Pornography: Interview videos," by Nick Corcodillos, Ask the Headhunter®, October 14, 2014. http://www.asktheheadhunter.com/7537/hr-pornography-interview-videos

191. "A Cousin Of Siri Is Coming To The Recruiting Field," by Todd Raphael, ERE Recruiting Intelligence, September 8, 2016. http://www.eremedia.com/ere/a-cousin-of-siri-is-coming-to-the-recruiting-field/

192. "The Enemy in HR," by Robert X. Cringely, I, Cringely, September 28th, 2014. http://www.cringely.com/2014/09/28/enemy-hr/

193. Scott Aaronson, an associate professor of EE&CS at MIT, wrote a famous blog comment about his fear of being perceived as a nerdy heterosexual male found gross by females, which triggered a lot of online discussion. Overview: http://www.chronicle.com/blogs/wiredcampus/mit-professors-blog-comment-sets-off-debate-over-nerds-and-male-privilege/55461, then read the invaluable Scott Alexander's commentary on the incident: http://slatestarcodex.com/2015/01/01/untitled/, and then read http://slatestarcodex.com/2014/08/31/radicalizing-the-romanceless/.

194.   http://www.asw4autism.org/pdf/Changes_to_ASD_Criteria_in_the_DSM_5.pdf

195. See Apple's EEO-1 Form for 2015: http://images.apple.com/diversity/

pdf/2015-EEO-1-Consolidated-Report.pdf

196. "Rev. Jesse Jackson continues push for diversity in tech industry," by Marissa Lang, San Francisco Chronicle/SFGate, April 22, 2016. http://www.sfgate.com/business/article/Rev-Jesse-Jackson-continues-push-for-diversity-7304554.php

197. "Silicon Valley Capitulates to Jesse Jackson Shakedown," by Carl Horowitz, National Legal and Policy Center, May 30, 2014. http://nlpc.org/2014/05/30/jesse-jackson-takes-shakedown-campaign-silicon-valley-extracts-concessions-timid/

198. "Cypress CEO Responds to Nun's Urging a 'Politically Correct' Board Make-up," by Cypress Semiconductor CEO T. J. Rodgers, May 23, 1996. http://www.cypress.com/documentation/ceo-articles/cypress-ceo-responds-nuns-urging-politically-correct-board-make

199. "Slack Is Our Company of the Year. Here's Why Everybody's Talking About It," by Jeff Bercovici, Inc. Magazine, December 2015. http://www.inc.com/magazine/201512/jeff-bercovici/slack-company-of-the-year-2015.html

200. "Slack's director of engineering, Leslie Miley, doesn't believe in diversity quotas," by Matthew Lynley, TechCrunch, September 12, 2016. https://techcrunch.com/2016/09/12/slacks-director-of-engineering-leslie-miley-doesnt-believe-in-diversity-quotas/

201. "Jesse's New Target: Silicon Valley," by Roger O Crockett, Bloomberg, July 11, 1999. http://www.bloomberg.com/news/articles/1999-07-11/jesses-new-target-silicon-valley

202. "Intel pledges $300 million to improve diversity in tech," by Andrew Cunningham, January 6, 2015. http://arstechnica.com/business/2015/01/intel-pledges-300-million-to-improve-diversity-in-tech/

203. "Intel plans job cuts across the company, internal memo says," by Mike Rogoway, The Oregonian, June 4, 2015. http://www.oregonlive.com/silicon-forest/index.ssf/2015/06/intel_facing_disappointing_sal.html

204. "Kafkatrapping," by Eric Raymond, Armed and Dangerous, July 18, 2010. ""Your refusal to acknowledge that you are guilty of {sin, racism, sexism, homophobia, oppression...} confirms that you are guilty of {sin, racism, sexism, homophobia, oppression...}." http://esr.ibiblio.org/?p=2122

205. "There Is No Diversity Crisis in Tech," by Brian Hall, censored at Forbes online but republished by Techraptor.net, October 7, 2015. https://techraptor.net/content/there-is-no-diversity-crisis-in-tech-by-brian-hall

206. "From kafkatrap to honeytrap," by Eric Raymond, Armed and

Dangerous, November 3, 2015. http://esr.ibiblio.org/?p=6907

207. "Why Hackers Must Eject the SJWs," by Eric S. Raymond, Armed and Dangerous, November 13, 2015. http://esr.ibiblio.org/?p=6918

208. "Silicon Valley Has an Asian-people Problem," by Razib Khan, The Unz Review, February 6, 2016. http://www.unz.com/gnxp/silicon-valley-has-an-asian-people-problem/

209. "HR Department Benchmarks and Analysis 2015-2016," Bloomberg BNA. http://www.bna.com/uploadedFiles/BNA_V2/HR/Products/Surveys_and_Reports/HR%20Department%20Benchmark%20and%20Analysis%202015-16_Executive%20Summary.pdf

210. "The hidden reality of payroll & HR administration costs," PwC (PriceWaterhouseCoopers LLP), 2011. https://www.adp.com/~/media/Solution%20Builder/Documents/PWC%20TCO%20Study%202011.ashx

211. "Top Diversity Executive Salaries," Salary.com, August 29, 2016. http://www1.salary.com/Top-Diversity-Executive-Salary.html accessed 09-20-2016.

212. "The Rise of the Chief Diversity Officer," by Sylvia Ann Hewlett, Harvard Business Review, October 17, 2007. https://hbr.org/2007/10/the-rise-of-the-chief-diversit

213. "Certification," Society for Diversity. http://www.societyfordiversity.org/certification/, accessed 09-20-2016.

214. "Certification (CCDP/AP): Cornell Certified Diversity Professional/ Advanced Practitioner (CCDP/AP)," https://www.ilr.cornell.edu/human-capital-development/certificates/diversity-and-inclusion-professionals/certification-ccdpap, accessed 09-20-2016.

215. http://diversityofficermagazine.com/

216. "Engaging White Men to Drive Diversity and Inclusion," by Carole Watkins, page 263 in *The Rise of HR: Wisdom From 73 Thought Leaders*, edited by Dave Ulrich, William A. Schiemann, GPHR and Libby Sartain, SPHR, published by the HR Certification Institute, 2015. http://www.octanner.com/content/dam/oc-tanner/documents/ebooks/HRCI_TheRiseofHR-dual.pdf

217. "HR: Think Big and Bold," by Brigette McInnis-Day, page 391 in *The Rise of HR: Wisdom From 73 Thought Leaders*, edited by Dave Ulrich, William A. Schiemann, GPHR and Libby Sartain, SPHR, published by the HR Certification Institute, 2015. http://www.octanner.com/content/dam/oc-tanner/documents/ebooks/HRCI_TheRiseofHR-dual.pdf

218. "Salesforce CEO Marc Benioff announces new chief equality officer," by

Ron Miller, TechCrunch, Sep 13, 2016. https://techcrunch.com/2016/09/13/
salesforce-ceo-marc-benioff-announces-new-chief-equality-officer-at-
techcrunch-disrupt/

219. "Diversity Metrics, Measurement, and Evaluation," by Marc Brenman,
Workforce Diversity Network, 11-24-2012. http://
www.workforcediversitynetwork.com/
res_articles_diversitymetricsmeasurementevaluation.aspx

220. "Sexual harassment training may have reverse effect, research suggests,"
by Sam Levin, The Guardian, May 2, 2016. https://www.theguardian.com/
us-news/2016/may/02/sexual-harassment-training-failing-women

221. "A Point of View: How Much Should Diversity Training Cost?" by
Mary-Frances Winters, July 17, 2014. http://www.theinclusionsolution.me/
a-point-of-view-how-much-should-diversity-training-cost/

222. "Diversity Policies Rarely Make Companies Fairer, and They Feel
Threatening to White Men," by Tessa L. Dover, Brenda Major, and Cheryl R.
Kaiser, Harvard Business Review, January 4, 2016. https://hbr.org/2016/01/
diversity-policies-dont-help-women-or-minorities-and-they-make-white-
men-feel-threatened

223. "Why Diversity Programs Fail," by Frank Dobbin and Alexandra Kalev,
Harvard Business Review, July 2016, p. 52. https://hbr.org/2016/07/why-
diversity-programs-fail

224. ibid. (Dobbin and Kalev)

225. "Why Diversity Training is Ineffective," by John J. Sarno, Esq. http://
documents.jdsupra.com/22508b98-c30e-4066-ae84-8cd0f6b27940.pdf

226. Shibboleth, after a Hebrew word (meaning shock of wheat) which
foreigners could not pronounce. "A word, especially seen as a test, to
distinguish someone as belonging to a particular nation, class, profession
etc." Saying the expected things in the correct way is now a survival
requirement in public life, and a corporate spokesperson who says
something politically incorrect now will attract abuse, boycotts, and
demands for cleansing from activist groups. For example, the well-meaning
"All Lives Matter" is now taken as evidence of racially insensitive thoughts.
https://en.wiktionary.org/wiki/shibboleth

227. "Entryism... is a political strategy in which an organisation or state
encourages its members or supporters to join another, usually larger,
organisation in an attempt to expand influence and expand their ideas and
program." Originally referring to Trotsky's strategies for small, motivated
groups to take over larger political parties. The connotation is that these

people share an ideology which would not be able to gain much support (or, as in this case, support themselves in a free market) unless cloaked by a larger, more respectable organization. Entryists enter, work themselves into positions guiding the organization, then direct the organization to their own policy goals. https://en.wikipedia.org/wiki/Entryism

228. "Don't fuck up the culture," by Brian Chesky, Medium, April 24, 2014. https://medium.com/@bchesky/dont-fuck-up-the-culture-597cde9ee9d4#.o03k874m8

229. "Is It Time to Outsource Human Resources?: Professional employer organizations help free up business owners' time to focus on generating revenue," by Toddi Gutner, Entrepreneur Magazine, January 14, 2011. https://www.entrepreneur.com/article/217866

230. "Benefits Outsourcing: Focus on the Employee Experience," by Joseph B. McGhee, PHR, SHRM, February 11, 2013. https://www.shrm.org/resourcesandtools/hr-topics/benefits/pages/benefits-outsourcing-employee-focus.aspx

231. "Google under scrutiny over lobbying influence on Congress and White House," by David Smith, The Guardian (UK), 18 December 2015. https://www.theguardian.com/us-news/2015/dec/18/google-political-donations-congress

232. "Google age-discrimination lawsuit may become a monster," by Patrick Thibodeau, Computerworld, June 30, 2016. http://www.computerworld.com/article/3090087/it-careers/google-age-discrimination-lawsuit-may-become-monster.html

233. "Labor and Employment: Roundtable," Callawyer.com, April 2011. https://www.fenwick.com/FenwickDocuments/Roundtable_LaborEmployment_04-11-2011.pdf

234. "The Congressional Review Act, rarely used and (almost always) unsuccessful," by Stuart Shapiro, The Hill, April 17, 2015. http://thehill.com/blogs/pundits-blog/lawmaker-news/239189-the-congressional-review-act-rarely-used-and-almost-always

235. "Freedom of Contract," by David E. Bernstein, George Mason University Law and Economics Research Paper Series 08-51, http://www.law.gmu.edu/assets/files/publications/working_papers/08-51%20Freedom%20of%20Contract.pdf

236. "Playing the Name Game: Newscasters with Anglo-sounding last names are switching to ethnic handles. It gets them work--but some ask if it's ethical," by Scott Collins, Los Angeles Times, August 18, 1996. http://

articles.latimes.com/1996-08-18/entertainment/ca-35229_1_minority-reporter

237. http://bastionofliberty.blogspot.com/2016/08/feminizations-and-productivity.html

238. Comment by DysG at Instapundit, August 11, 2016. https://pjmedia.com/instapundit/241048/

239. Comment by Molon Labe.

240. "Why Cisco chooses acquisition over R&D," by Jennifer Scott, Computer Weekly, November 19, 2012. http://www.computerweekly.com/news/2240171835/Why-Cisco-chooses-acquisition-over-RD

241. "Friends at Work? Not So Much," by Adam Grant, New York Times, September 4, 2015. http://www.nytimes.com/2015/09/06/opinion/sunday/adam-grant-friends-at-work-not-so-much.html

242. "The Path From Harvard and Yale to Goldman Sachs Just Changed," by Lindsay Gellman, Wall Street Journal, June 23, 2016. http://www.wsj.com/articles/goldman-rethinks-campus-recruiting-efforts-1466709118

243. "What Your HR Department Could Learn from Hayek," by Harrison Burge, FEE (Foundation for Economic Education), August 22, 2016. https://fee.org/articles/what-your-hr-department-could-learn-from-hayek/

244. https://en.wikipedia.org/wiki/Bootleggers_and_Baptists

245. Deprez, Esmé E.; Hogue, Millie (October 27, 2014). "Arkansas liquor stores join churches to save dry counties". *Bloomberg Politics* (Bloomberg News).

246. "Head Start Impact Study and Follow-up, 2000-2015," U.S. Department of Health & Human Services, Administration for Children & Families, Office of Planning, Research & Evaluation, http://www.acf.hhs.gov/programs/opre/research/project/head-start-impact-study-and-follow-up

247. "A Randomized Control Trial of a Statewide Voluntary Prekindergarten Program on Children's Skills and Behaviors through Third Grade," by Lipsey, Farran, and Hofer, Sept. 2015, Vanderbilt Peabody Research Institute. https://my.vanderbilt.edu/tnprekevaluation/files/2013/10/VPKthrough3rd_final_withcover.pdf

248. From "Off The Wall: The Right of Free College," Mike Rowe, 3-28-2016. http://mikerowe.com/2016/03/otw-rightoffreecollege/

249. "One of the World's Largest Solar Facilities Is in Trouble: California's Ivanpah concentrated solar power plant has underdelivered on its energy contracts and now has a year to shape up, or it could be shut down." MIT Technology Review, by Richard Martin, March 18, 2016.

https://www.technologyreview.com/s/601071/one-of-the-worlds-largest-solar-facilities-is-in-trouble/

250. "Ivanpah: Time to End the Subsidies," Cato Institute 11-11-2014 by Nicole Kaeding. http://www.cato.org/blog/ivanpah-time-end-subsidies

251. http://www.energy.gov/lpo/solana

252. http://www.energy.gov/lpo/mojave

253. "Solyndra times five: What's up with the $2.65 billion in federal loans to Abengoa?" Watchdog.org, Dec. 4, 2015. http://watchdog.org/250161/solyndra-loans-abengoa-2/

254. "Bootleggers, Baptists, and McClendon," Power Line Blog, Steven Hayward, March 4, 2016. McClendon appears to have committed suicide-by-car the day before, ramming his vehicle into a bridge abutment at high speed the day after he was indicted on charges of bid-rigging in acquiring drilling leases. http://www.powerlineblog.com/archives/2016/03/bootleggers-baptists-and-mcclendon.php

255. "What Do FanDuel And Sheldon Adelson's Online Gambling Ban Have In Common? This High-Powered D.C. Lobbyist" - Online Poker Report, Dustin Gouker, October 14, 2015 http://www.onlinepokerreport.com/18514/fanduel-hires-rawa-lobbyist/

256. "Bootleggers, Baptists, and E-cigs: Unlikely allies from the tobacco wars try to fight off a game-changer." By Jonathan H. Adler, Roger E. Meiners, Andrew P. Morriss, and Bruce Yandle, Cato Institute's Regulation, March 2015. http://object.cato.org/sites/cato.org/files/serials/files/regulation/2015/3/regulation-v38n1-3.pdf

257. https://en.wikipedia.org/wiki/Tobacco_Master_Settlement_Agreement

258. "Issue Brief: Tobacco Securitization Bond Issuance in California," CDIAC #08.04, California Debt and Investment Advisory Commission http://www.treasurer.ca.gov/cdiac/reports/tobacco.pdf

259. https://en.wikipedia.org/wiki/Tobacco_Master_Settlement_Agreement

260. "When bootleggers and Baptists converge," Washington Post, Apr 22, 2015 https://www.washingtonpost.com/opinions/when-bootleggers-and-baptists-converge/2015/04/22/2b6f0ffa-e85a-11e4-9a6a-c1ab95a0600b_story.html

261. "The new 'restaurant math' of Seattle's $15 an hour minimum wage is starting to 'break the system'" - by Mark J. Perry, AEIdeas, March 3, 2016. http://www.aei.org/publication/the-new-restaurant-math-of-seattles-15-an-hour-minimum-wage-is-starting-to-break-the-system/

262. https://pjmedia.com/instapundit/230266/

263. Bootleggers and Baptists: How Economic Forces and Moral Persuasion Interact to Shape Regulatory Politics. Cato Institute, September 2014.

264. "In America; A Sea Change On Crime,"
by Bob Herbert, New York Times December 12, 1993. http://www.nytimes.com/1993/12/12/opinion/in-america-a-sea-change-on-crime.html

265. "Stereotype Inaccuracy: A Belief Impervious to Data. When are liberals anti-scientific?" by Lee Jussim Ph.D, Psychology Today, August 1, 2014. https://www.psychologytoday.com/blog/rabble-rouser/201408/stereotype-inaccuracy-belief-impervious-data

266. "Are Racial Stereotypes NOT Really About Race?: How wealth and environment influence stereotypes, by Douglas T. Kenrick, Psychology Today blogs, Sep 02, 2016. https://www.psychologytoday.com/blog/sex-murder-and-the-meaning-life/201609/are-racial-stereotypes-not-really-about-race

267. "Where microaggressions really come from: A sociological account," by Jonathan Haidt, September 7, 2015. http://righteousmind.com/where-microaggressions-really-come-from/

268. https://en.wikipedia.org/wiki/Systems_of_Survival

269. "I have one of the best jobs in academia. Here's why I'm walking away," by Oliver Lee, Vox, September 8, 2015. http://www.vox.com/2015/9/8/9261531/professor-quitting-job

270. "Why Aren't There More Women Futurists?
Most of the big names in futurism are men. What does that mean for the direction we're all headed?" by Rose Eveleth, The Atlantic, July 31, 2015. http://www.theatlantic.com/technology/archive/2015/07/futurism-sexism-men/400097/

271. Eveleth.